Buttermilk Book Publishing

Myrtle Beach, South Carolina

Copyright T. Allen Winn 2020

All Rights Reserved

This is the second memoir written by T. Allen Winn. All stories are nostalgic memories of his past.

Typecast in Times New Roman

ISBN 978-1-7331576-4-3

Don't Sit Naked in a Grits Tree, More Nostalgic Nonsense Vol 2

Dedication

John Speed Hall (June 4, 1952 – May 14, 2020)

One of my best friends died tragically while riding his Harley. Struck by a drunk driver head-on just a few miles from home, 2020 impacted our lives like no other year. Speedy played into his fair share of my nostalgic memories growing up in Abbeville, S.C. I will forever miss him but cherish those adventures we managed to get ourselves into when we were young and thought we were bullet proof.

Edward Joseph McMenamin (October 6, 1942 – May 31, 2020)

May of 2020 claimed a second good friend. I met Ed, originally from Philadelphia, at Tupelo Golf Course on the Grand Strand after I retired in 2015. He and Martin welcomed me into their group and for the next five years we played weekly at Tupelo. Eddie contributed to many golfing stories documented in *The Perfect Mulligan*. He refused to take a mulligan or a gimmie putt, playing out each shot, each hole, each round. Ed, the founding father of the Tupelo Boys, made his mark as a loyal friend.

Francis Woodbury (August 5, 1954 – October 9, 2020)

Francis and I were employed at Metglas, Inc. in Conway from 2005 until I retired in 2015, but I continued working part time there through 2018. She always brought a smile to my face when we visited in the warehouse where she worked. We became close friends, so much so that she shared a true story with me, one of paranormal origins. With her permission that story was the basis of *The Hardwood Walker of Port Harrelson Road*, and documented her horrific childhood memories of something not of this world that haunted her and her sisters. I last spoke to Francis in 2019 during a visit to Metglas. 2020 took a lot of the good ones.

One final dedication is to the Thomas boys, Dale, Andy, Scott, and Sam, and to Brandon Scott. No, they are alive and well. They are my grandchildren by marriage but grands just the same. When I published my first nostalgic book, *Cornbread and Buttermilk*, it laid the groundwork for a wonderful reunion we had 25 years in the making.

Foreword

Documenting nostalgic moments through memoirs is something I have profoundly recommended. After the release of *Cornbread and Buttermilk, Good Ole Fashion Home Cooked Nostalgic Nonsense*, I now more than ever firmly stand behind that belief. I have stated previously how it is important to listen to your elders, those telling you stories we often take for granted. When they are gone, so are their stories of precious moments. Not taking time to write this stuff down is sinful. I am carrying it a step further, lesson learned from my last memoir. I am in that 'getting old as dirt' category now. Writing down what is most memorable to me is significant. When I am gone, so are those memories. There are those snapshots in time that have touched your heart, those unforgettable and often lesson teaching incidents that you have imbedded in your memory. Possibly you have shared them or maybe you have not. Write it, type it, video record it, but for goodness sake do it, not only for you but for those you wish to share them with and do not put this off as tomorrow might be too late.

In *Fostering Four and Much More*, in the last half of my *Cornbread and Buttermilk* memoir, I shared my personal journey down the foster parenting path. Low and behold, by doing so, it opened another pathway for me, reconnecting with four, no, five. Posting the release of the book on Face Book resulted in me being contacted by five incredibly special young men. One by one I received heartwarming messages and chats from those responsible for my venturing into the world of foster care. For those of you who have not read the previous memoir, you might be a tad lost by what I'm about to recant. In Fostering Four I specifically disclosed what prompted me to become a foster parent. Four boys, ages six to ten, abruptly handed over to social services by their father. They were grandchildren by blood to my then wife. They were placed in foster care. The only way my wife and I could hope to remove them from their current situation was for us to become certified foster parents. Even then we weren't guaranteed that they would be placed with us. We gambled and it paid off. They were placed in our care and so began one of the most challenging and rewarding times of my life.

After almost a year under our care the boys were eventually returned to their mother, absent from the household when they had been originally delivered to social services. A year or so later my wife and I divorced. I forfeited my relationship with these four, plus a fifth boy belonging to another one of my wife's daughters, losing all contact with them.

Unfortunately, the divorce left me few options for continuing me to be part of their lives. Looking back now, I did not even try, assuming the divorce removed me from all possible contact. I did not divorce them, did I? As fate would have it, a far greater plan was in the works twenty-five years later. Things have a tendency for working out for a reason. Several of the boys contacted me via Face Book to thank me for being part of their lives when their lives were in turmoil. After reading my memoir they remembered things too. They shared with me their memories of me with them and how I impacted their young lives so many years ago. Tears flowed freely each time I read what they had sent me. It served as a validation that I had made the right decision to do what I had done, even though I had written about my experience without their acknowledgment. Still, hearing it from them impacted my life in ways they could never imagine.

From these shared memories we decided to have a reunion over twenty years later, the boys now men. Up until now I had only seen one of them. Andy came to my first book signing in Abbeville in 2011. It was a tearful reunion then too. They shared their memories of nostalgic moments with me on Face Book. Together we journeyed through the worlds of *Superman, The Teenage Ninja Turtles* and even *Peewee Herman*. Little Caesars' Pizza, collecting baseball cards and the Atlanta Braves tomahawk chop as all were part of their memories. Andy told me that I was responsible for him collecting cards and forever loving the Braves. Lizardman tales as told by me about the creature seen in Bishopville scared them as I had intended it and, yes, they still remembered me telling them. Even weekly trips to carry off the trash in my pickup, covertly used as an excuse to drop by the Hawaiian Frozen Ice Shack, have a place in their hearts as it does mine. Road trips to Cherokee and to the Columbia Zoo were on the agenda, shuttling them there in the leisure van.

Fostering Four plus One More, the Reunion
25 years in the making

Those Thomas brothers, the ones filling the pages of Fostering Four in my Cornbread and Buttermilk memoir, got wind of my book when published. As mentioned, Andy had been the only one of the four that I had laid eyes on in twenty-four years. He had come to my first book signing of Road Rage at Uptown Girls in Abbeville four years prior to my release of the memoir. He approached me at the book signing. He had been a skinny little nine-year old when I had last seen him, barely coming chest high to me. We hugged, me having to reach up to him this time, roles reversed, a mountain of a young man towering over ole Papa Tommy.

Through our brief encounter Andy told me how I had made a positive impact on his childhood, bringing tears to my eyes. Me of all people, had influenced his life in such a good way. I figured their heads had probably been filled with bad tales and he and his brothers had long forgotten me being a part of their lives. The oldest, Dale was ten years old at the time. After my first book release, it would be another four years before I would publish the memoir that changed everything.

Once I had published Cornbread and Buttermilk in 2015 and I began posting excerpts of chapters and stories, Andy sent me a chat on Face Book to tell me he had a copy of the book and had shared it with his brothers. The fire had been stoked and they had begun remembering some of those very same memories I had shared in the book. I never considered myself a role model by any stretch of the imagination but to these boys I had apparently left a lasting impression that I had not realized. The one that really shook the tree arrived via a Face Book chat a short time later. Greg, the youngest and only five years old at the time when we had them in foster care, sent me a photo and the most precious note. I cried when I read it. I cried and barely choked out my feelings when sharing it with my wife.

Greg, now going by Sam, that escape name he used as a mere five-year old, had snapped a photo of what he called 'his top shelf' at his home. There sat the Pewee Herman ventriloquist doll that he had been given all those years ago along with a Superman action figure, another of those characters the then Greg used to pretend to be. Venturing into his imaginary world had helped him escape the world of being abandoned and turned over to foster care by his father. Underneath the photo Sam shared what he remembered about those days with Papa Tommy and his grandmother.

That's the third tier of my bookshelf – a collection of my favorite things. Peewee made the cut as a reminder of the best part of my childhood.

Dale called and summarized an excerpt from your book - I'll be sure to order a copy

I have vague memories of the time before Grandmother and "Papa Tommy," but sharply remember the uncertain roller-coaster that came after. As a man, I'm now able to understand, perhaps forgive, the ones that made that ride so bumpy. I can even appreciate those rough experiences as a stark testament to the "go-with-the-flow approach" when life is out of your control. Sometimes it simply is.

But thankfully, I'm always in control of my home décor. Yep, on my bookshelf, in my home, I keep a reminder that there's always something good in the mix. It's funny; now, just looking at a plastic doll can conjure so many fond memories from 25 years ago. Long trips to the land of the Indians, Cherokee, NC – short trips to trash dump – chopping thin air and chanting the Atlanta Braves tune while pulling for some guy named John Smoltz - the nice, distinct smell that only comes from the interior of a roomy conversion van - a yellow Sesame Street cloth that was only brought out to accompany Little Caesars pizza – "Glo Worms" charged by the light fixture before bed. Too many to mention...

Just wanted to send a quick Facebook message (as stale as that may seem) to let you know that the impact you had on us Thomas boys does not go unnoticed or unappreciated. Hope all is well or well is all hope.

-Greg... or Sam

Back at you Sam. This is my whatnot in my author cave with my Peewee and other favorite memorabilia, Braves stuff included.

How can I add anything else to that? But, as the info commercial goes, 'But wait, there is more.'

The Mighty Greg before he became Sam

Eventually Scott, the next to the youngest of the four sent me a brief but short message that he too had his memories and appreciated the life spent at the Winn country home. Dale, the oldest, is the only one I did not hear from, but he does not use Facebook. I will give him a pass because he is the owner of the book that got the ball rolling. I am so inspired and uplifted by these boys reaching out to me that a plan began developing in this old brain of mine. I contacted Andy, the front man and frequent user of Facebook and suggested maybe it was time for a Papa Tommy and Thomas boys' reunion. I told him to be sure to invite *Lizard Man*, Cousin Brandon. I planted the seed and Andy cultivated it. Eventually we had a date and a place.

Judy and I ventured to Abbeville where we prepared to meet Dale, Andy, Scott and Sam Thomas, Brandon Scott. The Village Grill on Trinity Street had been chosen as the reunion destination. Sadly, Dale was unable to make it due to a previous commitment. Andy, his wife and child, Sam and his girlfriend, Scott, Brandon, and his son, were in attendance. After exchanged hugs, again, me reaching up to all these fine-looking young men, being the runt of the litter now, with the exception of being taller than Brandon, the feeling was indescribable.

I had bagged a few little surprises for the boys. Unbeknownst to them, twenty-five years ago when they returned to the custody of their mother after a year in foster care, had never received their Christmas presents that year. Their mother, for reasons defying explanation, denied us from seeing the boys for about six months after she had gained custody. We were not the bad guys. We had rescued them from being placed with strangers by becoming certified foster parents.

These four boys loved the Teenage Mutant Ninja Turtles. That Christmas before they returned to that mother, we had bought them turtle action figures. Guess what, ole Papa Tommy still had those turtles. They had never been opened and were in the original packaging. Twenty-five years later the Thomas boys were about to receive their Christmas presents. I even tossed in one for Brandon. Also included in their little goody bags were photos I had dug up of them during the time spent with us. I had also written a story or a poem for each boy back then, including Brandon, capturing their traits at the time.

To say the least, I choked through the tears when I gave the bags and watched as checked the contents. I then explained the significance of their gifts. After all, these five boys were my very first grandchildren, even if by marriage. Sam said his turtle would land a spot on his top shelf with Peewee and Superman. During the meal we began to share tales we remembered. The boys brought up stories even I had forgotten. Nostalgia, you just can't beat it.

I had forgotten about a nightly ritual we called the night train. When time for bed we would line up in the den, Papa Tommy assuming the position of the train's engine. The boys would fall in behind me, each train car locked in place with hands latched onto the hips in front of them. I would call out all aboard and sound the train whistle and then we would rumble down the tracks of the hallway with designated stops at their bedrooms. What can I say, they brought the kid out in me and I loved living it through them?

Andy reminded me that I had been the fastest runner alive. We'd have races with the boys pitted against one another around the house. Then I would race them. Before arthritic knees I was quite the sprinter, holding the title of fastest man alive in the house on the hill on highway seventy-two. Andy had twisted his ankle before arriving for our little reunion. I accused him of fabricating that little excuse to avoid a rematch in the parking lot. Even with bad knees, I was confident I could take him. Guess we will never know.

Of course, we relived the Andy and Dale streaker episode, none of us able to explain what had inspired them to become streakers that one night after bath time. We also recanted the Sears catalog episode, Scott remembering everyone thinking he had cut out those lady pictures from his grandmother's catalog. I had always thought Dale had stepped up to take the blame for Scotty. Scott confirmed that Dale had been the original culprit. He said, because he was the shiest of the four, he tended to get blamed unfairly. Scott had been the one who always seemed to be in his own little world, skipping and humming. This seemed to be his perfect escape mechanism, that of the perfect loner in times unfair to kids.

Scott brought up an episode that I had forgotten. It had to do with a toy rifle he had received, and he had done something that warranted us taking it away from him as punishment. We had never given that gun back to him and years later he found it in the attic of the house where we had lived. He mentioned that a large rock had been tossed in the swimming pool and he gotten blamed for that one too. Being so quiet and introverted he had never been one to argue or stand his ground to prove his innocence. I regretted that we had treated him unfairly. He tossed in one last memory of how the others had ridden with me to get pizza and how he had missed out on that adventure as well. Given these unfortunate events I told him how proud I was that he had gone on to serve our country and was now attending Clemson.

Andy, Papa Tommy, and Scott 1988 in that Pool

All the boys had fond memories of the leisure van and its captain chairs, traveling to various destinations like the mountains of Cherokee and Columbia Zoo. I was the fifth kid, six counting Brandon. Of course, I had terrified Brandon with tales of Bishopville's Lizard Man, the myth of the legendary creature just coming to light back then. He and I still use the code name, Lizard Man, when corresponding on Face Book.

Andy asked if I had planted the blueberry bushes at the home place on seventy-two, the very place he now lives. I had gotten them from the Clemson Extension when we lived there. He said they were always loaded with blueberries and would save me some. Of course, that brought up more memories of the boys helping me in my vegetable garden, them picking various veggies before they were ready to be picked. I quickly educated them to when each crop was ready to be harvested.

Sam told shared a great story about their Uncle Ben Thomas. He and Andy had come up with this scheme to pull a prank to scare Ben. Sam had an authentic Gorilla outfit. Andy distracted Ben while Sam snuck up on hi with the ape suit. Prank gone bad, Ben grabbed a shovel and was about to whale away at his nephew in the chimp suit. Joke was on them. Ben was a fearless monkey slayer.

I discovered just how creative Sam was, listened to stories of how his videos had won various awards in the Lander film festivals. He was currently opening a film studio on Trinity Street in Abbeville. I told him that hoped to visit it once open. Since then I have viewed numerous films he has produced.

I thoroughly look forward to the next reunion, hopefully to include Dale. The best of times can be the least expected. I do indeed love my Abbeville grandboys and am proud of each and every one of them, considering the obstacles and hurtles they faced to get where they are now.

Pictured (Andy, Sam, me, Brandon, Scott and little Brandon)

I could not exclude Dale, the eldest of the Thomas brothers, who couldn't make the little reunion, so here's the best I could do for the photo opt.

Papa Tommy is still proud to be called their grandpa after all these years. In the back of the book I have included some silly poems I had written for the boys in those Papa Tommy days.

Old Folks Are Us

Digging in the dirt watching the garden grow.
Makes Granny happy, Papa says so.
Fishing and hunting put food on the table.
Squirrel dumplings and fried catfish when Papa is able.

Old Folks living the life inside us.
Following in footsteps knocking off the rust.

An ax, hickory stump and kindling for the stove.
Heating up the house fending off the cold.
The smell of burning coal drifting in the air.
No place like home coziness always found there.

Old Folks living the life inside us.
Following in footsteps knocking off the rust.

That old time religion feeling the Holy ghost.
Sunday's around the dinner table missing it the most.
Cast iron skillet cornbread, butterbeans in the pot.
Granny's fixings on the table serve it while it is hot.

Old Folks living the life inside us.
Following in footsteps knocking off the rust.

Churning peach ice cream in the shade of a tree.
Listening to the radio sipping ice cold sweet tea.
Country rides to nowhere family piled in the car.
Counting cows for fun while never riding far.

Old Folks living the life inside us.
Following in footsteps knocking off the rust.

Granny, Papa, Mama, Daddy been gone for a spell.
Leaving us with wonderful memories to tell.
Always listen when elders have something to say.
When they are gone the stories will be too one day.

Old Folks living the life inside us.
Following in footsteps knocking off the rust.

Life has come full circle digging in our own dirt.
Aches and pains are common no end to the hurt.
Children listen to the tales told by an old cuss.
Remember you will be old one day just like us.

Old Folks living the life inside us.
Following in footsteps knocking off the rust.

By T. Allen Winn

Because memories can be spurred unexpectedly, come as flashes, anytime and anywhere, these stories (chapters) are in no chronological order. When significant I include a date or time frame in my nostalgic journey. Now, prepare for more nostalgic nonsense.

Chapters

Don't Sit Naked in a Grits Tree
Pass the Hash Please
Got My Goat
Sopping a Possum
Some Like it Hot
Waffling in America
Don't Do This with a BB Gun
Bugamania
I'm Not Marlin Perkins
Deer Me!
The Truth and Nothing But
Baboon Buffoon
Bush Whacker
Free Comes with a Price Tag
It's Howdy Doody Time
Just Like a Good Neighbor
Oh Christmas Tree
Looking For a Few Good Snowmen
It's Eleven O'clock Do You Know Where Your Children Are?
BNG
This Is A Weather Alert…Really?
We're Not in Kansas, Toto
The Wild, Wild World of Cow Pasture Sports
Lounge Lizards and Gigolos
The Good Old Garnet and Gold
One Is an Only Number
The Perfect Square

Twas the Four Days of Dickens
Tailgating for Dummies and In-laws
Going Coastal
Better Be Glad You're Not My Young'un
Skating, Surfing and Skiing
The American Car
Around a Table, Not a Knight's Tale
Charlotte's Web
Not your Average Duncan Donut
Remembering Chad
Heart of the Tiger
Hub and Spoke
Hail to the Heroes
Home of the Braves
The Kudzu Palace
Seeing is Believing
Is that you Marilyn?
Do-Overs Are Not for Dummies
The Little Red Jeep (Hurricane Dorian)
Sleeping Beauties Caught in the Act
Perfect Pair, Nice'uns in their Day
Politically Incorrect

Don't Sit Naked in a Grits Tree

Sounds southern and fitting, doesn't it? My wife, who was raised on a farm or at least that's what she claims, once got snookered by a Clemson agricultural story. In the segment they were talking about harvesting grits from a tree. Judy heard the segment on the television and dropped what she was doing to watch it. At the end they announced April Fool. She also enjoys sharing an incident involving her oldest sister, Brenda. She and her husband Raymond were living in Illinois at the time. They stopped by a mom and pop grocery. Brenda asked the lady behind the cash register did they have any grits. The lady climbed a ladder to reach something high on a shelf and turned and asked, 'Hominy?' To which Brenda replied, 'Just one.' They were indeed hominy grits, the bag layered in dust. I have a vivid imagination but sometimes you just cannot make this stuff up.

No. This is not where the title of my second heaping helping of nostalgic nonsense originated but it just seemed relevant. I often joke that I had to give up drinking Bourbon because I ended up naked in trees way too often. No. I never woke up in a tree naked, but the brown liquor in my past life did often contribute to memory lapses, memory loss or just plain embarrassing and regretful moments. That was then, this is now. I no longer partake of Jack or any other similar brown liquids. Originally, I had planned to title the second edition of nostalgic stories, *Pass the Hash, More Good Ole Fashion Nostalgic Nonsense Served on a Slice of White Loaf Bread*. While catchy, it is a page full for a book title. This plan became derailed or should I say influenced while we were visiting friends August 2019 in Princeton, West Virginia.

We were having supper (not dinner) with Tom and Laura, Bernard and Paulette, Jack and Pam. While discussing an assortment of craziness, including some of my books and various short stories, Jack proposed the grit title. I liked it and decided to change the title of my next nostalgic book. It was a catchy phrase. It reminded me of the title of one of the late great Lewis Grizzard's books, *Don't Sit Under the Grits Tree with Anyone Else but Me*.

While among friends, you can always count on humorous stories being shared. This group was in rare form. Two couples reside in Princeton while the third live a stone's toss across the state line in Virginia. We had met these fine folks during our church's Snowbirds and Seagulls program in January of 2019. First United Methodist church in Myrtle Beach has sponsored this program for over thirty years; a way to welcome the winter visitors to the beach (snowbirds) into the fellowship of locals (the seagulls) by offering Tuesday golf outings and several dozen or so

Thursday's of additional fellowship at the church, meals and entertainment included. The church also provides a Monday night service specifically catered to our visiting friends that arrive in January and remain until around March or April. Okay. I have laid the groundwork for some nostalgic tales related to our newfound friends.

I will start with Jack and Pam since Jack inspired the title for this book. As the story goes, Jack and Pam were on vacation, about to board a train on the subway. They had noticed a grungy dressed man, possibly a homeless character, as they approached the boarding terminal. They entered the train and car and the man ventured inside as well. No, Jack and Pam weren't stereotyping or looking down on this guy. It was just an undeniable observation on their part. Somewhere along the way, the man reached his destination and exited. It was then that the two noticed he had left an odd package on the floor behind. Suspicions got the best of them. Could this man have been a terrorist, leaving a bomb behind? They remained in the car, watchful but didn't react. I would have called authorities and gotten out of there if possible. Luckily, they survived their commute, no explosions. On another vacation, the duo was entering another country and the immigration clerk apparently had a weird sense of humor. He accused Jack of attempting to smuggle a woman, Pam, into the country illegally. He finally smiled, giving up the ruse after seeing the panicked look on Jack's face.

Let us move on to Tom and Laura. Laura was on a trip. She explains, while in an airport, on a shuttle tram, she thought she was standing in front of a mirror, but she did not see her reflection. She panicked, thinking she was having some kind of 'out of body' experience and had possibly died. The tinted glass simply offered no reflective characteristics. Primping can take on a scary experience when no one is primping back. Eventually, she determined that she was still among the living and not a ghost just yet.

Laura then shared a Tom story. Tom is a retired Baptist minister. He is a one-man treasure trove of hilarious episodes, many of which I have included in my published book, *The Endless Mulligan*. They were having lunch at a local mom and pop restaurant when a new waitress flopped down beside Tom, commenting they she recognized him. Tom did what most of us would do and pursued the conversation, asking her where she had worked before being employed at the restaurant. It seemed like a perfectly innocent and logical follow up. She smiled, saying she used to work at Southern X-Posure Gentleman's Club. Tom, now red faced, found himself in a most precarious position. After she left, he quickly quipped that he used to be the one that polished the poles there. Obviously, or as far as we know, Tom has never set foot inside the local strip club. Preachers are supposed to be honest and trustworthy, right?

I first met Tom on the golf course during one of the church's Snowbirds and Seagulls captain's choice outings. He and I were cart buddies. On the back nine at Arrowhead Golf course, Tom retrieves a pack of Oreos from his golf bag. After finishing them, he looks over at me and asks if he has any cookie crumbs in the corners of his mouth, explaining that he normally does. I looked and he did indeed have Oreo crumbs smeared in his mouth corners. I did what any mother, or in the case, golf buddy would do. I reached over and cleared the residue with my fingers. We became remarkably close friends that day. He now carries a woman's compact in his golf bag. No, I'm not kidding. I have seen it.

Another time, we were playing at the Thistle Golf Course in Sunset Beach, N.C. After the round, and after the round while unloading our bags at my car, I couldn't find my street shoes in the car. I wondered if I had left the car unlocked and someone had stolen them. They were gone. It had to be the only explanation. It was then that I heard this little chuckle coming from behind me. Tom held up one of his feet and he was wearing my shoes. Honest mistake. I don't think so. Tom wears two shoe sizes larger than my 10 1/2. How did he get them on his feet? Understandably, he had not brought his street shoes. I had picked him up at his beach condo and he had already been wearing his golf shoes. When I dropped him back off, he retrieved his street shoes from his car, and they looked remarkably like mine, enough so that he had stretched them over his big feet. We have gotten some mileage out of this one for sure.

We have met some amazing people while traveling. October of 2019, we took a bus tour trip to Kentucky and visited a horse race farm in Lexington and toured the Ark Experience and the Creation Museum before venturing into Ohio Amish territory. On this trip we met Ezra and his wife Nancy Gough from N.C. Ezra was a hoot. He would play the harmonica for us, belting out almost any tune. Ezra liked to backpack, and he was older than me, in his 70s. He said he was once hiking the Appalachian Trail and he would do portions of it and then his sister would pick him up before dropping him back off to continue the next day. Three young men hiking had passed him on the trail. They had exchanged pleasantries before continuing their trek. He arrived at the pickup point and the next day his sister dropped him off further up the trail. Later that day, the same group of young men caught up with him a second time, bewildered as to how he could have possibly gotten ahead of them again on the trail. Ezra left it to their imagination.

Ezra asked a park ranger once what animals should he fear the worse on the trail. The ranger responded, people. A bear once reached up in a tree and broke the strap holding his food stash. He also told me he once had a dream about encountering a bear while backpacking. It was unusual to see bears but mostly they gave you wide berth. In his dream, the bear approached and began following him. Finally, the dream version of Ezra climbed a tree and the bear followed him, mere branches below Ezra pulls out his harmonica and belts a tune, either calming the beast or scaring him off. Hope he never has to test that theory for real.

Ezra met Nancy after both had been widowed. He said she married him so that she would have someone to work her farm. She cannot get rid of him now, not unless she can trade up for someone to take on his chores. Ezra looked at me one morning and told me that I looked good. Following that up he added I bet your wife didn't tell you that.

Another gent we met on this trip was named Melvin Lutz. Like Ezra, he was full of himself too, both friends. Melvin taught classes at Gardner Webb, Greek, to be specific. Melvin told me that he was on another bus trip once when they visited the site where SAS shoes are manufactured. Someone asked what SAS stood for and Melvin told the inquirer that it was the acronym for 'Sex After Sixty' and that he owned three pairs. He then clarified that SAS was San Antonio Shoes. Ezra and Melvin were seated in a mall with other travelers, appropriately so, underneath a sign designating the seating area as 'The Do-Nothing Club.'

On another occasion, Melvin asked me how many bites were taken from the apple in the Garden of Eden. I had no clue, so he explained. Eve ate, Adam too and the devil one, totaling eleven bites, $8 + 2 + 1$. On a somber note, while writing this piece, Ezra posted on Facebook to pray for his Nancy as she had been diagnosed with pancreatic cancer. My mom died from this dreadful cancer. Prayer warriors were in full force. Sadly, Nancy lost her battle with cancer in 2020.

Our coach driver on the Kentucky trip was Tim Wyatt. And yes, Christian Tours calls their buses coaches. Costing hundreds of thousands of dollars each, they are not buses by a long shot. Tim entertained us as well. He claimed to have driven all types of buses before landing his current gig. His toughest by far had been driving a school bus. He had even driven a prison bus. He warned the prisoners if they ever considered jumping him to think twice. He would intentionally wreck the bus and take at least two thirds of them out with him. He once told the kids on his school bus while passing a prison bus; behave, stay in school, or end up on that prison bus. He once took a selfie of himself in an old stand-alone phone booth and then texted it to his wife. It was lost in translation, his wife thinking he had texted it to her from that booth, asking him if he had tried to call her first.

These were not some of my ancient nostalgic tales, happening in 2019. but there is no hard fix on how long-ago nostalgia must happen to qualify. If it is memorable, it is nostalgic. If they trigger special moments, then they are worth sharing, if for no other reason than to preserve them. An acquaintance told me recently that she had begun entering some of her life story on her computer, thinking that the tragedies that she had experienced might help others. I suggested that she purchase a pocket recorder and make entries as she thought about them and had the time. Often life doesn't always offer opportune moments to flop down in front of a computer. Capture them now. Transcribe later. Preserving your past, your moments are no more complicated than that. Use that recorder for your elders, listening to the stories that only they know. Remember, when they are gone so go the stories and the opportunities. Never take life for granted. None of us are promised tomorrow, another second or minute. Leave others something to remember and stories to bring smiles to their faces. Tomorrow might be too late to start. Okay, enough said. Get ready. My oldies but goodies begin next, the second plateful and an assortment of silliness and heartfelt nostalgic nonsense.

Pass the Hash Please

Hash, a southern tradition, is something I grew up eating. Of course, I had my fair share of other southern traditions such as cast-iron skillet homemade cornbread, churned buttermilk, macaroni pie, homemade potato salad, banana pudding and lemon meringue pie. I need a bib to contain my drooling. What is hash you might ask if you are not southern born and raised? It is not to be confused with hashish that one smokes to become high, that is for sure. You will not get busted for trying good ole homemade southern hash. It is not to be confused with that canned corn beef hash, diced or chunky with potatoes. I turn my nose up at that. Most true southerners would.

John and Ruby Bowie, my grandparents, had their own special recipe. It probably had as much to do with technique as ingredients. Sorry. It remains a family secret. Papa and Granny are both gone now as is Mama who inherited the gift of hash making from them. Mama, an only child as am I, ensured the rite of passage. The secret was passed on to me. Mama took great pains in retrieving the information from her parents, writing down the recipe and laying claim to the tools of the trade before their passing. Put your pencil and pad down. I did not say I was going to share it with the world. It would not be a family secret if I did now would it?

I'll tell you this much. Papa's traditional hash contained chicken, beef, pork, onions, vinegar, salt, pepper, potatoes and other ingredients not to be disclosed. We'll talk about his non-traditional hash later. Granny usually did the meat preparation, slow cooking a pork roast, a beef roast and breast of chicken, plus cooking up the other fixings, onions, potatoes, etc. These meats were drop off the bone tender by the time they finished their cooking cycle. The meats were allowed enough time to cool before beginning the grinding process. Yeah you heard it right…grinding.

Modern technology had no place in the Bowie household when it came to making homemade hash. Forget powered grinders or food processors. They were prohibited, plain and simple. An old-fashioned hand crank grinder (**The 20 Blue Glass made in the USA**) did the job of preparing the meat. Nearly every kitchen had one back in the day. These contraptions were cast iron. Theirs had a silvery finish and it had to be clamped to a surface to secure it for use. Papa had fabricated a special table, the only one in the house that would work with the grinder. He bolted it to the table securely before beginning the process. The various meats were hand fed into the hopper while cranking the handle. The screw impeller pulled it through and ground up the meat. Sometimes I got to turn the crank. I still have that table and the grinder, inherited so to speak when my Mama passed away. Both the table and grinder are still in tip top shape. One must respect and protect one's heritage.

Lots of folks make the mistake of using electric food grinders or processors but the old-fashioned way cannot be beat. Food processors do too much chopping or blending, not actual grinding. Electrical grinders often introduce too much friction and can change the texture of the meat. That alone can ruin good hash. These old folks knew what they were doing. You cannot improve on perfection. Papa had been making hash for much of his eighty years. Making homemade hash is not for everyone. It is not something that is done frequently either. That is why quarts of the stuff are made at a time and then frozen for later. You just can't make a little bit.

One must remember, times were hard back in my grandparent's day. Sometimes they had to supplement the meats the best they could. Improvising was an acceptable practice. Chicken wasn't hard to come by because they raised their own. I remember, as a youngster, Papa and Granny having a fenced in chicken yard bordering the back ally behind their four room mill house. Papa picked out a lucky candidate and then took the chicken over to the hickory chopping stump, the same one he used for cutting kindling for the coal pot bellied stove. Graphic warning…he whacked off its head with an ax. He then tossed it into the yard until it stopped flopping around. Papa plucked it and prepared it for the pot. I witnessed this process many times as a mere child. It was cool back then, but times were different in those days.

I mentioned that when times were hard and regular meats were not always available or affordable, what do you do? You improvise and sue what you have available. Papa often substituted venison, goat, squirrel, or rabbit in place of the pork or beef roast. Hard times required both creativity and versatility. My grandparents were survivors of very harsh times growing up in the early 1900's. Money was often tight. They didn't always have the luxury of chain grocery stores. Food for the table depended on improvising and being thankful for what you could get. Most of us wouldn't have fared well back in their time. We're too spoiled and soft. My wife, Judy was always reluctant to eat Papa's hash because she didn't trust what he might use for the meat. Raised on a farm herself it seemed odd she was so picky about eating. Truth is Papa would never trick someone into eating something by pretending it was something else. It wasn't his way. He wanted you to enjoy what you ate. He never pushed it on anyone. It just meant more for him and more for us if you passed on sampling the good stuff.

One of my most memorable hash events occurred in the mid 1980's when I invited my boss, Kirk Husser, to join me for lunch one weekday at my grandparent's house on South Main Street. They lived less than ten minutes from Flexible Technologies where we both worked. Husser is not exactly a good ole southern name. Kirk had originated from Pittsburg, a far piece from Abbeville, and not exactly known for producing hash. He was a gamer though and willing to give it a shot. The plates, silverware and glasses of sweet tea were waiting for us when we arrived. Fixings included a loaf of white bread, homemade slaw, a plate of sliced tomatoes and a favorite Bowie treat, a bowl of sliced cucumbers, bell pepper and onions soaking in vinegar and oil. A southerner's meal fit for a king was laid out on the kitchen table, a place where our family gathered at their house.

Kirk commented on how he thoroughly enjoyed lunch and even had a second helping of hash. Papa and Granny grinned from ear to ear, appreciative of his thoughtfulness. We got back to work, and Kirk began explaining to coworkers his entrée at the Bowie's home. He said that while tasty, he could not quite grasp the concept of taking perfectly cooked meat and running it through a grinder and then plopping the finish product on a plate with a spoon. He described how it resembled some sort of brown pre-chewed mush. I slapped him on the back and welcomed him to the south, telling him that next I would have to introduce him to cornbread and buttermilk or maybe squirrel dumplings.

In the south hash and barbeque pulled pork go hand in hand. There is nothing better than a good ole fashioned pig picking combining hash, pulled pork and spareribs. While I still have that original grinder and table, we have not made any hash since my mama passed away in 2004. I could never part with those tools of the trade though. We do still have that original recipe and I suppose the passing it down ends with me. Ferguson's in Abbeville makes and sells a hash very comparable to Papa and Granny's. When we visit Abbeville from Myrtle Beach, we often buy several quarts and take it home and freeze it. Kinfolk coming to the beach bring us quarts to confirm their reservation at our house; that and fresh tomatoes when in season. Thank you, Ferguson's. Papa would like yours too.

Yep, making hash was a craft perfected by our elders, master chefs of southern cuisine. On the next 4th of July, I would wager that a quart of Ferguson's hash will be on our menu. Pass me a couple of slices of that white loaf bread and plop enough juicy hash on top to cover them. Salt and pepper it and we're good to go. It is better than eating a 'fat pill'. I can visualize sitting around that kitchen table and swapping yarns, family fellowship at its best. Boy do I miss them and times at their house. Pass the hash, please. Below are photos of the grinder in its original box and the grinder affixed to Papa's crafted table.

Got My Goat

It seems like my fondest memories growing up include ones spent with Papa. All are not those as seen through the eyes of a young boy. Papa and I had our share of adult times too, male bonding, grandpa, and grandson. We had a knack for making the simplest task an adventure. We never planned it. It just happened. Papa had a gift for comical moments. What made him even more genuine was that he could laugh at himself. No one enjoyed a good old friendly ribbing better than him, even if he was the butt of the laughter. He was toothless unless he inserted his store-bought teeth, which he rarely ever did. One thing was for certain, he would offer up a contagious, gut wrenching, knee slapping laugh when his funny bone had been properly tickled.

I was in my early thirties and had just purchased my second ever owned home, giving up the city life for that of living in the country. *The Green Acres* theme song comes to mind. I had five acres of land, mostly grown up except for a couple of acres of yard around the house. A push lawn mower was all that I owned to tackle the landscape. Not to worry, Papa thought on it a while and with a grin he flicked those suspenders on his overalls, pushed out his chest and said, 'Hon, you need a goat.' What in the world was I going to do with a goat? I did not know anything about raising a goat. I had never owned any sort of farm animal, let alone a Billy goat. Papa had raised his fair share, most of them ending up in hash or the stew pot, or whatever else you do with processed Billy or Nanny.

Papa was not going to be talked out of me having a goat. I wasn't sure when my say so had vanished. He explained that a goat was an eating machine. It could be moved from one area to the next allowing it to clear the briars, Kudzu, honeysuckles or just about anything green or editable. The land was not fenced so how was I going to keep a goat on it? I am a greenhorn, not goat herder. I wasn't even a descent sodbuster yet, even though I had high ambitions to eventually plant my very first garden. Papa's plan was simple. Park the goat where I wanted to plant the garden and let it clear it off for me. There was no need arguing with the man in denim Camel overalls. He was convinced I needed a goat, so I reckon a goat I was going to get.

So, where do we find a goat, I finally asked him. Papa had an answer for everything, a worldly man, at least when it came to Abbeville and the adjoining counties. He and I would ride to Mount Carmel in McCormick County where people he knew had a goat for sale. We would haul the goat back to my house in his 1961 Apache 10 Chevy pick-up. It sounded simple enough. One goat, at Mount Carmel prices, fifteen dollars, the ride there and back free, and the time spent with Papa on this little adventure, priceless. Goat hauling, we were headed first thing Saturday morning. I'd meet Papa at his house which was sort of on the way to our destination. I tried to convince myself that having a goat might just be fun. After all, I did live in the country now. Who knows, first a goat then some chickens…but I'll save the chicken story for another chapter. The similarities are uncanny.

Saturday morning arrived soon enough. I eased into the shotgun seat of Papa's truck and we were off to fetch us that goat. A coil of rope rested in the truck bed for tying the goat in place once we picked it up. The trip took about forty minutes. Papa rarely ever exceeded fifty miles an hour in the old pickup. We eventually arrived at our destination. A black lady met us in the yard, addressing Papa as Mister John. She apologized for her husband not being there and then pointed to a large, fenced area, saying the goat was inside. I assumed the goat would already be corralled in some sort of holding pin. That was a bad assumption on my part.

I spotted the goat, all black except for some white on its face and one leg. Papa said, "It's a little bigger than I expected". What was that supposed to mean I wondered? The lady told us we would have to catch it. I am no goat herder and I'm certainly not a seasoned wrangler. This was quickly going south. Reluctantly, I forfeited over my fifteen dollars. Papa smiled and said, "Hon, go in there and get your goat. Here's the rope. Just tie it around the ole boy's neck". Obviously, this was going to be a one-man job. Papa had no intention of entering the arena. I felt like one of those rodeo clowns, naked and without a barrel for protection. Little did I know I was entering the lion's den. I needed a goat like I needed a hole in the head. What could I do? I had paid the price for a goat that I now had to get. The old, seasoned veteran was not going to help me. Kind of like when I landed my first fish; I was on my own.

The black Billy eyed me when I entered the gate. At least he did not snort and stomp his feet like one of those black bulls. I was elated because I was certainly no matador. Heck, I didn't even own a red cape. I had but one strategy in mind. Somehow corner it, but then what? Visualizing another rodeo scene, I pictured myself wrestling the goat, bulldogging it to the ground and tying its feet to beat the clock. Who was I fooling? Just cornering this hardheaded foe was going to be a challenge. It takes one hardhead to know the other. Game on. The goat didn't want to be cornered and he had too much running room. Papa grinned and cheered me on. Apparently, I was the morning's cheap entertainment. The goat did not like it any more than I did but I owned it fair and square, bought and paid for. The goat just didn't know it yet and I'm not sure he really cared.

I did not have a stopwatch going but obviously I was setting no record-breaking time in capturing my purchase. I wasn't sure if I had eventually tired my adversary out or Billy was setting me up. Somehow, I managed to corner him and grab the goat around the neck. Then the real battle began. I learned quickly that goats can buck like wild broncos and they do not do this quietly. The bleating was blood curdling. I think goats are double jointed. I had dropped to my knees, tussling with Billy on the ground. The goat was held firmly in my death-like headlock. Now what? Somehow, I had to get the rope around the goat's neck. I looked over at Papa for help. He just nodded, signaling I had gotten him. I had flashbacks again of him just standing there when I landed my very first catfish. A tiny tot, I dragged that cane pole and five-pound fish on the bank while Papa was beaming with pride at my one-boy accomplishment. He had no intention in helping me then or now. It was me or the goat. The jury was still out on who might win this one.

Somehow in the wrestling match I did manage to loop the rope over the goat's head. I had him or maybe not. A goat on the opposite end of a rope doesn't mean that the goat is in a particularly cooperative mood. Tug of war ensued. These critters can dig in, that's for sure. It commenced to yanking me about with ease. Getting the hang of it, I eventually got the goat on the short end of the rope. This was not going to be like walking a dog though. Slowly but surely, I advanced the goat toward the gate. Papa at least opened it for us. How kind. There is justice to those who wait. Roaming freely in the yard was this huge white tom turkey. It had its feathers flared wide open, strutting about as if it was courting a hen. I had never witnessed this behavior. It was a pleasant distraction from my wrangling duty.

The turkey strutting was quite graceful to watch, but that was before it took a dark and priceless twist. For whatever reason, ole Tom didn't take a fancy to Papa. It began following him, still in strut mode. Papa told the black lady, "Don't worry. It's okay. I've raised my fair share of turkeys." That was before Tom had begun pecking and snatching at Papa's overall legs. Papa still remarked, "It's okay". Then the foul became even more aggressive, pecking his overalls with vengeance. I'll never forget Papa repeating, 'It's okay. It's okay. No, it's not". The black woman intervened, swatting ole Tom with a broom. The turkey, unfazed, was still trying to get back to Papa. I couldn't help him. I had my hands full with Billy.

My goat and I eventually made our way back to the Chevy. Papa was keeping a watchful eye on the butterball from hell. Leaning against the truck and rubbing his chin he said, "Yep. This here goat is a might bigger than I figured he would be. This rope ain't going to work to secure him in the truck bed". Great! I had forked over fifteen bucks to wrangle a goat and now we were not going to be able to take him home. I wasn't sure if I could ask for a refund. Papa assured me it would be all right and then said, "Hon, you're going to have to hold the goat in your lap". Whoa, I didn't sign up for this, Pilgrim. There is no way this goat was going to be a happy travel companion, not in my lap. Papa, the innovator, has a solution for everything, even if it is at my expense. He had me sit in the seat and scoot towards the dashboard. Now he decided to help me, sort of. He positioned the goat strategically straddling my legs, its front and back legs dangling on either side to prevent it from gaining a foothold. Somebody ought to be paying me to haul off this goat. Did I mention how goats are not the best smelling animals?

Soon we were off and heading back to Abbeville. Let me tell you that there is nothing worse than having a stinky goat held to your bosom and in your lap, bleating at the top of its lungs. It sounded like a child being beaten and tortured. That goat never let up for the entire drive. As we reached town Papa advised me that we needed to stop by the hardware store and purchase a chain long enough to secure the goat. Ace hardware store was located just off the Abbeville Court Square. Of course, he goes inside leaving me with the bleating goat still in my lap, in the truck, in the parking lot and in plain sight. It sounded like I was slitting its throat at the slaughterhouse. Those passing by or parking nearby gave me wide berth, eyeing me like I was some sort of pervert. It's not just every day you see a man by himself in the cab of a truck holding a loud and fretful goat in his lap. You would have thought the goat had visions of being the main ingredient in a pot of Papa's hash. Don't think the thought hadn't passed my mind a time or two.

Finally, Papa returned with the chain. My new grounds keeper had so far cost me a grand total of $33 and some change. I hoped the investment paid off at some point, and that I could reclaim my dignity. Last leg of our journey and the goat continued its bleat fest. Once home, the plan unfolded under Papa's leadership. One end of the chain was affixed around the goat's neck and the opposite end of the fifteen-foot chain was attached to an old truck tire. The goat would not be able to tow the tire but would be able to graze within fifteen feet in any direction. Once that terrain had been cleared it would be as simple as relocating the tire for new grazing territory. We watched the goat eat its keep. After about fifteen minutes, Papa suggested I reposition the tire. Sounded simple enough, right?

I approached the tire. Possibly ole Billy envisioned our last wrestling match or maybe he feared he might become a hash causality. He launched in the opposite direction, leaping off a short embankment. The swivel in the chain snapped. The goat realizing its newfound freedom, hauled goat butt across the field. After a long search we found neither hide nor hair of my goat. My investment amounted to a mere fifteen-minute rental, not to mention the images forever etched in my memory. Papa asked if I wanted to go get another goat. I said this one had already gotten mine. The next week was the 4th of July. Did Billy end up in someone's hash? The family got a lot of mileage out of my little episode giving me a 'Stubborn as a Goat' tee-shirt, a goat on the front and my name emblazed on the back. My next birthday was themed with a goat birthday cake. Humor is in the eye of the beholder. I still was not in a laughing mood. Life with Papa was always an adventure and forever priceless. He would whoop and holler every time the story was recapped. Guess I learned the meaning of 'Got your Goat' or in this case, maybe not.

Me with my Stubborn Old Goat birthday shirt and Papa

Sopping a Possum

In a grandson's eyes, growing up in the fifties and sixties, I walked in the shadow of my Papa. He was a famed and fabled rabbit and squirrel slayer. I never came close to matching his expert shooting. When not hunting rabbits with beagles he would place rabbit boxes in fields for catching old Peter cotton tail. The rabbit box is a rectangular wooden trap with a trip wire door. It is placed strategically and was Papa's technique for thinning out the ever-exploding cotton tail population. I was in my forties back then and the famed hunter was no longer walking among the mortals. Papa at the ripe old age of 90 had gained his wings. I carried on the tradition of trapping rabbits with a friend of mine. Sylvester Burton constructed the boxes. I placed several of the wooden traps on my five acres, baiting them with apples and periodically checking them. Sharing the bounty with my friend and grandmother, alternating between the two, the boxes provided plenty of rabbits for stewing, fricasseeing, frying and dumplings. The problem with these boxes is they can often attract other critters besides rabbits. The aromatic sliced apples strategically placed in the rear of the trap are just too mouth watering to ignore for wildlife seeking an easy meal.

On one such occasional, when making my afternoon rounds, I noticed a tripped trap, the door closed. I peeped inside and found a very ugly and hissing possum grinning back at me. I called Sylvester and asked if he would like me to bring him this nasty looking critter. He expletively turned down the offer. He suggested I give another friend, Melvin Peterson, a call, remembering that he did partake of the possum cuisine. Now let me clarify that Sly, my rabbit box buddy, is black as is Melvin and I am white. Sly nor I would consider eating a possum but Melvin, born of the old school, had lived through hard times apparently, and eating often meant you could not be choosey. Papa and Melvin could have been best friends for sure. I gave Melvin a call and he chuckled on the other end of the phone saying he would be there in ten minutes to take old fuzz face off my hands. I swear I heard him smacking his lips anticipating the forthcoming meal. Let me clarify that Melvin eats chicken feet or footsies as he calls them. They do sell them prepackaged in some grocery stores. I've seen them.

Melvin, like most folks in this southern setting, hunted for a hobby. He raised rabbit dogs, aka beagles, and just so happened to have his beagle hauling cage on the back of his old pickup truck. He lured the possum out of the box and into the cage. He advised me to burn out the box to remove the possum's odor. I asked him what he planned to do with the scrawny blackjack possum. He told me he would clean out its system with bread and milk, fatten it up for a couple of months then have it with sweet taters and onions. A Sunday dinner fit for a king, so he said. I witnessed him smack his lips firsthand this time. Mine remained dry and chapped. I just told him not to invite me over.

I saw Melvin from time to time and he still had that possum in the beagle cage on his truck. He had never gotten around to relocating it in a pen. The possum had put on a few pounds and appeared almost groomed, not greasy like I had last remembered seeing it. After the allotted couple of months had expired, I saw Melvin at one of our local hangouts, a country store of sorts where many a yarn was spun by hunters and fisherman alike. I peeked inside the beagle cage, but I didn't see Mister Blackjack. The cage was empty. Destiny had run its course I suspected. Taters and onions had garnished the meal. I asked him how the old boy had tasted. He stared at the ground and acted right peculiar. He him-hawed around and finally said he did not eat him. I quizzed him further asking why. He said he couldn't. I asked what had happened to the critter then. He told me he had set it free. I didn't get it. Don't get me wrong. I am sort of glad he didn't eat it. I just didn't comprehend just why he had turned the critter loose after priming him for the pot.

Melvin told me that he had hauled that possum around with him everywhere. He said that he had even begun talking to it, paying it more attention that he did any of his beagles. He would share his meals with it, throwing it extra scraps. He said he could not harm a pet and that is what it had become. You don't garnish your friends with taters and onions he told me. That just isn't right he spoke with conviction. I swear I saw him tear up just talking about that possum. I told him not to ride any chickens around in that cage or he would have to give up chicken footsies. We both laughed. I am confident that possum is out there somewhere grinning and missing his friend too.

Some Like it Hot

First thing that popped into my mind when I used this title was Marilyn Monroe standing over a subway grid and her skirt blowing about as she takes in the cool breeze. It's the wrong movie, even though I cherish that visual. That scene happened in the *Seven Year Itch*, not in *Some Like it Hot*. In *Some Like It Hot*, Marilyn's character, Sugar, confides that she has sworn off male saxophone players, who have stolen her heart in the past and left her with "the fuzzy end of the lollipop". Tony Curtis and Jack Lemmon, in drag, co-star.

Humor me. Nostalgia can often be the ramblings of an ole coot, stumbling and bumbling his way to an eventual point to be made. If you've read my memoirs previously you should expect this approach. I hardly ever draw straight lines. Nostalgia has a beginning though. The Lord gave you two ears and one mouth for a reason. Listen twice as much as you talk and perhaps, you'll learn something, especially when your elders speak of those days long passed. I qualify as a candidate for those senior discounts. I get the perks now, a rite of passage thing.

Hot spicy food and seasoning is an acquired, if not an inherited taste. For me possibly it is a combination of both. As a kid, I didn't eat hot spicy food, not unless dared. Don't dare me to do anything or you'll come up on the short end of the stick; or maybe I will, depending on how stupid the dare is. Mama always had a fondness for hot food. She particularly loved hot garden peppers. Papa mostly grew banana and bell peppers in his vegetable garden but had a couple of cayenne pepper plants specifically for her. I think she was the only person in the immediate family at that time that ate them. During our 1959 west coast driving trip to Uncle Floyd and Aunt Jane Bowie's home in California, our Pacific coast relative introduced jalapenos to her taste buds. It was love at first bite, a sizzling and steamy hit. I was only six, too young to be interested in anything green and vegetable related.

Upon our return I think she asked Papa to add jalapeno plants to his spring planting. I don't think they were readily available on the east coast side of the country. Of course, back then what did a tiny tike like me really know or care about a garden, other than playing in freshly plowed dirt. Throwing dirt clods could be fun until Papa caught wind of our exploits and chased us out. He did not take kindly to us throwing his good dirt out of his garden spot. Also, there is just something special about newly tilled dirt between barefoot toes.

Cut off jeans, barefooted and shirtless, it just didn't get much better. Back then we didn't have to worry about the dreaded fire ants. They hadn't arrived yet. Once the rows had been laid out, plants planted and seeds sowed, our playground was basically off limits. Trespassers would be prosecuted. That is if Papa caught us red handed and could run us down. Digressing, but nostalgia is just that. In this case it is my choice how I tell it. When you write yours, you are in charge to do as you wish. For now, it is my rules, my way.

We did a return two-week road trip to California in the 1960's, June timeframe, taking a northern route there, and a southern route back. This time, as a teenager, I remembered more details. On our way back and through south Texas we skirted the Mexican border. If memory serves me, we were in El Paso. Riding along the streets we could see warehouses here and there. Possibly we were lost, which was not uncommon with Daddy behind the wheel. There were five of us, my parents, Cousins Billy Joe and Leila Campbell and me of course.

I had taken a Spanish class in school that year and could speak and read just enough to be marginally dangerous. I began reading signs on warehouse murals, trying to assist in pointing Daddy a way out of town. I stumbled onto one advertisement on the side of a building. Apparently canned jalapenos were stored there. One catch though, it was just across the border. Mama said she wanted some to take back, cravings kicking in. Daddy and Billy Joe, minus me, crossed the border to see if they could purchase some. This was a different time. Crossing the border wasn't a complicated process. I decided to stay put and protect the women folk, having had my fill of border crossings after we had walked from San Diego into the outskirts of Tijuana. The little excursion had scared '*the you know what*' out of me. I had never been happier to set foot back on American soil.

Not too long after they had ventured into Mexico, they returned, each carrying a case of canned jalapenos. This should be enough to last mama for a while, given she was the only consumer at the time. I am not sure what triggered me to begin eating hot pepper. I cannot remember that *tah-dah* moment. It just happened. As I began having my very own garden, I always included cayenne and jalapeno pepper plants. I had so many I pickled peppers in jars of vinegar. Peter Piper did not pick them though. I did. Eventually it was not a rarity for me to have hot peppers as garnish with meals, including breakfast. My obsession had worsened more so than Mama's I dare admit. I soon began seeking out the ultimate hot peppers to plant in my garden.

I stumbled onto the habanera; way hotter than any pepper I had ever experienced. Green they were a firestorm and formidable challenge. Allow them to ripen to a yellow or red color, there was no contest. On a dare of course from one of my whacko friends, I bit into one, realizing way too late that I should have declined the dare. My lips, tongue, and anything it had come in touch with paid the price tenfold for such reckless stupidity. Never letting them see you sweat had never been more difficult to pull off. The experience was painfully pleasurable, just realizing I had survived the consumption ordeal.

I ran across a posting in the local newspaper boasting of a new habanera-carrot salsa recipe. Using a food processor, it required the following ingredients: carrots, tomatoes, onion, bell pepper, cilantro, lemon juice, garlic and one lone ripened habanera pepper. Add corn or black beans if desired after completing the blending process. Oh man, this was the best dip with chips. Not to stop there, I would often add a second habanera pepper for those liking to kick it up a notch. Some could not handle either version, one or two peppers. For the ultimate mother lode, add a third pepper. Only I could eat that version. Most of time I had to curb it back to one pepper per batch.

As an adult I earned the reputation of eating hot food, making blazing fire hot BBQ sauce, concocting hot spicy soups and chili beans. Contrary to belief, I don't want everything I eat spiced with hot sauce. I'm selective but that doesn't prevent people from always buying me every hot sauce imaginable for birthdays and Christmas. You can only eat so much of this. Bottles and jars don't empty as quickly as steak sauce, catsup or mustard. Soon the pantry was overflowing with every brand imaginable.

Friends Dave and Hilda gave me a jar of Dave's Hot Sauce once. It wasn't his brand, a novelty of course, his name being the label's brand. Dave had moved to Oklahoma but Hilda, with her mom in tow, had delivered the birthday present to us when we still resided in Greenwood. I sampled a mere droplet to test it. Hell had plenty of fury as delivered by whoever Dave might be. Never let them see you sweat. I manned up, eventually commenting how good it was, once I regained the ability to talk. Hilda later decided she would try it, pouring a tad too much into a spoon, inserting it into her mouth before I could stop her. We thought we were going to have to take her to the emergency room. It was painful to witness her agony. Her mom could not believe I had allowed her to taste it. Allowances couldn't be rendered because it had happened so quickly. Recovery time wasn't quick. Dave's Hell Sauce could only be used a few tiny drops at a time for any sort of seasoning thereafter. That bottle lasted forever.

Another story comes to mind. Wife Judy and I had stopped for breakfast at a mom and pop dinner on our way back from Lake Greenwood to Myrtle Beach, having visited the Sammy and Judy Cannon for the weekend. We like trying new places as opposed to food chain establishments. A gent checking out had a large Styrofoam cup of grits. He paused to pop the lid and apply a generous portion of Texas Pete to them. When asked, he said for us to try it, adding that we would like it. We did. Now we cannot eat grits without it, always asking for hot sauce after breakfast is served in diners. Tabasco or Texas Pete, most southern waitresses ask. Texas Pete please; there is a difference. We will settle for Tabasco if it is the only choice. I am not an oatmeal or cream of wheat guy so I'm not sure if it's applicable to either. Northerners, you decide.

Chicken wings, I like mine as hot as they come. When I order off any menu, I tell the waitress to bring the hottest thing you have. This is often met with disbelief or stern warnings. They come with names like three-mile-high, ass kicking wing sauce, colon cleaner, spontaneous combustion, dumb-ass hot, and rectal rocket fuel to name some of the more creative ones off the shelves and at some restaurants. Dave even has Gourmet Insanity sauce as well as Gourmet Hurt'in Habanera now.

The best I have found in any of the chain fast food places has to be the Insane Sauce @ Zaxby's. Every time I order it, I am met with stares of disbelief, *are you insane*? I'm quizzed if I have ever had it before or am I sure I want it. One guy even wanted to shake my hand saying he had never seen anyone order it before. He confessed he had tried just a bite once and would never do it again. Enclosed with the wings in the car on the short ride home will open your sinuses, a bit of heaven from my tilted perception.

Memories are often etched in stone and in this case singed in what remains of the liner of my stomach. Some do like it hot but be mindful, many do not. Sweat beading up on your forehead or top of your head can equate to a pleasurable experience if turning up the heat to your palette was intended. My sister-in-law said she does not understand why I don't suffer from chronic heartburn and acid reflux. I rarely ever do. I am more apt to have acid reflux from drinking milk before I go to bed than any hot stuff. I think back on my Mama. I have seen the sweat beading up on her, her flapping her tongue about, seemingly fanning the flames, but it never slowed her down. Her mantra, as mentioned numerous times, *I'll eat anything that doesn't eat me first* and, in this case, set your innards to blue blazes. Bless her heart. If she were here today, she would nod her agreement. Hell's hot peppers reside with her in heaven now. If rain pouring down on a sunny day is the sign of the devil beating his wife, then, maybe, those hot summer days with the temperature reaching a heat index of 113 is mama sharing habaneras with the Lord.

The following is from an interview I gave that was posted in the Charleston paper, The Post and Courier.

Lowcountry Chileheads talk hot habits

By Teresa Taylor The Post and Courier, Wednesday, September 17, 2008

Peppers, the hotter the better, I always say! Growing up in Abbeville and now living in Murrells Inlet, I inherited my love for hot peppers honestly. My grandparents, having a large garden, always included a variety of hot peppers, mostly cayenne and jalapenos. I carried on the tradition as an adult with gardens of my own, expanding the varieties to include Anaheim, Tabasco, Thai-Hot, Serrano and the ultimate butt burner, Habanero.

I've witnessed my mom popping hot peppers in her mouth, glowing red-faced with beads of sweat bleeding from her forehead, then smiling as she popped another in her mouth followed by a good old chunk of homemade Southern cornbread (not that sweet-cake flavored stuff), the real deal.

So, what do I do with these peppers? Eating them freshly plucked from the plant along with any meal (including breakfast) is a requirement of my diet. Pickling the cayenne and jalapenos in vinegar and a mason jar help me survive the winter months. Making a habanera-carrot or cucumber salsa is always a crowd-pleaser. One habanera is used if the general population is partaking, two are used if everyone likes it real hot and a third is added if I'm the only consumer. I always freeze at least one Ziploc of habaneras to have them readily available in the non-growing seasons. Just wash them, freeze them whole and grab them when you need them.

Tabasco peppers are used for our pepper sauce. Just add vinegar to about 30 or so yellow-red peppers in one of those funny little glass pepper sauce pourers and pour over your turnip greens, collards, cabbage or whatever else tickles your fancy. Replenish the vinegar as needed, keep refrigerated. Use your imagination for the other varieties of hot peppers as they can be interchanged at will. Hot peppers are hot peppers!

Y'all keep it hot out there and remember what goes in the mouth will always go south.

Thomas Allen Winn

Chef Tomas, Habanero Extraordinaire

Waffling in America

The buffet is open. Eating out can be quite adventurous, often entertaining, or just plain frustrating and irritating. The following is just a smorgasbord of memorable events in no particular order. Let's start with the obvious and work our way through the buffet line. The most interesting people tend to end up in Waffle Houses, sort of like that middle of the night crowd walking the aisles at Wal-Mart. So, we're at the National Square Dance Convention in Charlotte. Dancers must eat after all those squares and rounds. Plus, it's priceless going out afterwards dressed in our gaudy attire. The waitress seemed to be struggling with our order, taking it and eventually delivering it. Obviously, all had been lost in translation or she couldn't read her own scribbling. After considerable send-backs and approaching two hours in the booth, we asked her if this was her first day. She responded, "*Lordy no, worked here nineteen years.*" Bless her heart, just saying. Our busboy was almost as entertaining, possibly even her inbred love child. He seemed to be fanatical about mopping and mopped the same little spot over and over while he kept a watchful eye on a couple of guys and a dog outside. Out of the blue he turns to us and says, "*Whatever you do, don't look that dog straight in the eyes.*" Then he just walked away. Words of wisdom have never seemed weirder.

Another Waffle House, this time in Atlanta, nametag said Floe. She seemed to be in her very own Waffle World, dancing about, singing in a not so pitch perfect tone while stressing and talking about hurricane Ike brewing in the Gulf. Oddly, we were on our way to Branson, Missouri after just leaving the Grand Strand. Maybe Floe was offering us a premonition. The next day after we arrived in Branson, what was left of Hurricane Floe passed through our tourist community toppling huge trees and knocking out the power in the area? We slept through it. We did not realize it until the next morning when we ventured from our condo and saw the aftermath. We were informed at Shirley's Diner in Kimberly City that it had hit. Our resort was one of the few places in Branson that had power due to backup generators. Go figure. We leave the beach after a near miss with hurricane Hanna and fall victim to hurricane Ike in Missouri eight hours after we arrive. The community across the lake from our resort remained without power for five days. Glad we were not in Kansas.

Waffle House, Tennessee, Boo is our overly tattooed waitress. It says it right there on her name tag, Boo. Waffle House franchises must hire wannabe singers or karaoke outcasts. Boo belted out anything from Patsy Cline to Taylor Swift and other stuff we did not even recognize in her bluegrass twangy voice. In ten second intervals she would just bust a gut laughing; at what we had no idea. She was a wealth of information (TMI to be exact.) She warned us to stay clear of the leftover milkshakes, unsure what that meant until she explained. One had already done a powerful number on her, nature calling way too many times on her shift. She graphically shared her stomach woes. I had to ask myself, why I would order a leftover milkshake.

That's Aunt Lillian's booth...

Stewarts in Anderson, South Carolina, is a mom and pop local hangout with the Waffle House-Huddle House basic floor plan. Once upon a time I think it was a Waffle House. This was Aunt Lillian's favorite place. They even had a designated booth for her. Strangers were eyed suspiciously. The locals, everyone in Stewarts, including the cooks and wait staff, would turn their heads and follow your every move. It almost seemed orchestrated. Eventually after accompanying Aunt Lillian numerous times, we were accepted and ignored. Then, we could join in on the stares at any newcomers. We dearly miss Aunt Lillian, sharing a booth with the angels now. Stewarts is no more.

Aunt Lillian with Granny (Ruby) Bowie

Lizard Lady of Mount Pleasant, South Carolina…

We were at this restaurant overlooking the waterway, amazing scenery, a romantic setting, just kicking back and enjoying the ambiance. A nice enough looking couple were just seated at the table next to us. An appetizer resembling a backyard ring toss had been delivered by the waitress and positioned center stage of their table. Stacked high on the peg was breaded and fried calamari rings. The lady plucked one from the peg and looped it with her tongue. The entire thing vanished inside the open cavity of her mouth in one clean motion, freezing us in an awe inspired gaze. The gent unfazed by her feat plucked one and ate it quite boringly. She worked her way down the peg, the rings becoming larger, her technique remaining the same. Nostalgic anomaly, something you just don't forget.

Free styling in Savannah, Georgia…

Let's stick with the calamari theme. Judy and I accompanied by her sisters Norma, and Charlotte, brother-in-law Jerry, were vacationing in Savannah. We were taking in the sights and southern charm, strolling along the river front. Darting in and out of shops can awake one's appetite. We were assessing various posted menus, having not yet settled on a venue. A waitress outside one of the eateries sported a tray offering samples to try. Judy and I passed when offered and continued our trek. Behind us Norma, Charlotte and Jerry, not ones to turn down free eats apparently, plucked samples from the tray and plopped them in their mouths.

Judy caught sight of this and promptly stated, "I can't believe any of you would eat…" and before she could finish her sentence, they each began instantly reacting to her comment. Jerry plucked the sample from his mouth and promptly placed it in a nearby trash receptacle. Charlotte spat hers into a napkin, looking wild eyed, still unsure what she had just tasted. Norma, *'bless her heart'*, and to our embarrassment, began spewing the contents of her mouth onto the quaint cobblestone streets of Savannah. Judy and I picked up our pace to distance ourselves from the despicable display unfolding behind us. There is something not so appealing about a woman gagging loudly while spitting the contents of her mouth onto the street among other tourists.

Almost in unison they asked us what they had just put in their mouths. We informed them they had just sampled calamari. "What?" We clarified it in terms even they should understand, telling them they had just tried fried squid. They thought it was onion rings. You can't make this stuff up.

Tell me this isn't alligator...

In-laws, outlaws, branch kin, all can be easy sport and quite entertaining, especially since I am a seasoned instigator. No brag, just fact. A couple of carloads of my *in-lawed* family were partaking of supper in a local mom and pop spot near Six Mile, South Carolina. Brenda, another sister, had picked the location. Various appetizers had been ordered. I tend to follow in my mama's footsteps and will eat anything that doesn't eat me first. Some say I always order weird stuff off the menu. I just like trying new food items. Alligator is not a new food item for me. It's just not something you often see on an upstate menu where no gator population exists. But there it was, Gator Bites on the menu. I ordered them of course.

Upon their arrival they were passed about along the other appetizer selections. Most of the group passed on trying them. Charlotte, oh yes, the very same sister-in-law, popped one in her mouth. Realizing others were given her astounded looks, she asked what she had just tried. Brenda informed her that I had selected gator bites as an appetizer. Charlotte turned and looked in my direction and said, *"Tommy, tell me this isn't alligator."* To that I replied, *"Charlotte, it isn't alligator."* Judy elbowed me and asked why I had told her that. I replied, *"I just told what she asked me to tell her; that it wasn't gator."*

Martin Saylor's Steak and Biscuits...

Mama and Daddy, Jerry and Norma Solomon, Martin and Mary Saylor, Judy and I were on our way to Orlando, Disney World in the cross hairs. This would be our first stop before heading on a Bahamas cruise. My parents' travel van was our transportation for the ten plus hours drive. We preferred snacking instead of stopping for meals, making the trip quicker. Everybody brought a little taste of everything along. Martin began retrieving homemade biscuits and passing them to those who wanted one. Judy was the only one who passed on them. Jerry was munching down on one and commented how it was the best steak and biscuit it had ever had. To that Martin informed him that it was venison. Instant replay, Savannah, I had never seen mouths emptied so quickly. Jerry spat his into his napkin. At least this time Norma didn't spew the content onto the floor of the van. Deer steak between a biscuit, yummy, more for me I say.

Honey, you sure is thirsty...

The Singletons and we were having dinner at the now defunct Captain's Table seafood establishment in Murrells Inlet. No, I don't think it went out of business because of something we did. None of our relatives had spewed their food onto the table or floor. The water glasses were sort of tiny though, so goes the story retold. After about what must have been half dozen stops and refills at our table, the waitress finally commented to Judy, "*Honey you sure is thirsty*' in the gruffest southern smoker's voice. We all howled like a pack of wolves at that observation. I think after our little visit Judy appeared on a warning poster in the kitchen, the woman who drinks way too much water.

Potty Perfect…

Square dancing corners, fellow Merry Mixer's Roy and Mary Whitt often traveled with us to various events. Roy, heeding nature's call, visited the bathrooms quite frequently, most of the time before any of the rest of us did. He had a unique rating system, announcing his findings once he rejoined the group. He missed his calling. He should have been a restaurant inspector. Using that visual, Roy could have hung a rating shingle at the bathroom door entrances. Here is one more Roy story. While at the Flight Deck in Lexington, S.C., he cleaned his plate, no evidence of a morsel. He then asked the waitress for a to-go box. We busted a gut because he said it so seriously. Oh yeah, never allow Roy behind the wheel. He tends to drive in the direction that he is looking. That can be problematic when he is distracted by something left or right of the roadway. We love you, Roy.

MMM…

If one is going to participate in the drive thru option, one must also be prepared for the inevitable three **'M's"**. No one can appreciate the significance more so than the natural born klutz. Stand up, state your name…My name is Tom and yes, I am a recovering klutz. **MMM** can result where fast food is involved, or it can possibly just happen while eating in general for those prone to clumsiness. **M**eal **M**anagement **M**ishaps can strike at any given time and without warning. For example, Styrofoam cups with supposedly attached plastic lids can misfire when you least expect it. I had just retrieved my large size filled with sweet tea from the drive thru window while on my commute to work where I would be greeting visitors. While driving I reached for the cup in its convenient console cup holder. The lid popped off in reaction to my apparent manly grip. The content spewed onto my lap and khaki pants. I was now sporting a huge wet circle on my crotch giving the appearance I had bladder control issues. I was a short distance from arriving at work. No way was it going to dry in time. Even if it had somehow dried, it was going to leave an obvious stain. I prepared my disclaimer statement.

Same scenario, same outcome, with a bowl of chili this time; my peers and visiting customers were present to witness me flipping the bowl of chili into to my lap in a restaurant during lunch. Crotch stains prevailed once again on khaki pants. Maybe I should stop wearing khakis. These types of accidents never occur when I am at home and can change. Similar embarrassment, when water splatters on your crotch while washing your hands just before you exit the men's restroom. Most think it happened at the urinal. Men, as rumored by the female population, are labeled as inaccurate pointers when it comes to their bathroom visits. For those who squat, it isn't that we can't aim. Sometimes it just spews left or right instead of where we are pointing. That's my story and I'm sticking to it. And yes, I did waver a bit on the premise of my **MMM**, but sometimes you just must go where it takes you.

Hooters, my brother-in-law's favorite stop for a toasted cheese sandwich and curly fires should come with a warning, especially for Jerry. I treated him to a visit while he was at the beach during our brother-in-law weekend. The curly fry injured the back of his throat. How, I have no clue, but he could barely swallow afterwards. He said it had happened several times. Possibly he should focus more on his aim and consumption and less on the Hooter gals. Just saying.

You did what....

And another thing, if you're too cheap and frugal to order a drink from the menu, please just settle for water. Don't order extra lemons and then squeeze them into you water, add sugar and call it homemade lemonade. Yep, we had a friend who did exactly that. You might remember him from the Perfect Square's story earlier. Then there was our friend, Hilda who apparently thought I was the official beverage taster while on our Bahamas cruise. She always ordered diet coke and they always seemed to bring her regular coke. For whatever reason, she began asking me to taste it before she took a sip. It caught on because the waiter began plopping her glass down in front of me to do the needful before passing it to her.

Customers from a Mexico facility were visiting out facility. Lunch time arrived and my boss asked *"Where would you guys like to grab a bite for lunch? How about Mexican?"* He follows that up with, *"What do you think about them wanting to build that wall on the border?"* I know you didn't say that boss...

Years ago, we (wife and I) were at a little mom and pop spot between Rock Hill and Charlotte. The waitress took our drink order. Over the next thirty minutes or so she stopped by our table numerous times to ask if everything was okay. Finally, I told her, *"Yes the lemon was a nice touch for our water. Was she ever going to bring us our meals?*" She had forgotten to place our order with the kitchen.

That is not what I ordered…

On a cruise, Judy ordered chicken and when her meal was delivered the Cornish hen was belly up, legs in the air. Not going to happen, she ended up ordering something else. Judy, different cruise, I can't remember exactly what she ordered or thought she was ordering but accenting her plate was a pink crawfish. She screamed there was a bug on her plate. She reordered of course. Judy for breakfast usually orders bacon and egg whites and asks for both well done. More times than not, she ends up sending it back because it isn't cooked done enough for her. Now we help her and the waitress by stating, *"Burn it and if the smoke alarm goes off then it's ready."* She was eating blackened before blackened was cool and yes, the home smoke detector was often the timer.

King of the Wild Frontier…

Hot Fish Club, Murrells Inlet, South Carolina…Judy ordered decaf. We hear the waiter in the background singing D-cafe…D-cafe coffee to the tune of the Davy Crocket theme song.

Don't Do This with a BB Gun

Okay, rant time, sort of, so bear with me. I am old. I have earned the rite to rant. I grew up in a time when kids could be kids. We cherished that experience. Taking a line from that song in *Peter Pan*, most kids stood by their convictions, '*I won't grow up.*' As a juvenile it is our rite to experience the good and the bad, to make countless mistakes and have our fair share of boo-boos, as too many parents refer to our injuries. I hate that term by the way. Boo-Boo is Yogi's little buddy, not a skinned bloody knee. Getting a bloody injury was cool. Well, it was after you got past the painful part. It made us tough. Every kid I knew had the scars to prove it. We wore them proudly. That scene in the movie *Jaws* had nothing on us. We perfected it. That could have been any of us instead of Quint, Hooper and Brody sitting around in the cabin of the ship comparing their various scars while waiting the return of the Great White.

Kids of the fifties and sixties were adventurous. We were hardened, invincible and pert near bullet proof. Do not get me started on play guns. That is an entirely different rant. If we fell, we laughed, brushed ourselves off and got back up, even if our knee or elbow hurt like heck. Inflicting pain on our backyard buddies was expected. This was not bullying. It was horsing around with our friends. Did we get ticked off at one another? Sure, we did, all the time. That is why they call it payback. You must get even. The one who had done you wrong expected it, knew it was coming, didn't like it, but would take it; or might just one up you again. Sometimes the vicious circle could be endless. We did not care. It was called having fun.

Of course, we had those fragile little kids, whiners, the ones who could not take it or dish it out. Every era has them. They are the tattle-tellers, the snitches, the ones who cry if you touch them or look at them mean. We knew how to deal with them. They were still part of our neighborhood backyard gatherings. And yes, as depicted in numerous sitcoms or movies, they did get picked last. They knew it was coming, as did we. They expected to get picked last, but they got picked and remained part of our group. Leaders and followers and all those in the middle coexisted. We did not kill anyone. We worked through our differences. Sure, we teased, picked on and pushed around the weaker ones. I should know. I sure caught my fair share of it. I was little and nerdy, a long cry from the leader of the pack. I did my best to stay close to the middle of the pack though, safety in numbers.

We picked sides for most of our outdoor activities. Yes, as I've stated numerous times; we preferred playing outdoors. Inside was equivalent to solitary confinement. The team leader always had his or her favorites and it did not necessarily have anything to do with skill set. Unlike today, there were actual winners and losers of every event. We did keep score when scoring was part of the game. If you got whipped by a hundred to nothing, so be it. Second place was just last place. There was no consolation prize. No one's ego was permanently damaged. We were not traumatized for the rest of our lives, requiring adult therapy.

Wrestling and tussling were common terms and we pushed both to the limit. Jumping off stuff was something we did with vigor; just as climbing up things to get to the top. Landing on your pals, knocking the breath out of them was a frequent event. Sucking air, they would get over it. We stuck our hands in places we shouldn't have, but we learned by doing so not to do it again. Rocks hurt when you are hit by one, as does being plummeted by apples, pears, walnuts, snowballs, firecrackers, and bottle rockets. It still did not stop us, nor did our parents. They could not watch us every single second. Heck, they didn't want to, leaving us free rein to do pretty much anything we wanted to do. That's why they call it the great outdoors, the playground for those not so faint at heart. Swapping shoulder punches until one gave, so what. Pouncing on somebody's back when they least expected it; I got you before you got me. Kneeing someone's knees from behind, funny stuff, unless you're on the receiving end, and even then, the receiver often chuckles loudly, but plans the payback.

Sticks can put out an eye, but that did not stop us from using them. I don't recall having any friends that wore eye patches. If they had, it would have been considered cool, pirate like. Tripping was an art form. School hallways were specifically tailor-made for tripping unsuspecting targets. Ears were there for thumping, some more than others. There was nothing more painful than that pinch to the back of your arm. You weren't good at it unless you could leave a black and blue bruise. Messing up a guy's hair was fair game. Unfortunately, it did not work on crew cuts, but you could still give them a head-nookie. No pain, no gain, providing you were the instigator of course and we all were.

All balls could be used as weapons if need be. If it could be thrown it could also be thrown at someone. We sure loved those gravel driveways too. There was nothing better than throwing a handful of gravel straight into the air and then everyone running for the hills, hoping not to be a victim of gravity. It was just a deviation to playing dodge. I dare you. I double dare you. I even triple dare you. All challenges were met unless you were a total wimp. I met all dares. I embraced them, encouraged them. I was cheap entertainment, always up for a good dare. I still am.

Call me Tommy Dangerously. I had a reputation to live up to and did so quite well.

It was always fun to visit friends who had stuff that you didn't. Cousin Billy had a three-speed bike. I had only ever owned a one speed. It would go as fast as my legs could make it go, no extra gears to assist. There is a difference. Knowing where the brakes are is a critical detail when it comes to riding a multi-speed bicycle. Remembering that fact in an emergency can save your butt. Spinning that peddle backwards before crashing into the ditch and then bending the front tire and frame of your cousin's Christmas bike is unforgivable. Being able to outrun and out maneuver that same cousin on foot is priceless.

Rants and ramblings completed. Now I get to the BB gun debacle. This would have been when I was a mere teenager. My friend, Derrell Burdette, had this thing for guns. No, not cap guns or dart guns, not even water guns. He owned BB guns, something my parents forever said I was too young to have. My reputation, tarnished as it was, prevented me from owning a weapon that used BB's or pellets. My parents were smart. They could visualize the many ways I would probably misuse one of these projectile launchers. That is why it was good to have friends in high places. Derrell's parents apparently thought he was mature and responsible.

He had a BB pistol. Now, how cool was that? He now operates his own security system and teaches people how to shoot guns and obtain their concealed weapon license. Even back then, he went through the brief training orientation with me. Boring, I just wanted to shoot it. He instructed me how to load the BB's, aim down the site and shoot. Lined up were an assortment of bottles and jars. Let the shooting begin. He hit them every time. I didn't. I would have probably fared better throwing rocks at the motionless targets. I was an accomplished rock thrower. I eventually hit one or two, many BB's later though. What happens on South Main stays on South Main if I ever wanted to shoot it again.

Sometime later I was at another friend's house. Roger Davis, two years older than me, had a BB gun. He lived near the Abbeville Airport. Roger had one of those rifle style BB guns. He asked me if I had ever shot one. Big headed, I boasted I was quite good at it. Roger didn't shoot at unmoving targets though. He was into bird shooting. Any type of bird was fair game. This required stalking our prey. I had never stalked birds, but I didn't tell Roger. He quickly shot and killed a blue jay. He defended his kill by saying they were mean birds. He then gave me the gun, showing me how to cock the lever back to ready it for the next shot. The spring action was tough, but then again, Derrell had a BB pistol. You didn't cock a pistol. As hard as I tried, I couldn't cock it. Roger did it for me and again demonstrated the technique. He apparently had muscles that I didn't have yet.

He nailed another bird, a cat bird, a mockingbird, another bird deemed mean by the accomplished marksman. I'd never met any mean birds and now had witnessed two being slain. I did know those cat birds would dive bomb you if you were close to their nest. It was my turn again. Roger didn't cock it for me, saying I needed to do it. After a couple of failed attempts, I utilized my innovative skills. I rested the barrel end of the gun on the top of my barefoot while pushing down on the lever pump. Roger wouldn't let me stick the barrel in the ground saying dirt would clog the barrel. Smiling, beaming with delight, this technique appeared to be working much better. Catching me by surprise, the spring sprung back into place. Apparently, I was a tad trigger happy, my finger grasping the trigger as the lever closed shut. I was suddenly *Lucas McCain* from one of my favorite westerns, *The Rifleman*.

Instead of nailing one of those alleged mean birds, the BB discharged into the top of my bare foot, breaking the skin, and lodging quite nicely I must add. Remember, as mentioned earlier, one must get past the pain and never let them see you sweat. I remembered back to that time I was popping firecrackers with Ronny Smith in front of my Papa's house. Ronny lived two houses up the street from my grandparents. I had always placed the firecracker somewhere and then had lit the fuse. Ronny was lighting and tossing them. Not to be outdone, I did too. Beware of the short or fast fuse. I had taken the firecracker back even with my shoulder, ready to throw it, when it exploded in my hand and next to my ear. My hand was hurting and throbbing, my ear ringing. I smiled, walked away and went inside. Only behind closed doors did I scream and cry, begging Granny to make it stop hurting.

Back to my embedded BB…I exited the shooting range, but not before digging the BB from the top of my now bleeding foot. I remained cool, calm, and collected; at least until I got inside and out of view. Let the crying and sniffling begin. Peroxide, Mecuricome, and a Band-Aid later, I was almost as good as new. Sorry, for those of you that did not live back in the forgotten time. Mecuricome was in every medicine cabinet. It was dark red, an antiseptic containing mercury. Before the proliferation of over the counter first aid medicines and FDA regulations, Mecuricome was used worldwide and in Abbeville to treat minor cuts, scrapes, sores, and other external infectious conditions. The liquid was only sold in tiny bottles and one application by Q-tip was extremely effective.

I did not mention how this orangey stuff burned when applied. The adult administering it quickly blew on your wound once it had been dabbed on with the Q-tip. First though, peroxide was used to clean minor cuts, scrapes and sores before using the Mericuricome. If the injury bubbled, it was said to be clearing the infection and dirt from it. Oh yeah, a special touch, Mamas would often kiss the Ban-Aid after applying it, to make it better. I was not sure if the Ban-Aid or Mama had these super healing powers.

I never did own a BB gun as a kid. Come to think of it, I am not sure I ever fired another one after that foot episode. The exploding firecracker in my hand did not deter me from having a fondness for fireworks though. A cousin next door would eventually receive a pellet rifle from Santa. He was the same one who got the three-speed bike for Christmas that I crashed in the ditch. I decided to leave well enough alone. I couldn't outrun a speeding pellet if things went terribly wrong. I miraculously survived my childhood, living quite recklessly I must add but we all did back then. Kids race through their childhood today and become adult's way too early. What a waste? Take it from an adult. It's not what it's cracked up to be. What I wouldn't give to be back in the day playing king of the hill, when winning was expected, tolerated and built character. I can honestly admit I don't miss Mericuricome though. I am glad it is a banned miracle cure today. You can still kiss my Band-Aid and make it all better any time you feel impelled to do so.

Roger Davis November 4, 1951 – February 17, 2018

Roger the Mean Bird Slayer

A little side note, I did not know back then what BB stood for, but I do now. Some think it stands for ball bearing, but this is incorrect. Back in the day of the original BB guns, BB sized lead shots were used. Their size was midway between B and BBB size; thus, BB it became.

Bugamania

Why do most boys tend to have a fascination with bugs? Well, at least back in my day they did. Then again, that was a time before technology intervened. It sure seems like too many kids have a natural fear of insects now. My grandson when at the ripe old age of thirteen freaked out when a wasp or bee did a fly by. I did not even flinch. Still don't. Bugs are as much a part of our world as any other living creatures; probably more so. Okay. I know you are rolling your eyes thinking here we go with one of those "back when I was a kid" stories. Yep. You were right to think that way but then again isn't that what I'm supposed to be writing about here? My memories are not necessarily yours but maybe mine will trigger yours. If it does, my deed is done.

Bugs were cheap entertainment for us back in the fifties and sixties. I still enjoy a good bug encounter. No. Fire ants are not good bug encounters; not unless you are flooding a mound with water or gasoline or lowering the lawn mower blade on top of them. Sometimes a quick kick of their ant hill will do just to let them know you are there. Fire ants are a nuisance and are not representative of the bugs of my time. I know what you're thinking again, and no, this is not a movie trailer, *The Bugs that Time Forgot.* My bugs were fun bugs. We had unique ways of dealing with them. Reader beware though…my memories are about to become quite graphic and bizarre. Flip the pages to the next chapter if you are not on board with insect carnage.

As I have stated time and time again, we had no video games, limited television channels, three to be specific. There was no such thing as paid television, cable or satellite networks. The only satellite we were familiar with was the very first one, Sputnik, launched into orbit by the Russians in 1957. We were glued to the skies at night hoping to catch a glimpse of the only moving object in the heavens. Now the sky is peppered with the lights of planes, satellites, and UFOs. In my day bugs proved to be an intricate part of our everyday lives and a constant source of entertainment. So, you ask how insects entertain us. I'm about to bring you up to speed on that little secret. Maybe you'll better appreciate the little creatures as value added once you hear how we utilized their existence. I say we but I can only speak for me I suppose.

Let us begin with spiders. There is nothing more fascinating than those wondrous eight-legged critters. Too often spiders are pegged as evil. They are quite interesting if you take the time to really observe their antics. Think about it. They build those webs for snaring their dinner, designs almost uncanny to comprehend. In almost every nook and cranny around our house, especially underneath the window shutters were spiders, lots of them. Most were big old brownish fat spiders patiently waiting there for their next meal. The game evolved from the imagination of boys. "Hi, I'm Tommy and I will be your server."

Grasshoppers were in abundant supply back when I was a kid. All you had to do was walk and rake your bare feet through the grass and stir them into a hopping frenzy. With a perfected technique we could capture a limitless supply. Soon it would be feeding time at the old website. No. We are not talking internet. We are talking spider net. We would place a grasshopper in a web and the wiggling critter sounded the dinner bell. The spider would scurry from its hiding place and spin its prey into a tightly woven cocoon. It was fascinating to watch, nature at its best. How cruel, you must be thinking. Not at all for this served two purposes. We thinned out the grasshopper population that could wreak havoc on vegetable and flower gardens, and we fed the hungry little spiders a square meal. That explanation was for you, not me. I did it because it was fun to watch.

To make the match more even we would sometimes capture a bumble bee or honeybee with a jar. We would open the lid setting it free in a collision course with the web. Sometimes it worked but more often the bee would bounce off and fly away to pollinate another day. When the web did snare mister bee, the attacking spider didn't always have an easy go at it. Equipped with a stinger the bee could fire back sending the spider back to its safe haven under the shutter. After the bee tired from struggling, the spider would return to deliver its deadly venom. This was our miniature version of gladiators in an arena. Cable TV has a show that pits critters against critters. Guess we were innovative and ahead of our time.

The wasp was another worthy opponent. Here we assumed the role of American Gladiator. Aluminum awnings appeared to be the perfect place for wasp to build their nest. We had one over every window and entranceway as was the style on the homes where I grew up. The game consisted of dirt clods, small rocks or sticks and the, 'I dare you' concept. The objective was to dare your opponent to knock down the wasp nest without getting swarmed or stung. Call us crazy...debatable I suppose, but we were just thrill-seeking kids on a summer's day. Technique not that important. Just toss the projectile and run like heck. Objective number two; if you struck your target and dislodged it onto the ground, you had to retrieve the nest as a trophy of sorts. If attacked while claiming it, run like there is no tomorrow. If stung, just keep running and cry for mercy. If you missed, you sent the next guy in to try. Thrower beware. The wasp would be on alert next time.

We had two kinds of wasp: the large red ones and the little yellow guinea wasp. Ironically the guinea wasp could deliver the most painful stings. Once we were lucky enough to claim our nest, we'd pluck out the wasp larvae and find an active ant hill where we'd sacrifice them to the horde of hungry ants. Every game had prey and predator, nature's enemies, nature's way of survival. We were just assisting nature and expediting the process. That was just another sort of humane explanation for you. It was just fun for us, last bug standing.

Doodlebugs, aka Antlions were critters involving our play. The Evans home across the street offered the perfect place to locate doodlebug houses. Doodlebugs tend to locate in cooler, shady spots under crawl spaces of houses or other overhanging shelters. All we had to do was search for soft loose dirt and there we would find the funnels made by the little phantom creatures. We had two diverse games we played. One, we could capture ants and place them in the funnel where, like the spider, the doodlebug would detect their presence. Instead of scurrying up the funnel to claim their food, the doodlebug would excavate a landslide forcing the ant to slide to its doom. The doodlebug would capture its prey with powerful mandibles.

Game number two required singing while stirring a stick inside the funnel to capture the doodle bug. It went something like this. We'd find a small swig and begin stirring the bottom of the funnel creating a dirt whirlpool. At the same time, we'd sing, *"Doodlebug, doodlebug come and get your bread and butter because your house is on fire."* We'd repeat this until we captured the doodlebug. We obviously thought the song was the key in the apprehension process. These were indeed strange little creatures. For some strange reason we didn't feed them to anything. After palming and poking them with our fingers for a few minutes we returned them to their home, our version of capture and release. I don't know why but we seemed to respect the little fellers.

Another favorite insect game…capture a Praying Mantis in a jar and feed them an assortment of grasshoppers and other bugs. These double-jointed little bugs were quite fun to watch. They would cock their heads this way and that before they snatched up their prey with those barbed claws. Introduce a bee to the jar, and like with the spider, this often evened the match. Mostly the predatory Praying Mantis won the battle though. Every bug deserved a proper meal.

June bugs captured and then their leg tied to a string offered up our version of a motorized flying kite, no batteries required. These large almost iridescent anomalies were harmless but made great pets on a leash.

They emitted a motorized sound when flying. Like the doodlebug, we did not feed them to other insects. We would eventually set them free. Some bugs deserved a second chance, I guess. I have no rhyme to our reason for our diverse treatment of some insects.

We had our nighttime bugs too. The lightning bugs were in abundant supply during my childhood. Spring and summer, they began appearing at dusk. Flickering yellow taillights signaled their presence. We would capture them by hand scooping them from midair. We would then place them in a mason jar, the lid punctured with air holes. A jar full would be our natural version of glow sticks. While we did not feed them to any awaiting predators, they would still fall prey to us. We would sever their twinkling tails and write or draw on the sidewalk with the florescent abdomens. We never considered killing bugs cruel or unjust, just a way to use our vivid imaginations and provide cheap entertainment.

Think about it. How many of you never hesitate to smash any form of flying, crawling or jumping insect? We even pay to have exterminators make our houses as bug free as possible. Don't begrudge us for having uniquely done the same thing. We just combined it as half sport, half game because we had nothing better to do with our time. Just think of us as an early form of exterminator who really enjoyed our job. We worked for free. I do not remember hearing cries for saving the bugs. And for the record, none of us, at least that I am aware of, ever stepped up our game and did the same thing to animals. And no, none of us ended up serial killers or scarred for life. We did not evolve into merciless bullies. Most of us ended up normal adults. Seek your own second opinions if you are not buying mine.

I'm Not Marlin Perkins
but I did stay in a Holliday Inn Express

I am an animal lover. I always have been. Come on now, forget about that last bug chapter. I rarely ever meet any furry critter that does not like me or me it. Sure, it sometimes takes some give and take to warm up to one another, especially if the other is one of those snippy little Chihuahua lap dogs. They too often come with an attitude, little dog syndrome. They aspire to be the big dog on the block. Don't get me wrong. I have owned plenty of the little buggers but that's different. Growing up with one and meeting one for the first time is not the same. Dogs are supposed to be man's best friend, right? Some dogs have not read that rule book apparently. Enough about dogs. I like dogs but my tale has nothing to do with dogs. It's just more of my ramblings setting up the next story in my life. There are plenty of other choices for pet owners. Kids must always explore his or her options.

1959, I was six when I got my first pooch, a boxer bulldog. I know. I said no more dog stories and I meant it. I can fill an entire chapter on nothing but doggy tales and probably will. Unlike kids of today, those seemingly fused to modern technology and the electronic world, oblivious to what exists outdoors, kids of my time were innovators and were always enthralled by God's wild kingdom. Nature's wonders captured our interest. It could have been something as simple as catching toad frogs or turning over the rocks in the local creek to find salamanders and crawfish. It was our cheap entertainment. The great outdoors held a special place in our hearts. Indoors was taboo, a necessary evil, to be avoided at all cost. Simpler times were the best of times. We actually acted our age. Kids were kids and adults allowed us to be what we were.

I learned at an early age that one cannot squander an opportunity to capitalize on one's misfortunes. Whiny, sad, and pouty faces can be parlayed to one's advantage if one knows how to play the game. I was indeed a gamer, the master of illusion and drama. Could I make a face or what? Mama and Daddy were easy marks much of the time to a shyster in training. You're never too young to become a snake oil peddler. Snake! Hold that thought. I'll get to that a little later.

My folks loved vacationing in Daytona Beach or maybe it was because Daddy loved going to the car races. Daytona International was his favorite track and we were there almost every Forth of July. A two-week stretch would ensure that we attended the Firecracker 400 race and all the practice and pole qualifying sessions. Mama loved the beach life, so everything worked out for the best. Racing, body surfing or digging in the sand was all good from my perspective. I was a kid. What difference did it really make, providing I was having fun? This one particular year fun took an ugly twist for the fun innovator. Playing 'I dare you' was a main component of our antics growing up. To this very day, please refrain from daring an old man to do anything. I will take you down. Anyone who knows me knows this. I would have been the Johnny character in the song, *The Devil Went Down to Georgia* by *Charlie Daniels*.

On this Florida trip I had met a kid in the pool and soon we became best beach buddies. I seem to recall that he was from North Carolina, not that it matters or impacts this story one way or the other. One afternoon down by the shuffleboard court and near the various gym-set type contraptions, he and I were playing a deviation of dare and follow the leader. We'd swing really high and then launch ourselves from the swings, the furthest winning the contest. We would also try to launch the other guy from their seat on the teeter-totter. The playground also came equipped with one of those push type merry-go-rounds; kid powered of course. We'd push it until we reached new centrifugal forces and then launch our little bodies onboard, spinning until we were dizzy and daffy. Soon our imaginative innovation kicked in as it always does. A low wall was nearby, so enters the dare.

'Bet you can't jump from here to there while it's moving,' dared my new best pal? Not one to back down, I did the only thing I knew to do and said, *'Betcha I can.'* I assumed my position and he gave it one running spin. Not too fast though as we weren't seasoned acrobats. The wall was maybe three or four feet away. The jump was a piece of cake for a nine-year-old with my agility. Timing is everything though. I judged the distance for several rounds gauging my leap as the speed slowed. Truth or dare, it was now or never, do or die. I finally went for it. Judgment gave way to misjudgment. I gave it my best try and fell just short, banging my left shin on the wall. It was one of those numbing blows that stings like heck. I smiled and turned, shrugging at my pal, blocking out the pain and showing him my game face. I was greeted with a face of pure terror. My new pal pointed towards my leg.

I glanced down to see my shin sliced open to the bone, not really bleeding that much, but gory just the same. Strangely, I was in no real pain but the sight of it launched me into a full crying panic attack; something you never intend to do in front of friends. This wasn't a skinned knee or bruise though. I deserved a pass. Luckily for me a man nearby had witnessed the Dare Olympics and my failed attempt to win the gold. He scooped me up in his arms and managed to understand my wailing directions to our ocean front cottage. I know you're lost. You asking what does this have to do with the wild kingdom? Hold your horses, a favorite term back in my day that makes no sense for a non-horse owner. Okay, it means I'm getting to the end of this tale.

I was rushed to the emergency room and ended up with a huge 'check mark shaped' wound, requiring twenty something stitches. Did I mention this happened on day two of our two-week summer vacation? With my leg now bandaged I couldn't get in the pool or ocean. I'm a nine-year-old kid at the beach for at least twelve more days. How sad is that. But wait! How does one milk this little situation? I had always wanted a pet alligator; I had asked numerous times during previous visits only to be turned down. Yes, in the early 60's Florida pet shops actually sold baby alligators. It was not illegal back in the day that time had forgotten.

Being an opportunist, I lobbied whiny, pouty, and pitiful behavior to become the proud owner of a twelve-inch baby alligator. Back in Abbeville I would be the envy of every kid in the neighborhood. Hindsight, I should have charged admission for my Abbeville Alligator Farm. Like all pets, they are fun for a while. My gator's new home was a plastic baby bathtub. I was allowed to keep Chopper in my room. Yep. That's what I named him. Daddy even made a wooden ramp so he could climb out of the water when he wanted to, still secure in the tub of course. Catching grasshoppers and crickets to feed him was fun. He also ate little pieces of raw hamburger. Chopper was named appropriately. More than once he latched onto one of my fingers. Apparently, he did not read the owner's manual. Never bite the hand that feeds you.

Let me tell you, an alligator living in stagnated water with rotting hamburger meat can really stink. Plus, Chopper had become somewhat of an escape artist. Too often we had to conduct an all-out room to room search party. Soon Mama banished him to the screened-in side porch. Even out there wasn't far enough away for her. I had my prize pet for about a year. The luster had long worn off. My gator met his final end when Papa painted the inside of our house. Poor Chopper, cooped up inside, succumbed to the paint fumes and bought the big one. See you later alligator. He was history.

Tropical fish were the next non-dog species on my agenda. My folks gave in to my having a ten-gallon aquarium. I played the whiny, pouty and fretful card over losing Chopper. Fish are fun to watch, at least for a while. It is a double-sided sword having live bearers though. It's quite traumatic during the live birthing process when Guppies, Swordtails, Platy or Mollies devour their own as quickly as they pop out. I had experienced one of nature's wonders, the process of having babies. At some point, from either over feeding or maybe neglect, or the fish reaching their life expectancy, they just eventually go belly up. Fish do love fish though. Feeding frenzies are not uncommon in the tank. Like all pets, the responsibility wears off and parents inherit the burden. After the last fish croaked the aquarium and stand was stored in the attic.

Enter Emily and George, without my parent's permission this time. How does it go? It is easier to ask for forgiveness than permission. That should be the kid's mantra. I had again used my modest allowance for the acquisition of two mice and a cage. The cage was equipped with one of those little spinning wheels. Mama could not believe I had brought rats into her house. Lucky for me, Mama was an animal lover too. Soon I had her literally eating out of my hand, handling, and petting George (the brown and white spotted male) and Emily (the larger white female).

I had no idea just how fond mice are of that little exercise wheel. Mice are nocturnal little creatures. That noisy wheel kept me up at night. Even back then I was a light sleeper. Mama and Daddy could hear it from their bedroom as well. We eventually banished the duo to the kitchen and opposite end of the house so we could catch some shuteye. George and Emily soon outgrew the confines of their little cage. Not to worry. I still had the fish-less ten-gallon aquarium that would make the perfect home for mice. We relocated them to the den and happily got rid of that rackety wheel. Next, I would experience a new eye-opening nature event, the miracle of mouse birth.

Emily soon became a mom. I witnessed the blessed event, five times to be exact. It was no longer a mystery where babies came from, at least not in the rodent community. George was not a happy daddy. We had to break out the cage again and separate him from Emily and the kids. We had a growing problem, seven now instead of two. My parents were not too thrilled. They had something to be thankful for though. Cousin Stevie had bought a four-foot Boa Constrictor at the same time I had purchased the mice. Guess what? Its favorite menu item was mice. Nope. Mine would not be served up. I did help him catch wild ones in feed barrels in a neighbor's barn. Wild mice are not the friendly sort, let me tell you. You better wear teeth proof impenetrable gloves. His snake finally died. From what, we never knew. I eventually gave my mice back to the pet store.

Let us follow the snake theme. Picture a young man of eighteen courting his soon to be bride. I experienced one of those episodes of cockiness, a need to show off and demonstrate just how fearless her future husband could be. While visiting her grandparents on the outskirts of Elberton,

Georgia, we took a stroll in the countryside. It was a gorgeous spring afternoon on their tiny farm. The jonquils were blooming. Black bumble bees were buzzing about, and birds were singing and chirping. Nature had made us aware of her presence. Sneaking a little kiss here and there, tuning out our surroundings for more important things on my immediate agenda, I failed to notice one of nature's darker, sinister creations.

Stretched out and sunning directly in our footpath was a four and half foot serpent. It looked to be a harmless black snake, like I knew my snake species back then. Fear not my damsel. I will protect you from the fearsome creature. I did not say anything like that, but I would have been better off taking that approach rather than springing into irrational action. I had watched Stan and Marlin countless times wrestle those twenty-foot Anacondas on Omaha's Wild Kingdom. There was a method to their madness as I recalled. Apparently, I was having one of those maddening moments, an out of body experience, thinking I could be the next critter catcher. The snake stayed put, paying us little attention. I should have done the same, but no, it wasn't to be. Cue the 'Macho Man' music.

I searched around until I located a low growing tree branch the right size to do my bidding. I snapped it off, stripped the leaves and shaped the perfect tool, a forked limb. It was very similar to the ones I'd seen the famed snake catchers use. Never try this at home, right? I had never attempted this before but that was my little secret. My plan was simple and quite flawless, at least in my pea brain. I slowly but methodically trapped the serpent's head between the fork. As trained through my years of television watching, I slipped my right hand around the snake's neck. To be honest, I am not sure a snake has a neck. It seems to me that almost anything behind its head qualifies as neck.

With my right hand now firmly grasping my prey and left hand holding on to somewhere down the middle of its extended neck, I stood and sported my catch in front of my bride to be. She turned up her nose and backed away. It wasn't the reaction I had hoped for. Snakes apparently don't enjoy being held either and tend to go off script. Thinking back now, way too late, some of those snake captures on television were adventurous and scary. Snakes don't have feet but don't be fooled. This one was gaining a foothold. It was wrapping itself around my right arm, squeezing forcefully as it eased its head from my clutches. I quickly attempted to unwrap it and then repositioned my grip just to have it re-wrap its death hold on my arm.

How does it go? *Never let them see you sweat*. I did my best, but I was losing the battle. It was just a matter of time before the snake's head would be free. It was still wrapped around my arm. Somehow in one fluid motion I unraveled the rope on steroids, flinging it to the ground and back peddled to put some distance between me and that snake. One never knows just how angry a snake might be. Thankfully, it quickly disappeared into the weeds. I was never so happy to see nature's own return to where it belonged. I might not be Marlin Perkins and, no, I had not stayed in a Holiday Inn Express, but for that mere moment in time, I had done my best to show off in front of my future bride. To be truthful, the snake oil peddler had met his match. But that will remain mine and your little secret. What happens in Elberton stays in Elberton. That wasn't my last snake encounter. Snakes and chickens will be another chapter.

Deer Me!

I no longer deer hunt but once upon a time I did. I really didn't become an avid or fair-weather hunter until I was well into my late twenties. I had hunted a time or two but not enough to make me dangerous in the woods. One of my first memories of hunting, Cousin Billy Joe took me somewhere on game management land in Sumter National Park. He had me climb this prefabricated wooden deer stand where I sat bored out of my mind until darkness fell. I was a teenager. We don't sit still for long periods of time. Sometime just before dusk I heard what I thought was a pig grunting just out of eyesight range in the bushes. It could have been a Sasquatch, but Bigfoot was not familiar to me back then. I thought it might have been Billy Joe funning me, but he approached my stand from the opposite direction of the sounds. Knowing what I know and have heard now, that was probably my first encounter with a grunting buck.

I recall Daddy telling a story once about taking Mama with him while deer hunting at the Grove in Edisto Beach. The Newton's, our kinfolks in the low country, owned the old southern plantation. Daddy said she was non-stop talking, fidgety and slapping misquotes loud enough to be heard miles away. When the hunting dogs finally ran a deer in their direction, she yelled, telling him not to shoot it because it was too pretty. That's certainly not the Mama I remember; her mantra, '*I'll eat anything that doesn't eat me first.*' That woman loved venison prepared and processed in any editable form. Deer eventually transformed from pretty looking to pretty tasty.

As a young adult, I had a few experiences hunting the Grove and other low county areas with my cousin Louie, the passionate deer stalker and slayer. He was the legend of Adams Run. Adams Run is a curve in the road before heading down to Edisto. It's a stone throw from Hollywood, S.C. We spent one weekend at the Grove in an old house on the premises. I was just a mere teenager then too. We saw plenty of deer, but none close enough to make any shots. Our closest encounter came when we spotted about a dozen deer at the far end of a soybean field. A narrow patch of woods separated the field from a dirt road that paralleled most of it. Louie and I, concealed by the trees, were stalking along that road in hopes of getting close enough to make a shot. Just a few yards shy of reaching our destination a carload of trespassing boys came driving towards us sending the deer running off. Many of them crossed the road in front of the approaching vehicle. The smartasses pulled up alongside us laughing and asking if we had seen all those rabbits. Noting our not so amused faces and trigger-happy fingers they quickly whipped around and made a hasty exit.

One other low country deer expedition comes to mind. Cousin Louie had granted me permission to bring some of my pals to experience the deer hunt with dogs. Five of my Abbeville buds joined me. We loaded three each in two pick-ups and headed to Adams Run. I had my white Chevy Luv with a camper cover over the bed, perfect for stowing our guns and gear. The other truck trailed. Three of us were cramped in the front seats of each for the four-and-a-half-hour drive that took us more like six hours. I will spare the details of the six guilty as sin suspects or I'd have to invoke a parental reading warning. I will keep this version clean and just stick to the deer hunting theme.

My trips to the low country were few and far between so navigating the route often offered challenges. We sometimes made a wrong turn here or there, leading us to drive awhile in the wrong direction before getting back on track. One thing for sure, real men don't stop and ask directions. We never admit we're lost when we drift off the beaten track. What my buds didn't know wouldn't hurt them, providing I picked up a warm trail. Sometimes you just find yourself slap dab in the middle of one of those gotcha moments, busted and no way out. Attempting to covertly get this two-truck caravan back on track, making a few ill calculated strategic turns, I lead us into a precarious situation, one of those '*oh crap*' moments for sure.

Something did not feel right, and the warning signs reinforced my instinctive intuition. And when I say warning signs, I am talking real metal and posted warning signs, not those flashing loud and clear inside my head. We realized we were driving down the entranceway to the Savannah River Nuclear Plant. No problem. We would just find a place to turn around and I would eat a little crow. Then we would be on our merry little way, right? Wrong! Panic did not really set in until I saw the gate and the guard shack ahead. Why panic, just an honest mistake, right? Wrong again!

This next one would have happened in mid 70's. Picture this scenario. Six guys crammed inside two trucks, late at night, hauling ten guns, both rifles and shotguns, with enough ammo to ignite a small war. We had other contraband that could easily land us in the brig, struggling for reasonable and believable explanations. Thank goodness this was in the pre-terrorist days. Big Bubba stepped out of the guard house, armed and uniformed, awaiting our arrival. Hopefully, he would recognize us as harmless good ole southern boys who had just made an honest driving mistake. If he looked in the back of my Chevy, we would be guilty until proven innocent. This was before cell phones, so we had no way of communicating our plans or concerns to the trailing truck. Misdirected winging it would land us in deep dodo. There was nothing to do but cross our fingers and allow this to run its course.

I hate stereotyping a fellow southerner, but the guard was a beer bellied behemoth, most likely sporting size 32 pants, six inches below his true waist size, many inches rounder. His mouth was crammed full of a wad of Beechnut. He possessed the swagger of the sheriff portrayed by the late Rod Steger, straight out of the movie classic, *In the Heat of the Night*. He motioned for me to pull up directly underneath the bright lights. I rolled down my window and I do mean rolled down, no electric ones on the Chevy. He smiled and inquired, '*What you boys up to this late out'cher?*' Honesty is the best policy in these situations. 'We made a wrong turn on our way to Adams Run to visit my cousins to do a little deer hunting'. This was my best, a not so well rehearsed reply. He smiled, nodded, and gave me directions to get us back on track, wishing us happy hunting. Catching crap from my five partners in crime didn't faze me after skirting the chance to sport a ball and chain and pound rocks into gravel.

Oh yeah, we did eventually make it to my cousin's place and had a successful hunt, filling our coolers with fresh low country venison. I was armed with a borrowed long barrel, single shot, goose gun, nearly as long as I was tall. Standing my ground at my designated post I spotted the deer as it attempted to sneak by me just ahead of the pack of trailing dogs. Knowing I would only get one shot, no chance to reload, I took careful aim. The gun almost knocked me on my butt. Guess what? I had bagged my very first deer. Another valuable lesson learned. While in the clutches of buck fever one can suffer a skewed perspective. Gauging distance and size are not easy for the unseasoned hunter. Cousin Louie, trailing the tracking dogs, having heard the shot, arrived to investigate.

I stood there beaming, waiting for my Kodak moment with my bounty. Louie picked it up by its hind legs and then looked at me and said in his low country drawl, "*You done went and shot Bambi. I can't believe you shot Bambi.*" The deer maybe weighed forty pounds. For the record, it did not have any spots and it looked much larger from where I had been standing. My only saving grace was that it was a doe and not an immature buck. Louie's rants in front of my fellow hunters were laced with terms like greenhorn and Bambi slayer while confiscating my goose gun. I took it like a man. None of my other buddies had killed a deer yet.

My day would come in 1979. I would reclaim my dignity, my place among hunters. I lived in the country a few miles west of Abbeville on highway 72. My new home and six acres were a honey hole of deer activity. I did not own a rifle then. I only had a four-ten single barrel shot gun. My pal, Sylvester Burton, from work allowed me to borrow his 35 caliber, five shot rifle. Borrowing guns seemed to be a theme for me. First though, he must teach me how to successfully use it. He secured a paper plate in a tree fifty paces away and then took a shot. He hit the plate dead center to prove the gun sights were accurate. Now it was my turn. I fired over a dozen times and never hit the plate. He fired one more time just to prove I was a lousy shot and then wished me good luck, saying even an elephant would be a safe target. Cousin Louie would have been spouting, 'Once a greenhorn always a greenhorn.'

Some weeks later and a workday for me, already into the hunting season, I stepped out onto my deck overlooking a vast field below. I was barefooted and shirtless, letting the dog out before getting ready to head to work. To my amazement I spotted at least five deer in dawn's early light. I rushed back in the house, located the rifle and returned to the doorway. Utilizing the scope, I perused each critter silhouetted in the view finder. With my shoulder propped against the den's door facing I picked out the buck with the largest rack, recalling my inability to hit that plate at fifty yards. I then centered the crosshairs on the deer and pulled the trigger. The rifle recoiled. The scope nailed me above my right eye, blood trickling from the open gash on my brow.

After a brief recovery, I scanned the area with the scope once again and caught the white flicker of the fallen animal. Without thinking, still shirtless and barefooted, I ran with reckless abandon the one hundred fifty yards to where the prey had fallen. I had just bagged an un-Bambi like, nearly 200-pound, 10-point buck. I had almost missed my prize though. The shot entered just below the deer's spine. An inch higher and I would still be a certified greenhorn. Next challenge, drag the deer back up the hill and go purchase a deer license so that I could check it in. I still have the head mounted, stashed away in the attic though, no place to hang it where we live at the beach. I once had the deer feet lamp to match it but have since gotten rid of it. On the plague is engraved the date and the words 'Home Grown'. The deer still holds the record as my largest. Go figure. I nail the behemoth from my den door, three times further than all those missed paper plate shots, with a borrowed gun and no license. How priceless is that? You cannot make this stuff up. Well, you can but if I had, I would have made up a better story since I was in it.

Dec. 13, 1979

Hang in there for one last tale unless you do not hunt and support PETA instead. Having graduated to both a climbing stand and now having slain numerous deer, I considered myself a real hunter. While perched in a tree I heard my quarry approaching and waited patiently with my very own 30-06 automatic rifle. I also had a hunting license. The six-point buck stepped into the opening and I brought it down with a well-placed shot. Now trained, I stayed put and allowed the deer to undergo a peaceful departure before trailing it. To my surprise a second deer appeared. A doe stepped into my shoot zone. Boom, I had brought down deer number two with one shot. I climbed down, verified the kill, and soon located the first one. I dragged both to the creek bed I would have to cross and then walked back to the house to recruit help.

Low and behold, the only people I could find home were my parents. They were at my house in about fifteen minutes. Mama wanted to accompany Daddy and me into the woods. As we arrived to where I had placed the deer, she spotted them and remarked, *"Wow and they fell side by side when you shot them"*. For awhile I allowed her to believe I was just that good. I began dragging the buck while my parents took ownership of the doe, both weighing in the one hundred twenty-pound range. Mama had one last parting remark, one of those priceless unforgettable statements. *"Look at me, sixty years old and dragging my first deer out of the woods"*. She said this proudly too. She had come a long way since that time Daddy had taken her hunting. We had made the event a family experience. Bonding knows no boundaries. You can always depend on family in a crunch. Those of you who knew her, deer slaying put aside, can probably hear her saying these things. This one always brings a smile to my face. Funny, I am now in my sixties and remembering a wonderful Mama moment. Nostalgia is a wonderful concept. I wished I would have thought and snapped a few photos. How priceless would that have been. This was a time before cell phones.

The Truth and Nothing But

One rule in life is that you should never lie about food. What I am trying to say is that most everyone wants to know what they are eating. You should never trick anyone into trying something that they would usually not try if they knew what they were trying. My Judy always had a phobia about eating my Papa Bowie's hash. He and Granny made excellent hash, but she had heard rumors that he sometimes substituted the usual chicken, pork, and beef. This was partially truthful. As mentioned preciously, back in the old days when times were hard and money short, families did what they could do to put food on the table. That is why my grandparents always had a vegetable garden and during much of their early life raised chickens. I remember the old chicken house and pen behind their house on South Main when I was a kid. I have witnessed Papa many times selecting a hen and preparing it for Sunday dinner. Goat, squirrel, rabbit, snapping turtle, and deer had indeed landed on their table and possibly as a substitute in the hash. Papa nor Granny would never trick anyone into eating something they didn't want to eat. Now I could not say I would not put that past Mama though.

I've killed my plenty of deer and I always shared the spoils with my grandparents and parents. Nobody loved venison better that Mama. If she had it, she would often substitute it in spaghetti or for burgers. She might or might not declare it for those joining them at the supper table. Deer has no fat. You must add beef or pork fat when deer is processed. Venison is lean and a healthy choice. I don't quite get it. People will eat chicken, cows and pigs but somehow convince themselves that deer are not to be consumed. Have you ever watched chickens or pigs and their eating habits? But chicken, pork and beef are bought in stores some will argue. Sorry, those critters were not handfed, and they certainly weren't raised in a supermarket. Deer are so pretty they will say. How can you eat one? I have not ever seen a pretty chicken, pig, or cow.

Let's stick to the venison theme. My folks, Martin and Mary Saylors, Jerry and Normal Solomon, Judy and I were heading to Florida for a Caribbean Cruise. This is a more detailed version of an earlier story. We were traveling there in my parent's leisure van. It would be nearly a twelve hour in the middle of the night drive to make Fort Lauderdale. To minimize stops we had brought plenty of food to eat along the way. Snacks were in no short supply. When snacks were not enough, we had other provisions. Sometime during the night Martin fished out a Tupperware container with meat and biscuits wrapped with tinfoil inside, He asked who wanted steak and biscuits. Most were eager to have anything besides chips and candy. It was some good eating. During the meal, Martin asked how everyone liked their deer biscuits. Martin was not trying to trick anyone. He just figured that no one minded eating venison. Jerry began spitting the contents of his mouth into his napkin. I think Norma followed suit. Judy hadn't taken one, probably suspicious from the get-go. I figured there would be extra for the rest of us and I was right. Funny, it had tasted like beef steak until they had discovered it wasn't.

I think I have shared the Savannah fiasco numerous times, but it fits this narrative as well. Jerry, Norma and Charlotte sampling what they thought was onion rings but instead was calamari. Judy had turned to them and said, "I can't believe y'all are trying that." With the mere comment, Jerry and Charlotte quickly emptied the content from their mouths into their napkins. Norma, forgoing the lady like removal, began spewing hers onto the cobble stoned street. Be wary when sampling free food because it is free, right? Of course, Charlotte fell prey as well on that other occasion when she asked me to tell her that she was not eating gator tail and of course I obliged and told her what she asked me to tell her. Gator tastes like chicken to some.

I am a sucker for 'strange' food. When we are on cruises I can hardly wait until its escargot night on the menu. I will order two or three appetizers of snail. Most any night I will choose the stuff you don't see on the everyday dinner table. Most turn their noses up at my choices. Their loss. Judy ordered a seafood item once and then almost screamed when it arrived, saying her plate had a bug on it. It was a crawfish. She tells the story about when she was attempting to cook chicken livers for her son and passed out in the process. Speaking of chicken livers, it is a running joke during our CCU tailgate parties, that when we have fried chicken livers and some are left over, we'll just put them in our pockets, keep the warm and eat them later during the game. No. We have never done this. It's just a joke.

I remember Mama and her daddy, my Papa having brains and eggs for breakfast. I was a little too picky when I was a kid, so I never tried it. I should have asked them whose brains they were eating. Sometimes not knowing is better than knowing. Papa served up lots of odd food, remember. Fried or stewed turtle was a favorite. As was fried, dumplings or barbequed rabbit and squirrel. He even served up possum or coon occasionally. Mama earned her mantra at an early age, anything that didn't eat her first; food on that table when times were tough. I drew the line at cracklin cornbread. I didn't even know what a cracklin was, but I didn't think it belonged in black skillet cornbread. It was like eating cornbread filled with gummy bears. Same goes for homemade banana pudding; please don't add pineapple to pudding. Granny Bowie did this once and only once, after I protested. I still don't know what possessed her to it.

A cracklin is a fried piece of pork fat with a small amount of attached skin. It is generally considered to be part of soul food or Cajun cuisine. Cracklins are not frequently served as part of a regular meal unless they are served in cracklin bread, which is cornbread in which cracklins have been placed in the batter prior to its being baked or fried. Rather, they are a snack item which would typically be served at times other than regular mealtimes and are regarded as more of a delicacy or treat.

I love making oyster stew. It is a simple recipe; oysters, milk, butter, and there you have it. I like to add onions and corn sometimes. Judy likes oyster stew, but she does not like oysters. Go figure. She will fish through the stew making sure no oysters or portions of oysters land in her bowl. The farm raised girl can have some peculiar habits when it comes to eating and how she prefers her food. When ordering breakfast, she wants her eggs and bacon well done. Running joke, I tell the waitress to burn it, eggs, and bacon. I had never heard of anyone picking their eggs until Judy. Picking eggs? Do they grow in a garden? Nope, she and her sisters pick the un-egg like stuff from an egg yoke before they will use it. Me, crack it, add it, and cook it. She does not abide by the five second rule either. Drop any food, candy or otherwise on the floor, tile, wood or carpet and you can retrieve it within five seconds and eat it. Not her. Her daughter will. Figure that one out. Do not even get me started on using that hand sanitizer. She carries it in her purse. I grew up on dirt and germs. It makes you stronger I say. Years after writing this I must confess to eating crow. With the arrival of Covid 19, even I began using hand sanitizers.

We often make salmon stew, remarkably similar to oyster stew. A friend, Warren joined us once for supper and we served up salmon stew and saltine crackers. He had a couple of helpings. He would later tell girlfriend, Hilda, about how he liked the fish soup we had served him. Fish soup, really? Rest in peace Warren, our dear friend. And no, the stew did not do him in.

We often serve Spam. You can do so many things with Spam. Judy's sister, Brenda once remarked that I was the only one she knew who could turn Spam into a gourmet meal. It can be fried with eggs for breakfast or sautéed with peppers and onions for supper. Spam was apparently such a treasured item that when our home was broken into in Murrells Inlet, among the items stolen along with jewelry, guns, and computers, was Span from the kitchen pantry. You must respect a thief that would steal Spam. Okay, now don't tell me you have never had Spam or know what it is. Google it.

This is a photo of a can I have commemorating the 70th anniversary of Spam. The 'use by date' is March 2007, 13 years ago. I guess you could say it is a collector's edition, displayed on a kitchen shelve in out home. It makes for a great iconic and nostalgic conversation piece. I wonder what it might bring on eBay, vintage '07. I can't say it would be like a fine wine though, not after 13 years in that can. It is a keepsake. Maybe it will be handed down for generations to come. Wouldn't that be hoot, fifty, a hundred years from now it still being in the family. Nostalgia reaches a new level. Spam, food even a thief cannot pass up.

I remember having Treet instead of Spam when I was a kid. Judy turns her nose up at Treet. I have tried to convince her that there isn't that much difference in the two, especially after they've been fried. She is not buying it though. I guess Treet might be the poor man's Spam. Both work for me but then again, I will eat anything, right, the stranger the better. Treet might be a bit healthier if you compare fat content and calories between the two. Still, no argument, it is Spam or nothing in our household.

Treet vs. Spam Evaluation

Items for Comparison:	Treet	Spam
Cost Difference:	40% less	40% more
Main Ingredients on Label:	Chicken & Pork	Pork with Ham
Ounces per Container:	12	12
Serving Size in Ounces:	2	2
Servings per Container:	6	6
Calories per Serving:	140	180
Fat Calories	100	140
Total Fat in Grams:	11	16
Saturated Fat in Grams:	3.5	6
Trans Fat in Grams:	0	0
Cholesterol in mg:	50	40
Sodium in mg:	820	790
Total Carbs in Grams:	4	1
Fiber in Grams:	0	0
Sugars in Grams:	2	0
Protein in Grams:	6	7
Vitamin A	0%	0%
Vitamin C	0%	0%
Calcium	6%	0%
Iron	4%	2%

Baboon Buffoon

Most kids are enamored with the animal kingdom unless they've suffered from being bitten, nipped or have been scratched or clawed. I guess some kids possess a natural fear of animals, sometimes for reasons unknown. My wife is terrified of birds but has no clue why. She has no recollection of a deeply embedded traumatic occurrence in her childhood like being flogged by a chicken or dive bombed by a Mockingbird. The mere sight of a bird or sounds from their flapping wings or chirpy attitude can send her into a tizzy. She cannot even enter a pet store that sells birds. I guess that's why I own an aquarium, a birthday gift from my beloved. Plus, it kept me from having man's best friend as a companion too. Luckily, I like fish.

Growing up I fell into the first category. I, like most children shared that fondness for God's fury, wooly, scaled, or feathered creations. I have rarely met an animal I didn't like or didn't get along with and have no real fear of any species of living and breathing creature. Yes, I have been bitten, nipped, clawed, and scratched but it never deterred me from my love for animals. If a dog just absolutely refused to be my friend, then I just chalked it up to their loss and moved on. Best friends cannot be forced. This goes for people too I suppose.

Petting zoos or the livestock building at the county and state fairs tugged on me like a magnet. I often opted to visit them first before riding any of the rides. With little scraggily arms and legs I would tug at my parents. I would manage a foot hold in the sawdust floors and drag them towards the next holding pen containing the year's prize winners. I was mesmerized by the award-winning pristine cows, horses, pigs and chickens. While my parents were offended by the smells, I pushed on to the next holding cage, oblivious to the manure and urine flooding their senses. Children apparently have immunity to offensive smells or at least we did back then. The wild and not so wild kingdom was my world.

When on vacation we frequented Daytona Beach. I begged almost every time to visit the Saint Augustine Alligator Farm. Again, the smells of a gator farm did not exactly cause my folks to cut cartwheels. Eventually they would pay my way and wait outside setting a time limit on my visit. Luckily, I was too young to own a watch or tell time. See you later alligator. In a while crocodile. Mesmerized, I enjoyed every second roaming the grounds.

I remember my very first circus at the Greenville, South Carolina Memorial Auditorium. It must have been in the early sixties. My Aunt Lorraine, my daddy's sister and her husband, Hub, took me to the

Ringling Brothers, Barnum & Bailey Circus, The Greatest Show on Earth. The three rings ongoing simultaneously overworked my little imaginative brain. The animal acts, especially the lions, tigers and elephants held my undivided attention. I simply loved that clown car with fifty zillion clowns climbing from inside it. What wonderful memories. I am so glad that I can still recall those special times in my life.

Zoos, now that is where I found my calling. I've been to the San Diego Zoo, New Orleans Zoo, Bush Gardens, The Original Lion County Safari in Florida and Disney's Adventure Land safari to mention a few. My first one was Atlanta Fulton County Zoo. That is where I made my mark as a zoo patron. It was 1966 and I was thirteen. My folks took me there after having visited Stone Mountain, The Civil War tribute, the Cyclorama, and an Atlanta Braves baseball double header at Fulton County Stadium. It was a jam-packed Memorial weekend. Uncle Willy, the gorilla was one of the main attractions. I had only seen gorillas in Tarzan movies and horror flicks. After having seen Uncle Willy, I now have a pretty good idea that those were men dressed in big old hairy monkey suits. Willy was the real deal, silver back and all.

I squealed like a little girl; well maybe not exactly like a little girl, as I visited the many houses as they called the various containment areas. The Cat House was a favorite. Of course, that one takes on a whole new meaning now, but back then it contained all the big cats. I never imagined tigers and lions could be so large. There was the Reptile House, the Bird House and my favorite, the Monkey House. State of the art back then, the Fulton County Zoo attempted where possible to place the animals in a natural habitat, replacing cages and bars with moats and trenches. The monkeys and primates were behind glass enclosures for viewing instead of barred cages. This provided unobstructed views.

I scurried ahead from one viewing area to the next, reading the name and description of the various apes and monkeys. I arrived at one with what I thought contained a colorful faced baboon with a very red rump. I read the plaque and it identified the primate as a Mandrill. I thought that was the name of a group of singing country sisters. Oh well. Sparing no details, it described the Mandrill as a male and stated that its big old red butt becomes more pronounced on males when they reach sexual maturity and become excited during the courtship process. It referenced it to glowing like a red neon sign when hunting their counter parts in the dense rainforest vegetation. By the looks of it this old boy had been around for a while and seemed just a tad too excited to me. It stated this specimen weighed better than seventy pounds, putting it very close to my size.

I'm not sure who instigated the ensuing encounter, me or Mr. Mandrill, but the line was drawn in the proverbial sand and the contest began. I opened my mouth wide in a yawn. It bared its intimidating teeth and mimicked my yawn. I opened and closed my mouth quickly and it replicated my moves. I blinked my eyes rapidly and ironically it did the same. I suddenly understood the meaning of the term 'making monkey faces. Not to be outdone, I placed my hand on my head and waved it, taunting my counter part, monkey business on. As if in a delayed reaction mirror, it followed my lead, placing its hand on its head and wiggling its fingers. Was I imagining it or was that butt of his getting redder? Oblivious to the world around me and the elapsed time, I barraged my new friend with every monkey motion I could throw at him. He never disappointed me and continued to mirror most of my moves. This was simply too priceless to be true. Dogs certainly could not do this. Having a Mandrill for a pet would be cool I thought.

Determined to not be out done, I took a deep breath, eased back and prepared to step up my game. That's when I noticed the reflection in the glass. I swallowed, turned around and discovered a sea of people standing behind me, including my parents, enjoying the show. They laughed, cheered me on and broke out into thunderous applause. My face must have turned redder than Mr. Mandrill's butt. Embarrassed to say the least, I searched frantically for an escape route. The shoulder to shoulder people offered little hope. I finally bolted, pushing my way through my audience and made an almost tearful exit from the monkey house. Mr. Mandrill had succeeded in making a monkey out of me that holiday weekend in hot Atlanta. I had thoroughly enjoyed every second of it, at least up until the moment the tourist had invaded our privacy. A mere child, I got over it as I'm sure so did my partner in crime. Two buffoons were caught up in the moment, a special and memorable moment at that.

A Mandrill, My Nemesis

Bush Whacker

Allowances are a wonderful supplement for those protected by child labor laws. Allowances should not be confused with government entitlements. Furthermore, having a weekly allowance from my parents did not ruin me. It did not make me think I was owed something for nothing as I grew older. I have never been on welfare or food stamps, so no deep seeded or skewed thinking was ever embedded in my little brain at an early age. I have earned my keep and worked for everything I have ever had in life. My parents raised me right. They gave me an allowance because they wanted to; not that I expected it or demanded that I deserved it. You did not demand stuff when I was growing up and if you talked back you better have just cause. Scratch that. Talking back was a bad idea on any terms, just because.

I think I might have received a buck a week in the beginning. I'm not sure how old I was when it started. My parents are not around today so I can't verify it. For sake of argument let's go with the dollar plan for now. Let me tell you. A dollar would go a long way back then to satisfy my needs. Remember that '*burning a hole in my pocket*' story in my Cornbread and Buttermilk memoir. It did not mean they didn't buy me the usual stuff like Cokes or candy, the occasional toy. This just meant I had a dollar that I could spend the way I wanted to, no questions asked. Possibly this instilled in me the value of a dollar. I have always been a good money manager throughout life, something I am proud of to this very day. Blame my parents. I do. I give them all the credit.

I received annual raises, a quarter here and there and was soon up to a buck-fifty. With age your needs increase and the purchasing of mere candy might not do it anymore. I had greater aspirations, things out there that caught my eye and fancy. Comic books were high on my priority list, as were those models you assemble. Then there was the walk-in movie theater on the square, which is now the Abbeville Opera House. Back then it showcased those Saturday matinees. As I matured my taste in toys expanded. This required saving up and pooling my resources. I often bartered with my parents, negotiating deals, doing chores not expected of me for the right price of course. Stuff caught my eye. I saw things that I wanted but I never asked my parents to buy them. What was a kid to do? A bank wasn't going to give me money. We had no neighborhood loan sharks, none that I remember. Money didn't grow on trees. I heard that mantra more times than I care to count.

Cousin Billy next door had discovered the answer. He mowed yards to make extra money. He was a big kid for his age, much larger than me. I was three months older than him. August must have been a fertile month for kids born then. I decided if he could do it, why couldn't I? Hurtle number one; I didn't even help with the mowing of our yard. I had never asked, nor had daddy ever prompted me to mow ours. We had a huge yard. Daddy mowed it with a Snapper rider. There was no way he was going to let me drive it. He had this pull cart for hauling brush and sometimes he would haul kids in it too. Once in a blue moon he would allow me to have a turn at the wheel. This was a far cry from cutting grass. That's what we called mowing the lawn, cutting the grass. Skinning this cat was going to be tricky at best. We didn't have a cat. We didn't even own what Billy used, a push mower. It was self propelled by big kid power. He had more horses under the hood than my scrawny little butt. Hurtle number two; if I pulled this off, whose yard would I mow? Billy had already laid claim to those on Hunter Street where we lived.

Where there is a will there is a way. Isn't that how the saying goes? The wheels were turning in my little problem-solving head. Papa and Granny Bowie lived midway up South Main from Hunter Street, within walking distance. Often, I did just that. Sometimes I stopped by on my way to or from Busby and Cox Groceries, the Candy Mecca. While sitting on the porch with Papa it dawned on me that he had a yard. I wondered if he would like me to cut his grass and if he did, what would he pay me? I worked it into the conversation, and he said, *'Sure Hon, you can cut the grass if you want to.'* Well, me wanting to was certainly a good start but he didn't mention any pay, nor did I. Luckily for me he owned a push mower. He put me through lawn mower training 101, filling the gas tank, checking the oil and then how to crank it with the pull rope.

The steps seemed easy as Papa walked me through them and demonstrated the technique. Open the choke. Position the lever on the handle. Prop your foot on the base of the mower and just pull the rope. Oh yeah and keep your feet away from the underside and the blade. Once it started you just adjusted the lever to control the power. It certainly sounded and looked simple. He switched it back off and prompted me to try. I followed his instructions to the letter and then yanked that rope. The rope yanked back, pulling it free from my hand...ouch with a capital 'O'. Papa laughed at my ill-fated attempt. I was cheap entertainment, but he was a patient man. He said, "Hon, try yanking the rope with both your hands." I envisioned a double ouch coming. Taking a deep breath, I did the double yank with almost the same result, losing my balance this time. He caught me before I fell. He demonstrated it one more time before having me try it again. I just couldn't get the hang of it. Moving on, he demonstrated the art of grass cutting.

He picked the flat part of the yard located between his house and the fence that separated his property from Mrs. Margie's next door. It appeared easy enough to do. Mow in a straight line and when you come to the end, tilt and turn the mower and mow the adjacent row back in the other direction. The key so said my instructor, "Make sure you don't leave any gaps and grass sprouts between mowed rows". I didn't know mowing had so many rules and instructions. After a couple of passes he turned over the handle to me. It came above my chest. I felt like I had placed my hands on the handlebars of one of those chopped easy rider motorcycles.

Head down, digging in and in a fully extended stretch, I managed to get this booger rolling. The turn was tricky, but I was sort of getting the hang of it. I had to develop my own technique for getting up close to the clothesline posts and assorted plant life scattered about their yard. A slight slope existed down to the hedgerow separating yard from sidewalk. Barefooted as I usually am during the summer, this became a treacherous feat. Even more death defying, crossing the walk that separated the other half of the yard without shutting down the mower. I must confess that I did make some sparks fly, the blade contacting concrete. Eventually I completed the mowing experience. I had cut the grass in my very first yard. Thankfully there was no edging or bush pruning required. That was way above my pay grade at that time. Speaking of pay, he gave me a buck-fifty for it. The groundwork had been laid. I had my first customer.

I must have done an excellent job. Mrs. Margie next door asked him if I'd cut her grass too. He signed me up. This was turning out better than I could have ever imagined. Using his lawn mower, his gas and oil, I became an entrepreneur. She paid me two dollars bringing my grand total to three and half dollars a week. Sometimes she would want me to skip a week. Man, grass can grow a lot in that extra week. Before summer's end, my great grandmother, Granny Holmes, just up the street, asked me to do hers. The yard was larger than Papa's and Mrs. Margie's combined. She only paid me three bucks, but I was up to five fifty most weeks. I was living large but now dreading my commitment. There is no joy and fun in cutting grass.

Still, my profit margin was great, no overhead, upkeep or gas to buy. Daddy eventually allowed me to use the Snapper to mow our lawn. One hitch, he didn't pay me. It was an expected chore. I had dreamed of motoring about on that rider but after spending a couple hours on it while my friends played, it had lost its appeal. Still, including my allowance, I was rolling in the dough, up to eight bucks most weeks, unless Mrs. Margie made me skip a week or rainy weather shut me down. Boy how that rain can make the grass grow too. Double the grass height didn't double my earnings.

I mowed yards for several years. Sadly, my customers never felt compelled to increase my wages. I never asked for more. I guess I did not qualify for cost of living raises back then. In the eleventh grade I acquired my very first summer job. Out of school for the summer is supposed to be a time of sleeping late and having fun, right? I cannot remember whose idea it was for me to work that summer, mine, or my parents. I am betting it wasn't mine. Now with a driver's license and no free gas, it was either earn my keep or walk. Two of daddy's sisters, Aunt Lorraine, and Aunt Cornelia, worked for the Little River Co-op. They wrangled me a summer job, working on the right-of-way crew. I had to rise and shine earlier than when school was in session. I sported brand new leather lace-up work boots, jeans, and work gloves. I was ready for duty, having no earthly idea what I had signed up for. What was a right-of-way, anyway?

Mr. John Pettigrew was my boss. Irvin Brown drove the bush hog and Jim Lyon was my mentor, point man for Irvin when he was mowing with the bush hog. Jim armed me with a bush ax, my tool of the trade apparently. I'd never used a regular ax, much less one shaped like the grim reaper's sickle. I soon found out that there is a wrong way and a right way to do a right-of-way. First, as you chop down at anything, make sure your feet are not in the line of fire. I scarred up my new boots quickly with misjudged swings. I was thankful I was not barefooted and toe-less instead. My superiors motioned for me to start clearing an area, failing to give me any guidelines or clear technique for doing so. The linemen crew pulled up in their truck, apparently there to critique the new recruits. There were five of us; Monty DeLoach, Allen New, Donnie Ray and Cousin Bobby Hagen. I was the only greenhorn in the bunch apparently.

I began flailing with reckless abandon, chopping, and dicing, missing, and ricocheting off saplings and brush alike. I was ten-yards-deep into the woods when it was brought to my attention that I was supposed to follow the power line, not make a path for a new one. At least not this time. I was also instructed to make my chops closer to the base of what I was chopping. They hadn't exactly put me through an orientation training film, nor had they provided me with a copy of *Bushwhacking for Dummies*. I weighed less than a 150 pounds back then, so technique did matter. One of the linemen said I looked like a mongoose with my wild attacking method. That name sort of stuck for the summer.

Another valuable lesson in the bushwhacking world, learn how to sharpen your ax blade. Chopping so close to the ground my blade found every rock buried underneath. I had sparks flying, like crossing the walkway with the lawnmower at Papa's house. And yes, there is a right way and wrong way to sharpen a blade with a file. And yes, wear your gloves because even a dull blade can and will draw blood. Eventually I got it down pat, mastering the whacking and sharpening techniques. I was gradually becoming a seasoned summertime worker. I was making a lot more than I had mowing lawns. Uncle Sam was getting his cut from my paycheck. I had been on the cash only plan until then. My earnings had not been taxed.

Valuable lesson number three; always survey your surroundings when approaching new areas. Hornets, bumble bees, wasp and yellow jackets are apparently attracted to building their nests on right-of ways. I should know. I got chased and stung by every one of them. Snakes, oh yes, there were plenty of snakes. Poison oak and ivy were in abundance and I'm highly allergic to both. Many trips to Cousin Ginny's were on my agenda that summer. She was featured in my *Talking out the Fire* story in memoir number one. Word to the wise; the summer heat isn't quite so fun when you're working in it. We capitalized on any opportunity to take a dip when nearby to a lake, river or creek. By summer's end I was tanned and toned. I had a few muscles for the first time. Oh yeah, my first day I discovered the value of making sure the cap on my thermos bottle was secure. It wasn't and it flooded my lunchbox and all contents inside. Soggy sandwiches really aren't too editable, even when you have worked up an appetite.

Lunchtime concepts varied but we always found a shady spot to park the trucks. Some ate while others napped. There were those among us that took the opportunity to explore or just horse around. Wrap your brain around the visual, Pre-cell phones, no calling or texting existing. Ah yes, but then there was the game of Smut. It was a card game played with the typical deck of cards. The one who lost the last hand ended up with the illustrious Smut Belt, an imaginary lineman's utility belt. You did not want to be the one who lost the last hand because that meant you had the honor of owning the Smut Belt until tomorrow's lunch break card game. It was sort of implied bad luck to possess it. Friday's were the worst, losing meaning you would have the belt over the weekend. For fairness, the last hand was always announced. I am no card shark. Call me Smutty.

I worked two summers for the Little River Co-op so I'm guessing mongoose eventually learned the ropes well enough to be welcomed back. I did have the opportunity to meet a host of interesting characters along the way. We were always invading folks' backyards and skirting their property when working those power line right-of-ways. Some would ask us favors like cutting down a tree here and there while others didn't really appreciate the service we brought or the infringement on their privacy. Sorry, we were just doing our job. Try remembering that when freezing rain brings those pine limbs down on the power lines. We were a preventive service.

One gentleman still sticks out above all the rest. We arrived at our destination. I can still envision him sitting on his front porch in that rocking chair on the old Anderson Highway. He wore his overalls and sported a Fedora hat reminding me of my dear Papa Bowie. It was early morning and we needed to pass through his yard to get to a stretch of lines in the pines behind his house. The conversation was brief and to the point.

Mr. Pettigrew exited his truck and walked up just shy of the porch, and said, "Good morning. I'm John Pettigrew, crew leader for the Little River Co-op. How are you doing?"

The man on the porch replied, "None of your damn business. How the hell are you?" He then smiled and invited our leader to join him on the porch.

From cutting grass to bushwhacking, there are always lessons along the way. For me, I learned the value of a dollar, earning my very own money and managing it to stretch as far as possible. Hard work does pay off if you are willing to give it a try. Sponging in the fellowship and friendship is a bonus. Teamwork is a must. Values are taught at a young age, but it does take a teacher, a mentor, loving parents, family, and friends. I have made my fair share of mistakes and have often lived spurts of my life with reckless abandon. I surely left my parents with grey hairs and much anxiety, but in the end, I do know right from wrong. The measuring stick in life hinges on one's choices. Choose wisely my friends; advice from an ole bushwhacker.

Free Comes with a Price Tag

Remember I told you during my episode of wrestling and lap totting goats that I would get around to another critter story. Tah-dah, this is that 'around to' moment. I cannot blame Papa this time for the precarious predicament I found myself in. Given his Tom Turkey adventure during the great goat round-up he would have probably loved this adventure. Apparently, I'm a sucker for free or maybe just lame brain ideas. A coworker of my wife was moving out of town so goes the story and he had a bunch of chickens he was trying to give away to anyone that wanted them. Papa and Granny had chickens during my childhood. Papa had raised goats too but what had that really gained me. Genealogy doesn't pass along the art of critter catching or raising if you catch my drift. Still, he did say they were free.

Before claiming the flock of barnyard narrow heads, I had too first come up with a place to house them. Papa's health had declined so I could not lean on him for his expertise. Granny did toss in a few pointers saying I needed a chicken coop and a fenced in chicken yard. I had an entire yard, nearly five acres, so why did the chickens need one too? What could be so difficult in fencing in a section, right? Post holes do not dig themselves. Stretching and extending chicken wire apparently is some sort of unique art form. I didn't have a copy of the chicken farmer's handbook, or one of those 'For Dummies' editions. Posts…check, post hole diggers…check, chicken wire…check, hammer, and heavy-duty staplers…check, wire cutters…check, blueprint…clueless, enough chicken wire…hopeful. It is nearly impossible to dig a hole in rock infested ground with dull post hole diggers. The pen was to be built around an old wood storage shed. Lucky for me there was a slew of small hardwoods scattered about providing shade to the area. Like connecting dots, I would utilize these trees as much as possible for the fence posts. The design would not be square or rectangular. It would be tree angular.

Painstakingly I constructed the not so perfect chicken containment yard, ultimately requiring the purchase of another roll of chicken wire. I don't even know how to begin describing my masterpiece. Breathtaking wouldn't do it justice. Zigzagging from one tree to the next nearest tree added to its uniqueness. Like I said, it wasn't square, rectangular or even octagon in shape. Plus, I still needed to construct a door of some type. Innovator extraordinaire, I somehow built a halfass frame and used an old wood screen door. Boy did that dress up the old hen yard. The bottoms of the crooked fence offered too many entries or exit points. The contour of the landscape was not exactly perfectly flat. I disassembled wood pallets and used the wood slats to secure the bottom of the fencing. This added to the already abstract design. Next, as instructed by Granny, I must construct roosting and nesting areas inside the shed. Lesson number IV. It isn't easy to build roosting and nesting areas when clueless as how to do it. Abstract apparently was my specialty but would it pass close inspection by the future feathered flock?

I purchased chicken feed and feeders and water feeders. Free was becoming quite expensive. Now all I needed was the chickens. I decided to go collect my flock. The owner said he'd toss in the transfer cages and suggested I plan to arrive about dusk when the chickens went to roost. Chickens were not night owls apparently. Who would have figured? Not me. I arrived with high expectations, like when I ventured to Mount Carmel to pick up my goat. The gent was not a home. A common theme for me continued. His wife pointed me to the hen house. There was no fenced in area. She also informed me that I might be a little early. I thought I was on time. She explained that the chickens were still free ranging and not on the roost yet. Rhode Island Reds and little black bantam chickens were up for grabs, literally. You got it. I just became the designated chicken wrangler. What a resume I was developing. There was nothing to do but wait for sundown. As darkness fell and as if by magic the chickens began filing into the house. Good news. I would have them trapped. Bad news. I had never caught a chicken. Worst of all, I was on my own, baptism by fire, Foghorn Leghorn…Greenhorn.

Chickens play possum when on the roost. Let the flogging commence. Upset one chicken and you have panicked the flock. Cackling and fluttering about, they weren't too keen on my play to apprehend them. Lucky for me the owner returned and tutored me in proper technique, clutching them by both legs and then placing them in the cages. While he corralled the red ones, I tried my hand at capturing the smaller versions, the black bantams. No one told me the little boogers could fly like a dang bird. Soon all of them were outside and up in the trees. I would have to settle for the full-size ones, four hens and a rooster. Tomorrow I would have to come back after dark for the bantams, six total, making me the eventual proud owner of eleven chickens. I did return and soon had them in their home, sort of. Each morning the bantams flew the coop and returned come dusk. So much for a fenced in chicken yard.

Never build the nest close to where the chickens roost. The eggs they lay become covered with chicken droppings. And, a wood floor collects chicken crap too, requiring frequent removal. Overlooking these minor inconveniences, we were rolling in eggs, regular and bantam size. I had enough to share with my parents and grandparents and other family members. I discovered soon enough that my family wasn't the only ones that loved fresh eggs and the taste of chicken. I also learned that cackling chickens in the middle of the night didn't mean that the chickens were wide awake without just cause. More than once I ventured with flashlight in hand to discover a possum nearby or inside the pen. I began taking my 4-10 single barrel shotgun along for those nighttime investigations. It's unnerving to find an ugly possum clutching a freshly killed chicken in his grinning jaws, attempting to climb up and over the fence. An eye for an eye, dead chicken, dead possum, and justice served. I constructed a chicken wire top over the fence, another roll of wire required. Free was sure an expensive lesson.

It did not take me long to figure out that that most everything the good Lord placed on this earth loves the taste of chicken. Remember that 'Marlin Perkins' adventure. I would not be making that mistake a second time. One of the chicken's nesting areas was just inside the old shack and directly to the right. I had become quite accustomed to blindly feeling about the nest with my right hand and scooping up any eggs as I entered. Let me tell you, it is an attention getter when you feel the eggs and they are on the inside of a snake curled in the nest. Action one…remove your hand immediately. Action two…back pedal as quickly as possible and exit the premises. Action three…locate something to do battle with the freeloading trespasser. Mistake number one…a dull hoe is not the best weapon of choice. I normally do not kill black snakes, but six-foot black snakes will continue to return to the scene of the crime until you do. By the way, they tend to travel in pairs to the buffet bar. Each year without exception I had to execute two huge black snakes raiding the henhouse. It made me wonder if these were some sort of magical mythical creatures that couldn't be killed.

Snakes were really the least of my problems. At least they only consumed the chicken byproduct. Possums, raccoons, foxes, hawks, weasels, dogs and cats and a draft pick to be selected in a later round claimed the Holy Grail, the whole chicken as their main course. Possums were the only ones I ever caught in the act though. The rest were as elusive as Bigfoot. Once while standing in the yard among my free ranging flock, a red-tailed hawk the size of the American eagle did swoop down and try to snatch up a chicken. It almost took my head off in the process. It banked off and flew away at the last second, apparently not spotting me under the canopy of trees. It took up roost in a tree about a hundred yards away biding its time. I retrieved my double barrel shotgun that I usually kept loaded and decided I would scare it off. Unfortunately, and bad for Mr. Red Tail, I had forgotten the shotgun was loaded with buckshot instead of birdshot. My deadeye shooting had improved. It plummeted to the ground. Upon closer inspection of the deceased predator, its talons were nearly as large as my hands…quite impressive.

Over the course of the next couple of years my flock increased due to secluded nests and hatchlings. Just as quickly the counts were offset by those consuming the flock. After about a four-year run, I was down to one surviving little black bantam hen. She hung in there until one day I found only feathers to mark she once existed. As crazy as it sounds, I was better with chickens than with goats. Owning any farm critters comes with challenges and a price tag. There is no such thing as free. I missed the crowing, the cackling, and the scratching about in the dirt and of course the eggs. What I don't miss is having chickens…other than battered and fried.

It's Howdy Doody Time

I am frequently accused of holding on to things way too long. For the record, in my humble opinion, I am not a pack rat and I'm certainly not a hoarder, but I do have a sentimental spot, worse so than most possibly. Lessons learned have landed me where I am. There is a rhyme to my reason. Nostalgia is not necessarily limited to one's memory. The past can accompany us throughout the present and into the future. My direct blood line is no more. My parents and grandparents have passed on. I am an only child as was my Mama. Losing the last of my immediate bloodline (Mama, Daddy and Granny) in an eleven-month span in 2004-2005 further pushed me to where I am today. Holding on to items, pieces of my past, is important to me. I don't give them up easily. Let's dive headfirst into my alleged addiction, shall we.

My Granny Bowie collected salt and pepper shakers. Yes, I have that collection boxed up, not displayed. Some are unique but that's in the eye of the beholder. I inherited them. I have my Papa Bowie's daddy's tool chest with an assortment of my great grandfather's tools inside. I never knew Papa's daddy, but I can tell by the assortment of tools that he was quite the carpenter and handy man. I have a mahogany bedroom suit. Mama and Granny had identical ones and I kept the best between them, bed, bedside tables, chest, and a dressing table. I slept on one of these beds most of my childhood. At the foot of the bed is a huge metal and leather traveling chest belonging to them. I still have most of Granny's handmade quilts. The huge pink glass lamp on the dresser came from my parent's living room. It is older than me. I remember it forever being in our living room. I have Granny's original garden hoe, a Papa custom made garden hoe with longer handle for her. I also have Papa's hand-crafted iron fire poker. Many chunks of coal and kindling have been poked with it in their pot-bellied stove. I have done my fair share of poking in my wood fire places.

As mentioned in the opening chapter, I have the original hand grinder used to make traditional hash, along with the table Papa made specifically to attach the grinder to. I have an assortment of other do-dads, what-knots, trinkets, gadgets, dishes, cooking utensils from my past and theirs. Much of it boxed up and in the attic. Someday I might sell it if I can muster up the courage to turn it loose. If you were to ask my wife, she would say it all needs to go. Do me a favor though. Don't ask her. Some items go beyond my immediate bloodline. Aunt Shug, Papa's only sister was quite artistic. She painted pictures, dishes, and other various items. I have many of her works of art. One of her paintings is the childhood Bowie family home. Was she famous? Nope, but she was the family resident artist. I can't leave out Daddy. He had this large Tupperware canister filled with a lifetime's assortment of screws, bolts, nuts, pins, brackets, odds, and ins, left over this and that. You never know when you might need one of what was in that magical container. I cannot count the times I have deep dived looking for that special something I needed. More times than not I found it or something close enough to do the job.

Television shows like American Pickers, Toy Hunter and the Antique Road Show have struck a vein in me. Nostalgic possessions can be treasure troves in the eyes of seekers, appreciative of their value and associated history. How does the Sinatra song go…*Regrets, I've had a few*? In the end I did it my way, too, sad to say. How I have let them slip through my fingers, let me count the ways. Toys. I am talking toys with defining moments, those one of a kind, wish I still had them, collectables. I owed a Howdy Doody doll. Some of you are scratching your head and saying, 'a what?' I grew up watching the *Howdy Doody Show*. I've fallen backwards into time. Humor me while I relive it as if it were yesterday. A distinctive feature on the show was the Peanut Gallery, on-stage bleachers seating about 40 kids. Each show began with Buffalo Bob's asking, "*Say kids, what time is it?*" and the kids yelling in unison, "*Howdy Doody Time!*" Then the kids all sang the show's theme song set to the tune of *Ta-ra-ra Boom-de-ay*.

It's Howdy Doody time
It's Howdy Doody time
Bob Smith and Howdy too
Say "Howdy do" to you
Let's give a rousing cheer
'Cause Howdy Doody's here
It's time to start the show
So kids, let's go!

Sorry, I forgot. Some of you have no clue who Howdy was, do you? He was a marionette ventriloquist doll, freckled face, dressed in a plaid shirt, denim jeans and cowboy boots. He appeared on a kid's television show with host, Buffalo Bob. The red haired Howdy had 48 freckles, one for each state at the time. Neither Hawaii nor Alaska was a state yet.

Meet Howdy

There were other characters, Clarabelle the Clown, Princess Summerfallwinterspring, J. Cornelius Cobb, Sir Archibald the Explorer, The Featherman and Chief Thunderthud, head of the Ooragnak tribe (kangaroo spelled backwards). Originally it was an hour show on Tuesdays, Thursdays, and Saturdays at 5 PM. The show eventually moved to Monday through Friday, 5:30–6:00. In June 1956, it began to be shown on Saturdays only, in a morning time slot (10-10:30), continuing until its final broadcast on September 24, 1960.

The final broadcasted episode was September 24, 1960 and was titled *Clarabelle's Big Surprise.* It was an hour-long episode looking back at highlights of the show's past. During the show there was an ongoing mystery. Supposedly Clarabelle the Clown had a big surprise. The rest of the cast attempted to find out what the surprise was, each interacting with the clown throughout the show. Mayor Phineas T. Bluster finally succeeded but promised to keep it a secret. Finally, in the closing moments, the surprise was disclosed through pantomime to Buffalo Bob and Howdy Doody. Clarabelle, who had never spoken before, had always used horns and hand signs instead. It seems that the quiet one could actually talk. Buffalo Bob called him out and challenged him to prove it because it would be his last chance with the show ending. Clarabelle faced the camera and the camera zoomed in for an extreme close-up. His lips quivered as the drum roll began and he simply said softly, "*Goodbye, kids.*" A tear could be seen in Clarabelle's right eye as the picture faded to black. I probably cried too.

I do have a point after all this, but I must tell it my way and I do eventually get to it. At that snapshot in time I had my very own Howdy Doody ventriloquist doll, a life-sized replica of the original, down to every little detail. He was my best bed buddy. I don't remember what happened to my Howdy. I probably outgrew it, and it was either given away or tossed away. Looking back now, boy Howdy, I wish I still had that little ditty of a collector's item. He's long ago gone to Howdy heaven I suppose. Back in the day we got all kinds of neat stuff. We played with it, outgrew, or broke it, and we moved on to the next greatest thing and didn't give it much thought. Who would have figured just how valuable old toys might someday be. Unfortunately, there are no childhood do-overs. There are only kick yourself in the butt regrets. I look back now and mentally recap the potential collector's item toys I have allowed to slip through my fingers, not realizing that I should have 'hoarded' them instead.

For Christmas Santa once brought me a real handcrafted metal and plastic Roy Roger's pistol and holster, boots, and western hat. Included was the Roger Roger's kid sized authentic guitar. Roy was one of those singing cowboys of my time, like Gene Autry. I have those rare photos of me seeing what Santa brought. In them I am dressed in my one-piece pajama jump suit, footed, and flapped on the backside. Yes, I have one with me holding my guitar. Santa even provided me with a Palomino colored rocking horse, reminiscent of Trigger, Roy's horse. The accessories are long gone but guess what; over sixty years later I still have that rocking horse. It is in excellent shape, no chips, or cracks, slightly faded but with the original stand and springs, perfectly workable. It has been loaned to Santa for cousins and even used with foster children over the years. Sometimes I just get lucky.

Yabba-daba-do…yes, I once possessed all the characters from the Flintstones, along with the town of Bedrock. An original Flintstones play set was released in the early 1960s and it came complete with the town of Bedrock. It included cars, critters. and other iconic symbols of the television series. Poof. I outgrew it and gone too. Cereal boxes of my day came with incredible toys inside, each brand trying to outdo the other. I retrieved my *Sky King* figure from one box. *Sky King* was one of my favorite TV series. It was sort of a modern western story, a horse replaced with an airplane, the Songbird. King usually captured criminals and spies or found lost hikers with the use of his airplane. King and his niece, Penny, lived on the Flying Crown Ranch, near the fictitious town of Grover, Arizona. I don't have my *Sky King* toy either…doggone it.

I can go on, but it is painful. I swapped my entire 500 count comic book collection to Darrel Tolbert for a weight bench set that I hardly used. Luckily, I did not collect baseball cards, or I might have bartered them away too. I once owned a vintage 1959 set of Mickey Mouse Ears from Disney Land but poof, long gone. I am sure there were many potentially collectable toys that have gone down the same path. So, what have I learned? I did begin a baseball card collection in the 1980's. I am sure there is no small fortune in them, even forty some odd years later. I have a couple of dozen of the Teenage Ninja Turtle characters in the original packages, vintage 1980's. I don't have Howdy but I do have a Pee Wee Herman ventriloquist doll, also vintage 1980's. Shogun Red and Miss Daisy dolls are still in my possession. These were Muppet type characters from the now defunct *Nashville Network* and *Buckmasters* shows. I am still hording 45's, 33's and even older style vinyl albums. Up until a few years ago I still had an 8-track player that worked and about a hundred 8 track tapes. Yep, I fell victim to one of those record club scams in the seventies. The player crashed and burned but I still have a handful of what I consider collectable 8 track tapes, if there is such a thing. Oh yeah, I have plenty of old and original board and card games. I'll save those for another story. It's Howdy Hoarder Time, y'all.

Just Like a Good Neighbor

Being neighborly is predominately a southern thing. No, that doesn't mean that living in the south you're guaranteed good neighbors. The Vegas odds might lean slightly in your favor, but I wouldn't necessarily take the bet. A mere babe in the fifties, my earliest memories are of our brick home on Hunter Street, just behind Langley Milliken Elementary School. The Bowie's, our cousins, anchored our left and the Argo's were on our right. Essentially, we knew everyone close by. I think it was some sort of requirement back then, maybe even an unwritten law, knowing thy neighbor. Directly across the street from us were Mr. and Mrs. Evans. Mr. Evans always sat in a rocker on their huge front porch. He had a fondness for my dog, Teco. For whatever reason he began calling him Tito. We never tried to correct him. Teco didn't seem to mind.

Just to their right were the Botts family, Bub, Carolyn and daughter, Susan. Carolyn was the Evans' daughter. Susan was older than me, very pretty. I think I had a crush on her. I had a lot of crushes growing up, love always in the air. Down the street and just pass Cousin Billy's were the Sorrows. Remember David, he was ambushed by Cousin Ann from the barrel in my first memoir while playing cowboys and Indians. Teco is responsible for the great bike wreck, David losing his front teeth. All he wanted for the next Christmas was his two front teeth. Sorry, that song just jumped into my head. The Timm's and McCurry's were at the end of the street. Toby Timm's had some sort of hearing problem and would finish sentences in a very high-pitched tone.

We had no official neighborhood watch back in the fifties and sixties, not even a formalized HOA. Neighbors had neighbors' backs in most cases, despite any differences or disagreements that might have occurred along the way. It was safe for us to play outside well beyond dark thirty with no fear of being abducted. Who would be crazy enough to do that anyway? It would be more like the *Ransom of the Red Chief* if they had. Strike that. We were little angels. Fibbing a tad isn't really lying. Ask any kid. Halos were the removable kind back then. One size fit all.

We had the largest yard on the block, so it was the kid gathering grounds. I thought I was just popular, but I really think they liked me for my yard. Yard envy was pert near incurable back then. Having large enough playgrounds to meet our needs was a necessity for most outdoor sports. Every yard was unique. Each had that certain appeal to us, a draw, the perfect something to distract us and test the limitations of our imaginations. Being neighborly we shared that wealth of options. The Evans had pecan trees and walnut trees, instant seasonal food and fun. The

Argos had a large Chinaberry tree in the front yard. The berries provided us with perfect ammunition. Trees seemed to play a big part in our lives back then.

People did not have to lock down their houses fearful of thieves lurking around every corner and behind every bush. Well, I do remember this one time that an act of thievery occurred. Uncle Floyd, after relocating here from California, started somewhat of a new tradition in Abbeville, decorating his house for Christmas like the county fair. He even piped Christmas music outside. He was ahead of his time for sure. People would make special trips to his house to view the decorations and listen to Perry Como or Frank Sinatra belting out traditional holiday tunes. Daddy, not to be outdone, jumped on the band wagon with his Hunter Street version. Each year, in true Griswold fashion, the spectacle grew. We had a telephone pole in the back with a yard light. Daddy strung strands of lights to give the impression we had a twenty-five-foot Christmas tree now erected in the backyard. These were large bulbs, not those tiny ones used today. I'd turn on all the lights at dark and Daddy would switch them off when he got off work from the second shift.

One night when he arrived home and from several blocks away, he had noticed the bottom third of the outdoor masterpiece was not lit. Mystery solved when he inspected it closer. We had a bulb bandit. Someone had reached as high as they could and had unscrewed and stolen the multicolored bulbs. The next day, using my sleuth skills, and judging from the height, I had figured that the culprit had been shorter than me. It hadn't been an adult, or if it had, the person or persons were tiny. Sherlock Winn was all over it. I began perusing the back forty. Low and behold I stumbled upon evidence of the crime. I found broken bulbs. Like breadcrumbs, broken bulbs scattered here and there provided the perfect trail leading away from our property. I crossed three neighbors' backyards until the trail ended at house facing the Cedar Springs highway. I now had a prime suspect in mind, innocent until proven guilty, right? It was time to light a fire under my little investigation. I was one shy of being the Hardy Boys. Okay, for the record, The Hardy Boys were fictional teenage brothers and amateur detectives back in my day, just like Nancy Drew from the girl side of the tracks.

Some days later I lured my prime suspect into our back forty. The boy was slightly younger than me, almost as big and his arm reach seemed to fit the profile of the bulb snatcher. Eventually I worked the caper into the conversation, even showing him shattered bulbs on the ground. I told him that I had followed the trail back to his house. I could see the guilt in his eyes, but he was admitting nothing. In these cases, there is supposed to be a good cop and bad cop to keep the suspect off balance. I was the only cop, so I did the only thing I could do. I pounced on him and beat the confession out of him. I submitted the evidence to Daddy. He contacted the boy's dad and he paid for the bulbs. I'll withhold the boys name because he is now reformed. But if you read this, you know who you are. Daddy did not embrace going all out Christmas decorating after that event. It took the special out of it.

South Main Street, where Papa and Granny lived was another example of neighborhoods spinning positive vibes. From South Main Street to the back alley and Maple Street and beyond, neighbors looked out for one another. If there was a death in the family, fixings a plenty were supplied. Those bereaving would not starve. Offering a helping hand where needed was something one never had to ask. In the twilight of his prime, when Papa was stricken with Alzheimer's, he would sometimes wander away from home and up the back alley. Smitty, the neighbor up the street would escort him back home. That's what neighbors did. They stayed involved. They cared. This was not considered being nosey. It was showing compassion and concern.

I lived the first seventeen years of my life on Hunter Street. We moved just before my senior year in high school to Marshall Avenue, just across the street from Granny Winn. We were now living among the elite, those living outside the mill village stereotype. Question, would we be perceived as invaders, not worthy of living in the upper crust so to speak. Winn's had already claimed their place on the street, so I guess we were accepted. Thieves did up the ante though, breaking into our house there. Their caper could have played out on a segment of dumb crook news. They stole Mama's fur coat thinking they had hit the Holy Grail. It was fake fur. They had passed on taking a much more expensive coat with a real fur collar and cuffs. My sleuth abilities never solved this crime. Either I had lost my touch, or the thieves were much smarter on this side of town.

My first owned home as a young adult was on Dundas Road. There I found myself with fellow Flexible Technology employees serving as bookends on either side of my home and another one just across the street. My first was a brick ranch with a chain link fence in the backyard. My fellow employees had brought home this large steamer from work and used it to clean their porches and carports. They asked if I wanted to use it before they took it back to work. This was a neighborly and coworker thing to do. I did have green discoloration on my back steps and patio slab so why not. That Saturday I went at it. The discharge stack on this thing was reminiscent of an old coal driven train engine. White smoke bellowed up and over my house. I paused to take a break, soon hearing a commotion on the street side of the house, sirens blaring. A couple of fire trucks had wheeled into the neighborhood. I asked one of the local firemen what was going on and he said they had received a report of a house fire. After they left, it dawned on me that someone had seen the steam snaking over my rooftop. I decided then and there my cleaning project was done.

My next home was out on highway 72, six miles outside Abbeville towards Greenwood. It would be my first taste of real country life. The theme song from *Green Acres* comes to mind. I had only one neighbor, just up the highway and opposite side of the road. My house was broken into twice. I guess it was easy pickings. There was no neighborhood watch in the rural outreaches. No one was ever apprehended. I did put my sleuth experience to use asking the investigating officers if they going to dust for fingerprints. They remarked, no need, it was probably kids. Do kids not have fingerprints?

The second break in instilled a new approach on my behalf. When I arrived home and realized that I had discovered the break in, I tossed caution to the wind. I entered the house seeking out my weapons first. All were still there where I had hidden them. I retrieved a loaded 30-06 automatic Remington rifle. I flipped off the safety and with rifle and scope pointed directly in front of me I did a room to room search. Luckily, my trigger-happy finger was never tested. I called the police. When they arrived, they spotted me with the rifle on the back deck. Seeing their uneasiness, I set the rifle down and identified myself. I told them this time I had already done their job for them, a complete sweep of the premises.

In 1995, Judy and I married planned to build a brand-new home in Saddle Hill, a Greenwood community. A friend with a bush hog cleared the lot and get rid of all the small pines. The next day at work I received a phone call from one of my new neighbors, raising you know what, very colorful language, threatening to kick my butt when I got home. There was a ten-yard-wide section of trees that separated our front yards. Apparently, all the trees belonged to him and I had cut them down. A civil discussion with him was out of the question. He was going to kick my butt. I arrived home and purposely strolled along the border, the scene of the crime. He never made an appearance. For the record I'm not a fighter but I had seen him and figured I could take him in an 'unfair' fight. I did the right thing. I had the section of land, his yard, seeded in grass and planted Leland Cypress trees down the property line. The design turned out genuinely nice, creating a privacy border. He never thanked me or ever said another word to me the nine years we lived there. One side note, other neighbors were extremely friendly, too neighborly. They always waved when they passed by while I worked in the yard. It was tough doing yard work when you had to return all those waves every time one passed. Waving is southern all the way. We wave at everybody. I think it's etched in our brains. Northerners don't get it, but we wave at them too.

Tree adventures tend to haunt our lives. We moved to Myrtle Beach within the year after the deaths of both my parents, three months apart. (Shameless Plug: The Caregivers Son Memoir). This was quite an adjustment for me, having always lived in houses with large yards. I was accustomed to having acres of land. Now we were moving to what I described as a postage stamp yard. Neighbors were up close and personal on both sides and a golf green and fairway were directly behind us. Between the house and the golf green were five huge pine trees. Neither of us preferred pines that close to the house. We had an HOA and neighborhood rules stated that one must get permission to cut down any trees larger than four inches in diameter. These were well beyond that, feet in diameter. My wife's philosophy, it's easier to ask forgiveness than permission. We had the trees professionally removed, even grinding up the stumps. The next-door neighbor, of northern persuasion, had them remove two of his. Even after planting two fifteen foot and one eighteen-foot palm trees in their place, very expensive price tag might I add, we were scolded in the neighborhood newsletter, not by name, but we knew who they were talking about. I guess you can't be tossed out of the neighborhood if you own the house and property. Oh yeah, and that house was broken into six weeks after we moved in the new neighborhood.

We were in Abbeville for the weekend at the Solomon's. We were having a leisurely Sunday morning before heading back to the beach. Judy's cell phone rang. She looked at the display and it was our home phone number. No, the crooks weren't calling us to ask permission to steal us blind; not even neighborly criminals do that. The voice on the other end said, "*Do you recognize this number? I'm Officer Smart-butt. I'm standing in your living room. Your house has been broken into.*" In tears, she handed me her phone. We made our return trip to the beach in record time, not even stopping for a food and restroom break. Our neighbors had heard the break-in but didn't investigate, so much for a neighborhood watch. These thieves stole guns, computers, jewelry and all the meat from the freezer. They even stole the Spam from the kitchen cabinet. Who takes the time to steal Spam? That's southern sacrilege behavior, isn't it? Stupid me, I asked the officer if he was going to take fingerprints and he said it probably wouldn't do any good. Am I the only one who watches cop shows? Maybe I should have rephrased my question and asked about DNA. Beach Barney was not very impressive, and we still hadn't got over that stupid phone call he had made from our living room.

Five years later, we eventually moved from the neighborhood, tiring of our house being bombed by golf balls from the second hole tee box. The par three green was directly behind our house on the Blackmoor golf course. I had told Judy when we moved in that it wasn't a good idea because people like me whomped the ball on those courses. Plus, with golfers, a mere pitching wedge from your back door, there is no privacy. Disgruntle golfers speak in colorful tongue and have no shame when it comes to looking through your shrubbery or flowerbeds for their expensive golf balls. The bright spot, I didn't have to buy golf balls, having collected over three hundred from the yard, at the price of one broken window and much damaged siding. We moved further south to Pawley's Island. There, I think every neighbor owned at least one dog. Judy met all of them while walking and knew every dog on a first name basis. Not to be outdone, I was tempted to net a couple of fish from my aquarium, place them in a Ziploc and take them for a stroll through the neighborhood. They'd have either thought I was bonkers or was the front man for Alan Funk and *Candid Camera*. Google it.

I'm not sure why we didn't just live in a double wide, something on wheels. After about four and half years we were on the road again, moving back northward this time. We downsized the house by 1000 square feet, cut my twenty-seven-mile work commute down to thirteen and moved into a gated community. Hopefully, no thieves lived there. The neighbors in Prestwick were the most neighborly of all our beach pit stops. Who would have figured that in a gated community? Even the HOA Gestapo was civil. And we have total control of our visitors. Be nice to us or we won't clear you for entry at the front gate. Seriously, remembering to let the guard know when friends or family are expected has had its fair share of hick-ups. I'm hearing that *Green Acres* theme song again or maybe the one from the *Beverly Hillbillies*. Nope, we don't have a cement pond, but I still do wonder where that chamber music is coming from just before someone shows up at the front door. Remember. Be kind to your neighbors. You never know just how many people might already be buried in their backyard.

Oh Christmas Tree

Everyone should remember the iconic song, Oh Christmas Tree. I can't sing a lick. I am the Barney Fife of singers, better heard from the inside instead of the outside. Be my guess though and belt it out to the lyrics provided below.

Oh Christmas tree, oh Christmas tree
Such pleasure do you bring me
Oh Christmas tree, oh Christmas tree
Such pleasure do you bring me
Every year this Christmas tree
Brings to us both joy and glee
Oh Christmas tree, oh Christmas tree
Such pleasure do you bring me
Oh Christmas tree, oh Christmas tree
Thy candles shine so brightly
Oh Christmas tree, oh Christmas tree
Thy candles shine so brightly
Each bough does hold its tiny light
That makes each toy to sparkle bright
Oh Christmas tree, oh Christmas tree
Thy candles shine so brightly

Oh Christmas tree, let me count the ways and the styles over the past sixty-seven years. Ready or not, let's begin in the 50s, my first recollection of Christmas and the tree decorated for the special holiday. Trees smelled back then. No, I do not mean that stunk. They smelled fresh and outdoorsy. I was a kid. I played outside more than I did inside. I knew what the outside smelled like. We only came inside at mealtimes, bedtime or during thunderstorms. The first tree I remember us having was a cedar tree. It was not bought. It was found. And no, the tree had not been lost but finding the right one was an adventure in its own. We would pile into the car if you call three of us a pile. Daddy, Mama, and I would ride the back roads in search of the perfect tree. Perfection was in the eyes of the beholders. Sometimes Granny and Papa Bowie would join us. Maybe we joined them. Papa always had a truck. I suppose, like us, they needed a tree too.

If they had tree farms back then, they must not have had any near us. Why buy a tree when they grew wild? All you needed was a saw and a good eye during the great tree hunts. Everyone manned a window and kept watch for a tree that would serve our purpose. Of course, I was little, so perception was not a strong point for me. I had no clue about big being too big or filled out meant anything. Daddy knew the right size to fit our house I suppose. I learned this quickly enough when I pointed out this one and that, him saying too big, wrong size, scrawny or other terms I probably did not understand. A tree was just a tree to me, one that would shade the Christmas packages in the living room and would mark the spot for the Santa drop.

Daddy always drove down those back roads, processing some sort of method to his madness. Thinking back now, we could have been arrested or shot for being trespassers. While the trees were basically free for the taking, taking was exactly what we were doing. I don't ever recall my parents asking anyone's permission for sawing down a tree. I don't remember them calling it stealing or even rushing to nab the tree before someone saw us. Maybe there was some unwritten seasonal guideline honored by the tree owner and the tree takers. Possibly, cedar trees were a dime a dozen and of no real value other than using them at Christmas. One thing for sure, they were sticky and prickly. You could always count on being zapped by sap and bleeding from scratches if you handled a cedar tree. Guess it was as much a part of the adventure, to sport the gooey and bleeding body parts. We got our tree, but the tree took a few parting shots while resisting.

Back to that method to Daddy's madness thing, I wouldn't learn until many years later where to find the easiest trees to harvest. Now, this didn't always mean you'd have the best ones but there would be much less dragging and totting. Most of our trees came from a pasture fence line. It was odd that trees liked growing in rows along the fence. I was just a kid. I did not try to rationalize the significance of this occurrence. While the fence line trees were accessible, they often came with a new set of challenges. Barbed wire. Yep. The best trees were often woven within the strands of barbed wire. Some were too wedged to be worth the effort to remove them. Barbed wire is worse than getting scratched by any angry cedar tree. Those barbs can inflict some serious harm. The best tree often remained the captive of the fence.

Eventually, we would return home with a near perfect tree according to my parents. What did I know? It was a tree, and it would soon be a decorated tree. Trees don't always cooperate when they are relocated from the outside into the inside. Doorways are not necessarily built for trees to easily pass through them. There is a right and a wrong way to doing this. Who would have ever figured? Never force them through a door headfirst, like a tree has a head. Daddy would be on the fat end of the tree and Mama and I would be on the skinny end. I am not sure I was really helping but they made me think I was. Family did stuff together when I was a kid.

Anything that could break was moved out of the way, as well as furniture in the pathway to the living room. Thankfully, we had a front door that opened to the living room, so that made this much easier. Inside now. More challenges. The thingamajig that held the tree upright never fit the tree trunk. Daddy would have to saw more off until it would fit in what he called the tree stand. Little screws and tightening bolts held it in place if we were lucky. Sometimes the tree ended up much shorter that what it was supposed to be after Daddy kept sawing off bottom pieces.

Now came the fun part, decorating the stolen cedar tree. I would say we borrowed it, but it was tough to return once sawed down. The lights were not those of today's time. These were large light bulbs, multicolored and with clips on each light socket to affix it to the tree branches. First things first though; untangle the string and test the lights by plugging them in. Unlike the lights we often use today, one light broken or not burning didn't keep others from working. You just screwed it out and replace it one another one. These lights were hot though and would burn you if not careful. Lights of red, blue, green, and orange were soon wrapped awkwardly around the cedar tree. Sometimes we didn't have enough of them and other strings had to be bought or these would be spaced as best as could be done.

Next came the Christmas ornaments. We didn't have all those theme-based ornaments of every kind that you can buy today. These were glass shinny balls, mostly red and green. You could always count on breaking a few. Ornament meets hardwood floor. Ornament always loses. Next were the silver icicles. We would start by hanging one icicle at a time. A tree can hold a lot of them. It was fun at first, but fun wears out its welcome quickly when kids are hanging them. Eventually Mama would let me toss handfuls onto the tree. I think she later repositioned those clumps I had tossed. A star would go atop the tree and then we were finished. A Christmas Tree was born and would light the way for ole Santa Clause hopefully, depending on which list I landed on, the naughty or nice one.

I documented one of the first Christmases I remember in my first memoir, *Cornbread and Buttermilk*. It was 1954. I had gotten my rocking horse that looked like Trigger, Roy Roger's horse. I had a belt with a pair western six shooters, cowboy hat and boots, and a Roy Rogers guitar. I still have that rocking horse.

Christmas 1954

My Rocking Horse Christmas 2019

Santa also took Rhonda Winn Singleton my rocking horse many years later when she was a kid. It was still in mint condition in 1964.

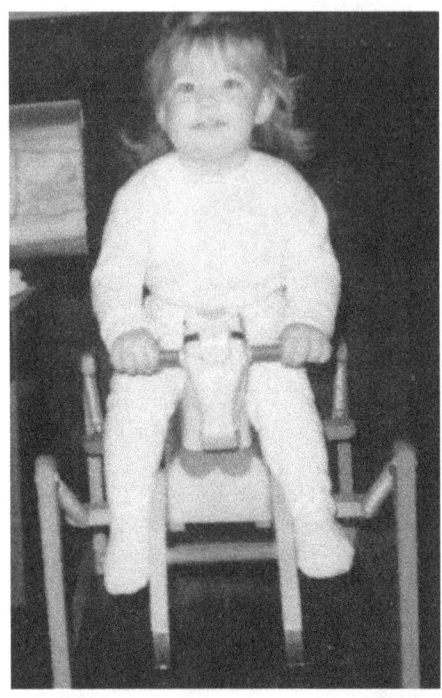

As I covered in first memoir, it is undeniably the worst way to start Christmas morning, waiting on all my grandparents to arrive before I dare venture into the living room to see what Santa brought me. It did not matter what time I woke up; I was forbidden to open those doors until they arrived. Grandparents have no sense of priority on Christmas morning. Suspense and patience are not something I practiced well. Begging and pouting got me nowhere. We could not go into that living room until Granny Winn, Granny Bowie and Papa Bowie arrived. I didn't get it then. Santa left me the goodies and none for them. Why was it so important that they be there? I get it now but back then it was just plain agonizing.

Papa Bowie, Me, and my First Bicycle 1960

Oh yeah, cedar trees shed. They shed a lot. The tree was decorated weeks before Christmas and wasn't undecorated until after New Years Day. No additional presents appeared under the trees for the week following Christmas. Everything was taken off the tree but the icicles. I'm sure glad we didn't have to take them off. That would probably have turned me against using them. Usually, you could count on breaking more glass ornaments and maybe some light bulbs before they were safely packed away until next year. It seemed to be a common tradition like telling a performer to break a leg before they performed. Break an ornament, break a light before all is done.

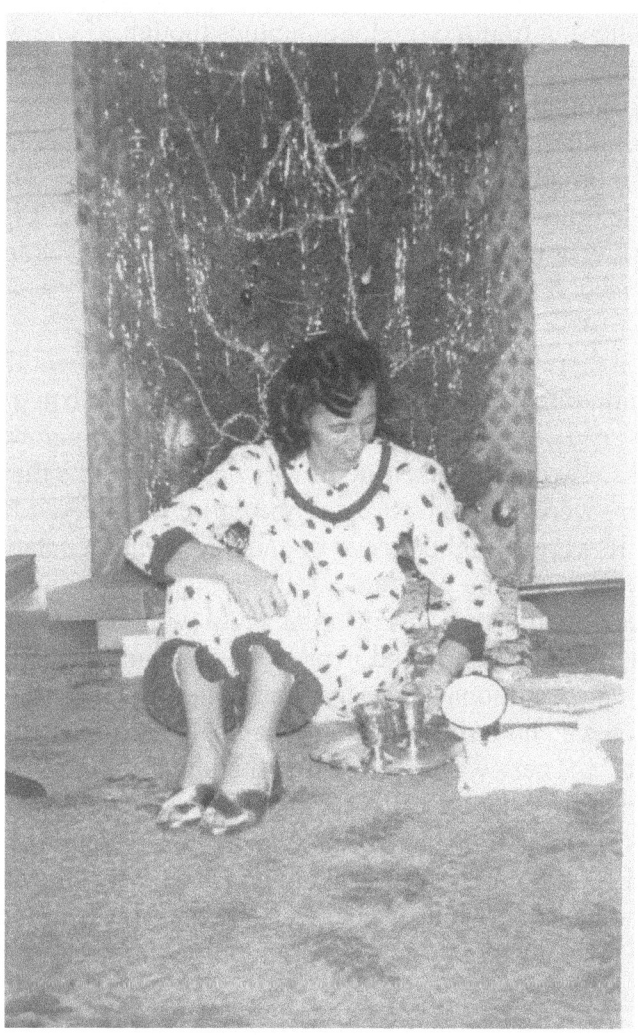

Mama (Mary Winn) and a Cedar Christmas Tree
(*think this was before my arrival*)

Somewhere along the way we graduated to a green artificial tree. With it came more challenges. First you had to align a skinny pole and fasten it in one of those tree stands. At least Daddy didn't have to saw any of it off to make it fit. Then came assembling the tree. It sounded fun at first. Every limb, and I do mean, every limb, had to be stuck in holes drilled in the tree post. But wait! You could not just put any limb in any hole. The tips of the metal limbs were color coded or numbered and they had to match the codes on the tree post. I hate puzzles. Always have. This was a big tree jigsaw puzzle. The fun wore off quicker than hanging icicles. One shinning light, we couldn't use the icicles on the artificial tree. If you put them on this time, you had to take them back off after Christmas. Why not just leave them on? I was disappointed, not really. We still used glass ornaments, but we no longer used the large lights. The lights were much smaller but multicolored. Sometimes though, if one went out, all the lights in the strand went out as well. Now, Daddy was the one getting flustered. Yep, you got it. The tree had to be disassembled after the holidays and the colored branches had to be sorted and kept together. And we usually broke more ornaments while hanging or taking them off. The companies that made ornaments must have been making a killing. Lights used the first time were never tangled. Somehow, they became tangled though before the next year.

Then there was one of my most favorite trees of all, the foil tree, made of aluminum. This tree was not assembled one limb at a time. It unfolded and was ready to place in its stand. Colored glass ornaments were still used, and some didn't make it to or stay on the tree like they were supposed to. There were no icicles because the entire tree looked like a giant icicle. There were no lights strung on the tree; none to untangle, replace, test or string. A rotating multicolor light thingamajig provided the color for the tree. Now this tree was just plain cool with the rotating color wheel. We had one and Granny and Papa Bowie had one as well. Granny Winn stuck with the traditional cedar tree but on her tree were these bubbling lights. I loved watching those bubbling lights. They animated the tree. It was alive, kind of. There was no more tree shedding in this version. Other than the assembly of the tree, it was a much easier one to decorate. I hated it when these eventually went out of style. They were popular from 1958 until the mid 60's. Some people held out and used them longer though. I think granny had hers longer than we had ours. It was just an easy tree to put up and take down and she had a tough time turning it loose.

Colortone Light

Our Aluminum Tree on Hunter Street 1964

The evolution of trees continued. Real bought ones became popular and they were not cheap. Trees were grown on farms or trucked in from other locations. These weren't cedar trees. They were fancy spruce and fir trees. I don't remember us buying any though. My parents still opted for the artificial kind, an investment that could be used year after year. These were becoming more believably life like though. They still shed little make-believe needles and could be as messy as a real tree. At least you did not have to water any of the manmade trees like you had to do for the cedar trees.

Bubble Ornaments

Mama had this little ceramic Christmas tree. She passed away in 2004 but I still have it and use it every year. Ironically, they are making a comeback and you can now buy what I call knock off versions, not the original versions. Of course, the aluminum trees have become popular again as well. Nostalgia knows no boundaries. Keep what you've got because it will eventually come in handy again.

Mama's Ceramic Tree 2019 At Our House

Not a tree, but I have my Granny Bowie's original Nativity scene. She passed away in 2005. It is nothing fancy. The manger is cardboard, and the figures are not expensive, but it belonged to her. Enough said. I also still use it every Christmas. Mama gave Judy and me two animated figures, Mr. and Mrs. Santa Clause in 1996 when we moved in our first house. They still work and we still use them.

Granny Bowie's Nativity Display 2019

Mr. and Mrs. Clause 2019

I must digress for a second though. Pre-Judy, I had a friend, Ricky Bryant, that didn't own a truck and he asked me to help find a tree and haul it home for him. This would have been in the late 80s. Yep. You got it. We went in search of a cedar tree. Ricky was not interested in the perfect tree. He wanted a cedar tree with character. Character in this case was what he called an ugly tree. We rode those old back roads in search of the perfect ugly tree and yes, we scoped out the pasture fence lines. I asked him why fence lines, remembering my daddy doing the same thing. He said, simple; birds eat the little berries off cedar trees and then they perch on places like fence lines and poop. The bird poop essentially contains cedar tree seeds. Thus, mystery solved. Cedar trees are aligned with the barbed wire where the birds left their business. How cool is that? We managed to find what he was searching for, a twisted and oddly shaped tree wedged in the fence. Finding it and removing it were two entirely different issues. A wedged cedar in barbed wire doesn't give up easily. It was a bloody battle, one for the records but we managed to retrieve that tree for him and his family. Character comes with a price but is ironically priceless in the end. They were happy so I was happy to have helped.

I did eventually venture twice to tree farms. No, neither tree was for me. I helped the Singletons once pick out a tree for the grandkids. It was a pick and pull, or I should say pick and saw. The kids made their choice, and we did the rest. The second tree experience was like the ugly tree adventure. I had the truck and my friend, Kirk Husser, wanted me to help him pick and haul one home from the tree farm. That was my first tree farm extraction, probably in the late 80s, early 90s. His daughters made the pick. He and I cut it down and I hauled it to their house, and I helped them put it up. In both tree incidences, more of the base had to be sawed off to fit in the stands. I don't know what happened for the ugly cedar tree but I'm betting it didn't fit the first time either. In all three incidences, the looks on the kids' faces were priceless, them involved in selecting the tree and taking it home. It warmed my heart as well, sort of like being the big elf off the shelf that helped.

Years in the grooming, I am now the adult tree owner. Over the many years I have always owned artificial trees. The first were 'the each limb' at a time assembly. Later the trees came in three or four sections, but you still had to bend and shape them after they had been stuffed and folded in their boxes for a year between usages. We mostly use all white lights. Over the years I have had blinking lights, twinkling ones, animated versions, and everything in between. And every year some do not work, even when the string is supposed to still work if one goes out. Highly over-advertised and overrated. Now they make the pre-lit trees, much easier but lights do stop working. I have graduated from the simple glass ornaments to handmade ones, souvenir ones, all kinds of crazy characters and shapes. For a while I had the little attachments that allowed the ornaments to rotate.

I stepped up that game when Judy gave me a stand that rotated. Picture a tree that revolves and tree ornaments that turn as well. We still have a six and half foot pencil tree that must be twenty-four years old. It's in the sunroom and our main tree is in the living room. The pencil tree was once used on our screened in back porch as my redneck tree. You would have had to have seen it to appreciate the artistry. Some years I had a tree in every room in the house, mostly the three or four footers but a tree just the same. I have always loved decorating for Christmas. Back in the 80's I decorated a twenty-five-foot cedar in my front yard. That one was tough to string the lights, but I managed to space them quite evenly. One foggy night a black man showed up at our front door, obviously intoxicated and lost, thinking he was at Lake Greenwood. The giant Christmas tree had been his lighthouse so to speak. It took some time before we convinced him he was in Abbeville County instead of Greenwood County.

We caroled back in the day, a time when I think I could actually carry a tune. It didn't really matter whether I could, or if I couldn't, kids sang, and adults nor other kids mocked us for trying. Christmas carols were a big part of life. Singing around a tree or in front of someone's house was expected during the fah-lah-lah-lah-lah season. It was a given in our family, just like giving gag gifts. A real pig's tail would make its rounds with someone's name on it. I was always given money by my parents to Christmas shop for them, my grandparents, or others if I could stretch my allotted funds. I remember once giving Mama a plastic pitcher shaped like a pineapple and four coconut shaped accessory cups. Everyone needed a set so I must have thought. She used them for a while, to pacify me I'm sure. I always wrapped my purchased goodies. No denying it, it wasn't a mystery which ones came from me, even without looking at the name tags. I was a kid. I could not cut straight with scissors. I never cut the wrapping paper the correct size for the shaped object. Folding and taping the paper was not a skill God gifted me with. Let's just say mine were unique but under that Christmas tree with all the perfectly wrapped ones. Milliken, where my parents worked, had their Christmas parties at the Abbeville National Guard Armory. Kids looked forward to any Christmas parties. Gifts and goodies, and a Santa appearance were guaranteed. There would always be a huge, decorated cedar tree inside the armory.

Oh yeah. We had Christmas parades; lots of them. Every town had one. We attended the Abbeville one for sure. Often, we traveled to Greenwood or Anderson. I even remember seeing at least one Greenville parade and possibly one in Iva. It all depended on when and if we had someone to take us; us being the parade craving kids. Santa and the Shriners always tossed candy to those watching, another perk of the way back when times. I have even participated in a few hometown parades; riding on floats, marching with the Cub Scouts and a junior marching band. During Christmas, traditions prevailed, and we embraced them. Families did this stuff together; no kicking and screaming from the children. We had no cable television, no video games, no internet, or social media then. That must be frightening to some of you reading this. Anything out of the normal was fun. I seldom attend parades now. Guess like anything, you outgrow the urge. I have attended a couple of Conway parades since living at Myrtle Beach. Mostly, we did this for the grand boys when they were young. It was forced family fun at best.

Another flashback to my youth; we rode all over the place looking at Christmas decorations each year, a family tradition hardly ever practiced now. The iconic giant tree on the Abbeville, S.C. hometown square was a favorite. For much of my life they assembled a tree frame over a tall civil war monument in the center of the square and then decorated it with real tree limbs and lamp sized multicolored bulbs. Another favorite tree was located on a pond just across the Greenwood County line when highway 72 was just two lanes instead of four. The tree was not in the pond but was mounted inside a wooden boat anchored in the center. It was a cedar tree, but there was something mesmerizing about that tree on the water. I've seen a lot of floating trees over the years, still special when they are spotted.

We would also ride to Williamson to view the many scenes and decorations in the city's Mineral Spring Park. It has been an upstate attraction since 1958. When we lived in the Saddle Hill subdivision during the 90's in Greenwood, a family had an upside-down tree decorated and hanging from the ceiling of their front porch. I liked that one, unique and original. I am an old softy for Christmas trees. Guess I will continue to have at least one or two if the old bones will allow me to have them.

> *Oh Christmas tree, oh Christmas tree*
> *Such pleasure do you bring me*
> *Oh Christmas tree, oh Christmas tree*
> *Such pleasure do you bring me*
> *Every year this Christmas tree*
> *Brings to us both joy and glee*

Looking for a Few Good Snowmen

Snowflakes falling, a young boy's fantasy comes true. Living in the foothills of the upstate of South Carolina for most of my life, snow was never a winter sure thing and rarely were there six-inch accumulations or deeper snows. We, more times than not, got what the forecasters called a dusting. Trust me. A kid cannot make a snowman out of a dusting any more than a kid can have a good snowball fight. Worse still are those dreaded ice storms, more prominent than the snows in the deep South. Those will bring down pine trees and the power lines along with it quicker than half dozen crews of pulp-wooders.

The other thing about our snows; it can snow six inches that morning and be completely melted by day's end. They rarely linger so at the first sight of a snowflake we kids were in our three layers of clothing, two pairs of socks, a ski mask, and gloves ready to take on the forces of nature. If it snowed during the day, we remained glued to the windows and if by night we constantly switched on the porch light to check the winter wonderland in the making. We could drive our parents completely squirrelly begging to go outside. It was almost as bad as those dreaded words while on a road trip, "*Are we there yet?*" Kids can be quite persistent.

About every seven or eight years we would be blessed with that one big snow, topping ten inches if we were lucky. Talk about absolute heaven. We would feel like we had struck the mother lode. Kids would have enough snow for everything imaginable. Snowmen, snowball fights, an endless supply of snow ice cream were all on the agenda. It was almost a certainty that we would miss at least one or two days of school. That is, of course, unless it snowed on the weekend. We had more time to play in it but those days away from school put us in the bonus round.

Snow ice cream, now there's a treat the entire family enjoyed. Rule number one, never collect snow with yellow stains or peppered with animal or bird tracks. Best place to harvest the snow was on an elevated table, the trunk or hood of an automobile or a low hanging roof. Rule number two, have all your ingredients ready before bringing the snow inside, milk, sugar and vanilla extract. Add snow and the ingredients in a bowl and blend them. Like magic, you had snow ice cream and usually an ice cream headache to boot. Brain freezes are not fun. Eating slow was not an option in our minds.

The neighborhood became a sea of children so layered with clothing it is a wonder we could move at all. Rollie-pollie figures speckled the terrain. Snowballs whizzed by just missing their targets while others nearly knocked us senseless. That once flakey and fluffy snow had been transformed into compacted lethal weapons, our version of paint ball years before it was ever conceived. Snow is for sledding too, so seeking out the best high ground was next on our agenda. Because we didn't reside in traditional snow country, hardly any of us owned a real sled. Improvising was required. Rounded tin tubs large enough to support a youngster's derrière were not necessarily our first choice but they can work provided our mothers had not realized we had snuck them from the kitchen pantry. Scrubbing the bottoms with wax paper improved the aerodynamics of sliding. That too we had to sneak from the kitchen.

Rounded metal trash can lids could offer safe passage down the hill providing they had no lift handle on top. Cardboard would work for a while until it became too wet then it abruptly disintegrated. The ultimate homemade ride had to be the famed Coca Cola bottle cap sign. When inverted it was the envy of backyard participants. Everyone waited their turn to try it. All vehicles were free wheelers, meaning you either slide until you came to a stop or you hit something or someone halting your forward progress. After the collision, most of us laughed. Only once in my life did I ever own a real authentic sled. My parents, a couple of adult cousins and I decided to head to the mountains one cold and wintry Saturday. Our destination was only two or three hours away and usually just a day trip. It began to snow when we were somewhere between Highlands and Cherokee North Carolina, the drive becoming so treacherous that my folks had to stop and place the snow chains on the car tires. The snow piled up quickly and we stopped at a local hardware store for reasons I can't remember.

What I do remember was seeing that wooden six-foot sled with metal runners in the store front window. Somehow, I convinced my folks we just had to have it, so they purchased one. We drove to one of the mountain side roads almost unrecognizable by the layer of snow. There we had the time of our lives, sometimes stacking belly on top of back three high as we soared down the incline. We repeated this trek over and over until becoming too tired to make the climb. Now that was spontaneous living. Somewhere above Ashville, North Carolina, we ended up becoming stranded and had to spend the night in a motel. We had only the clothes on our back. Stranded had it perks. It created a family bonding experience the old fashion way.

After we arrived back home, I was the envy of the neighborhood with my brand new authentic sled. Unfortunately, it never snowed again that year, so I had to wait over a full year before we received more than a dusting to enable me to wow my peers. We did not have any of those mountain back roads with long hills to do it justice. The bottle cap made it down our little hill better than my sled. The runner blades bogged down in the mere couple inches of snow. Quickly I grew tired of the sudden stops halfway down the hill. I would have to rely on my mountain memories, so it seemed. Framing this for my friends just wasn't the same though.

Given enough snow and enough help we could build some impressive snowmen. Every household tried to outdo their neighbor. Even the adults got in on the construction of the perfect creation. Just any snow didn't work. Too powdery prevented forming the snowball foundation. If it wouldn't roll up, failure was certain. Too slushy wasn't any better. Sort of like Goldie Locks and the Three Bears, you had to have that just right snow. Forming the base and foundation to support the next two sections posed the largest challenge. Lifting the middle section onto the base was a challenge. That's where an adult came in handy. While the third section, the head was the smallest, lifting it on top could be most difficult too. It became more complicated by just how large the snowman had become. Bigger wasn't always better but it made for great show in the front yard. Traditional rounded snowmen were prevalent but those rivaling ice carvings weren't uncommon. Mine were usually of the basic design; round base, round waist, round head, stick arms, rock buttons, rock smile, rock eyes, carrot or stick nose and some sort of hat and scarf.

Some stood straight and proud. Others leaned one way or the other teetering on falling over at the slightest breeze or elevation in temperature. It did not matter how they looked. We had our very own snowman. That's all that counted. Next, it was time to peel out of the many layers of clothing, wet from outer layer to underwear. Nothing felt better than cozying up to the open door of the preheated kitchen stove. Mama knew how to do this up right having prepared hot chocolate in a skillet on the oven eye and then topped it with melted marshmallows. Later we would have hot soup just like on the Campbell's Soup commercial. Once we had nourished our system and dried out for a spell, we layered up with dry clothing and headed outside again.

Our snowmen next had to survive the elevated temperatures and the snowmen assassins. The sun would test the integrity of our architectural skills and would whittle away at old Frosty, eventually reducing him into a mere puddle of his former self. If our masterpiece somehow dwindled but still survived proud and erect, the assassins would unleash their wrath kicking and plummeting on wintry friends. Snow blobs speckled the landscape until at last they were a fading memory. We do have our photographs, Kodak moments the early years. I do miss those childhood snowy days. We were the snow kings of Abbeville. Hope your smile is as large as mine is right now.

Young Tommy and His Snowman 1960

Cousin Billy Bowie and Little Tommy 1960

Billy and Tommy with Front Yard Snowman 1960

It's eleven o'clock, do you know where your children are?

I've babbled a lot about the Bowie side of the family. It seemingly is much easier to remember comic relief and memorable stories from Mama's roots. Not to worry though. The Winn side had their fair share of equally memorable moments. I just seemed to spend more time with my grand folks down on South Main than across highway 72 on Marshall Avenue. South Main was within walking distance of our house on Hunter Street. Plus, it was on the way to all the candy goody holes. I did spend many weekends with Granny Winn though. We would go to Greenwood to the movies and of course to Mister Quick or Rick's Barbeque. Who could ever forget the iconic voice of Melvin at the window of Mister Quick? The Bowie and Winn families were from opposite ends of the spectrum so to speak. Lifestyles and daily activities were much different. A kid had to learn how to adapt and adapting isn't a kid's strong suit.

Take for instance. I called Papa and Granny, Papa and Granny. Papa was my only Papa, but I had two grannies. During one stretch I also had a great granny tossed in for good measure. Thusly I referred to daddy's mama as Granny Winn and Granny Bowie's mama, my great grand, as Granny Holmes. It helped me when talking about them to differentiate, I suppose. Papa and Granny were good ole southern home bodies, as you have already discovered. They did not put on for anyone. They were genuine, same way all the time, no matter who was around. Everyone was greeted with a smile and a hug and an open invitation to have dinner or supper with them if you dropped by around feeding time. There was always plenty of food, no matter how many dropped by unannounced. If you left their house hungry you had no one to blame but yourself. They would always have something on the table.

Granny and Papa lived in L.A., Lower Abbeville, on the south side of Highway 72, the mill village section of town. Granny Winn lived on the north side of 72, and while still south of the town square, it was still considered to be the uptown side of Abbeville. I guess highway 72 was the division between the two, they *abided by boundaries* so to speak. Granny and Papa lived in that modest four room wood mill house while Granny Winn, Aunt Cornelia and Uncle Jerry lived in a ranch style brick home. Well, they did live in the brick house much of my life as a kid, having moved from another house about a mile away, still on the north side of 72. That home was a stone's throw from Milliken Textile Mill but not in the mill village.

Before I go on, let me be clear. I loved Granny Winn, but the love for her and the love I felt towards Granny and Papa was different. I could tell the difference at an early age, even though I did not really understand why nor could exactly explain it. Reflecting now, I do. I was Granny and Papa's only grandchild. That made it easier for me to be comfortable at their house. I could raid the kitchen cabinets or refrigerator with reckless abandon. At Granny Winn's, I was just one of many cousin fishes in the pond making the rounds. Plus, that warm and cozy feeling just wasn't there. I never quite felt right just going into her cabinets without asking permission. Another major difference, Winn's didn't typically greet you with a hug like at the Bowie household. They smiled and nodded. The environment there felt more structured, not laid back. Granny and Papa had only one kid, my mama. Granny Winn had eight kids, four boys and four girls. Maybe that made a difference in the lifestyle there and their way of thinking.

Granny Winn was a stay at home granny. I had never seen her work outside the household. Granny Bowie had worked in the mill until becoming disabled. Papa was a self-employed painter and provider. Granny Winn did take in sewing. The mud room, just off the kitchen and at the back-door entrance, was her sewing shop so to say. She took in sewing and got paid for it. She was an excellent seamstress and could make anything. To this day I have no idea why that tiny little sewing room was called the mud room. She didn't make pottery or excavate in the dirt there. Older and wiser and with the aid of Google, I have unraveled the unsolved mystery. A mud room is a small room or entryway in a house where wet and muddy footwear and clothing can be removed. It is usually tile or linoleum making it easy to clean. Well, it was an entryway and the floors were red tiled. Granny Winn must have converted it to her sewing room, but the name just stuck like mud.

Granny Winn was always prim and proper, exhibiting correct posture when standing or sitting. She was not Pentecostal like Granny and Papa, but she always wore a dress, no hair bun though. Granny Winn went to the beauty parlor weekly while Granny never did. Both grannies wore glasses. Granny Winn was educated and could read. Unlike Granny and Papa, book learning had not been a priority in their lives. Granny Holmes could read though, go figure. Cooking was noticeably different between the two granny's homes. At Granny and Papa's, you ate real food, good ole fashion southern home cooking seasoned and tasty. Everything seemed fresh out of the garden. Just the mere smells from the kitchen were a sure invitation. Tender loving care went into the dish preparations, no short cuts or dumping something in a pot from a can.

Granny Winn, sorry to say, was not a cook. Sure, she could put food on a table, but I guess the best way for me to describe it is it tasted like fake food. Forget any chance of homemade black skillet cornbread or even biscuits. Store bought rolls and loaf bread were more her style. They ate a lot of sandwiches if truth be known. Nothing ever tasted seasoned. They did not use fatback and I'm not sure salt or pepper were ever used. Forget fried chicken, rabbit, or squirrel. Don't look around for turnip greens, potato salad, fried okra or biscuits and gravy. Granny put special effort into making her banana pudding or lemon pie. Granny Winn's pudding was the instant mix kind and much to my disappointment, having had the bar raised down on South Main. Her potato salad, when she did serve it, was sweet tasting. Sorry, that is just too un-southern. We want our desserts sweet, not the regular food. Most weekly meals were served on paper plates and with plastic cups. Get this though, the plastic cups were washed and reused. Real glasses and dinnerware were only brought out for special occasions and during the holidays.

Eating events were structured at Granny Winn's as was most everything at her home, unlike the feeding frenzy and every person for their themselves at the Bowie household. There was the dining room table, especially reserved for Granny Winn, the higher-ranking siblings, with a few privileged spouses. No kids ever sat at that table. Table number two was the kitchen table. This was primarily made up of those spouses not allowed at the dining room table and if room allowed, an occasional older grandkid. The kids were banished to card tables set up in the den just off the kitchen. We didn't get to eat at the big tables, not until we reached a certain age and only then if a spot came open. Mostly this was attributed to certain families not being there or the passing of a member that opened a slot. We understood the pecking order loud and clear. It was the unwritten house rules.

Rules seemed to be part of every segment of Granny Winn's lifestyle. All meals were precisely served at a designated time and in perfect portions, hardly ever were there any leftovers like at Granny and Papa's. Snack time occurred the very same time each night. The ritual was always the same. Crackers and a plastic cup of Pepsi were served to those present. Coca Cola was not an option or allowed substitute. Occasionally they splurged with a serving of Borden's ice cream, and only because Uncle Dolph, who was a Borden's executive, kept them supplied. Like Pepsi, Borden's could not be substituted for another name brand, like Pet. That would be insubordination, something only a traitor to the family would do.

Did I mention assigned sitting? Yes, besides the dining pecking order, Granny Winn, Aunt Cornelia, and Uncle Jerry had staked out their spots in the den. The matriarch of the family would also anchor the couch end closest to the kitchen. I can envision her sitting there, puffing on a filterless Camel cigarette. I never ever saw her sit anywhere else. Those Camels and a box of matches would be within hand's reach on the end table. Secondhand smoke for grandkids didn't mean much back in the time before smoking was shunned as being socially unacceptable. Oddly, there were a scant few that she did not smoke in front of. I just wasn't one of them. Aunt Cornelia anchored the opposite end of the couch, a stack of newspapers marking her spot. She would have been prime subject material for that hoarder television series. Forget recycling, the attic was filled with old newspapers. You'd have thought it was the national archives. A recliner was staged in the small den just in front of the couch. That was Uncle Jerry's spot, unless booted by visitors. An uncomfortable long bench with cushions on it was located in front of the sliding glass door, reserved for the rest of us. That is unless you moved a chair from the kitchen into the den.

Aunt Cornelia was a throw back, always doing things a certain way, the poster lady for 'that's the way we've always done it'. She had a 'no color outside the lines' persona. I hope she had stock in post-it notes. She used them for everything. She and Granny Winn shared a bedroom, each with their very own bed but the yellow post-its were almost like wallpaper in the bedroom and adjoining bathroom. I think some of the reminders were older than a lot of us. Jerry's room was across the hall, our hangout most of the time. His décor was Clemson Tigers and Abbeville Panthers. Then there was 'The Pink Room'. That was the guest room and the only other bedroom in the house. You almost had to be privileged to sleep in there. It was never cluttered, almost shrine like. We were never allowed in there to play or make mischief.

House rules had no end but there was one that stuck in everyone's craw. The mud room door and main entrance to the house was on a timed locking mechanism, or so it seemed. If you spent the night at Granny Winn's, heed one warning and take it seriously. There were no exceptions. At precisely eleven PM each night that door would be locked. It was some sort of curfew. Be warned. You didn't dare test this one. That door would be locked. Ringing the doorbell or knocking was not a desirable option. Violators weren't tolerated. Most of the time Uncle Jerry would be delegated to let you in and you didn't want to disturb his sleep either. I always thought this applied to just kids, remembering the commercial of that time; *It's eleven o'clock, do you know where your children are?*

Trust me, if you stayed there, no matter what your age, the door locked at eleven. You were not given a pass key. Adults did not get it, but it didn't matter. A rule was a rule. It applied to everybody, no exceptions. Just like missing snack time, there was no makeup clause. I never actually heard an explanation for this lock down rule. I don't know if a specific incident triggered it or if it was just the way it had always been. Even after Granny passed on to the great beyond, Aunt Cornelia stayed firm to the house rules, even the eating and snacking arrangements. Aunt Cornelia collected those annually produced Hess vehicles and after she passed, each of her siblings, nieces and nephews received one, in mint condition in the original box. I inherited my dad's and still have mine, both in mint condition, still in the original boxes. Does that make me a hoarder I wonder? Does Howdy Doody ring a bell?

I have many photos of Granny Winn and all are the same. She would strike the same posture, perfect pose and never ever smile. It was almost like snapping a picture of a stone statue. As I have stated, I loved her, and she was good to me. I can't remember a time when she ever raised her voice to me. You know how it goes; perfection is a gift. Maybe I was just sneaky and lucky instead. I did sneaky very well back then. With her, I got to go to the movies, shopping and to eat out. Granny and Papa never attended a movie that I can remember; nor did they have the Saturday ritual of going to Greenwood or Anderson. That was something I only shared with Granny Winn, Aunt Cornelia ,and Uncle Jerry. Elvis and Disney were part of her regiment. She never missed releases of either. I am blessed to have had her in my life, to have known my daddy's mama. Thinking back, why would I have wanted my Grannies to be the same? While life with either of my grandparents was predictable, it was also vastly different and wonderful. I am granny-less now and all I have are those nostalgic snapshots and wonderful memories. All are good.

Granny (Amy) Winn 1967

Granny (Amy) Winn 1970

One final thought and an appropriate update...maybe Granny Winn was ahead of her time. Seems some governors and mayors in 2020 think that Covid-19 has an eleven PM curfew. Bars must be closed by then according to their unscientific based facts. Allow time to arrive home safely before the Covid hour. Cut it too close and the boogeyman will get you. This is called sarcasm folks. I get it. Covid is dangerous. I should know. I am in the higher risk category and blessed so far that the smart virus has not discovered where I live. And yes, I do wear masks when necessary and socially distance when I am supposed to. I possess common sense and understand the risks. I do not require an overreaching government to threaten or force me to do their bidding. I believe in and practice freedom. Now Granny Winn, she saw things differently, ruler of her roost. Back then things were much different, and kids had no rights. We did what we were asked to do, no lip. Elder respecting knowns no boundaries.

BNG

BNG, **B**efore **N**avigation **G**adgets we had Daddy. Back in the day of Daddy navigating the highways, his version of GPS was a tad different than today's' technology. Thomas (T.J) Winn had absolutely no sense of direction. Most men can make enough right turns, claim to not be wandering aimlessly and can usually eventually get back on track without stopping and asking for those dreaded directions. It's taboo in a real man's world to inquire how to get back on the beaten track. Not T.J. though. When he got off track, prepare for that three-hour tour. He would have been right at home on the S.S. Minnow. Let's face it. Daddy was a nomad, a wanderer, the very last person that needed to be behind the steering wheel when in uncharted territory. This was a kid's perspective at the time. I was not sure if he could read a map or a compass or if we had either then. Following directions or instructions, lost in translation I am afraid. I remember, when Mama would send him to the grocery saying we need bread, don't get any eggs. He would return with eggs and no bread. Not trying to sound cruel about my dearly departed Daddy but you've got to call them like you remember them. Fear not. I have the evidence to support my case. I will allow the jury to decide.

Where do I start down this venture off the primrose path? Columbia, the South Carolina State Capitol, was just a hair over an hour away from Abbeville. It might as well have been a desolate country as far as T.J. was concerned. Heading towards the Grand Strand usually took us directly through town. I am not sure if there were any bypasses back then, ways to skirt the city or if Daddy just figured the shortest way between two points was a direct line. He always forged ahead toward the bowels of the beast. One thing for sure, we were innocent passengers at his mercy and misguided routes. A kid did not have any say so, not that I could have assisted him being just a backseat window watcher. Mama on the other hand was supposedly the copilot. She would always reserve, or should I say restrain her opinions until we were hopelessly mired in deep dodo, circling the wagons so to speak. Lost was lost.

Columbia is a maze of criss-crossing streets. I only use the maze analogy because we may as well have been navigating our way through a Nebraska cornfield for all it was worth. Daddy utilized hit and miss methodology. It put a new spin on '*are we there yet*?' For well past an hour we traveled aimlessly through the streets of the state capitol. He was unable to locate an exit strategy for heading beach bound. I can't tell you how many times he drove by the capital building and the infamous Bull Street, Mama pointing out that fact to him during every drive by. As kids we associated Bull Street with the crazy house, the Lunatic Asylum, Bull Street &

Elmwood Avenue. Jokingly we would raze one another saying stuff like, 'Did you escape from Bull Street?' Or 'If you keep acting like that you'll end up in a padded cell and straight jacket on Bull Street.' Sorry, cruelty to our peers was just part of growing up back then. Thankfully, we were not required or expected to be politically correct. We could just be kids, be us and horse around with reckless abandon. Sorry, skirting off track but one nostalgic moment often triggers another one. Forbid a kid says anything about a gun now or points a pretend loaded finger. I digress. That is what I do when I ponder on those days where fun could be found in abundance.

Back to our journey to the center of the earth, Daddy's déjà vu route nightmare with Mama barking orders for him to stop and ask for directions. I don't think he stopped that many times. He opted for the blind hog will sometimes find an acorn. Somehow, we eventually got back on track and headed toward our vacation destination. Daddy, unfazed by the episode, tuned Mama out as he nonchalantly drove along as if the delay had never happened. Fast forward a week and the return drive. Lessons were not learned. We again found ourselves trapped in the Columbia twilight zone, riding and searching for a way home.

The construction of interstate highways would eventually remedy Daddy's doomed Columbia drive through experiences. Interstates posed a new can of worms though. Where there is a will there is a way. Unfortunately, the new four lane byways would just offer a quicker way to get to the lost world. I have examples to support this too. Daddy and antics like these would make it difficult many years later for us to identify that he had Alzheimer's. He had always been notorious for doing stupid stuff and I mean that as only a loving only child can say, having lived through the good, bad, and ugly of it.

In 1966 the Winn version of the Griswold Family East to West Coast two-week vacation was alive and not so well. AAA had laid out the route. We would, as was the custom back then, be traveling the back roads of America. We would take in all of what America had to offer including those oddities and once in a lifetime tourist attractions and traps. This was fun stuff for a teenager without a care in the world. It beat just hanging out with four adults. From Abbeville we would take a northern route to L.A. (not Lower Abbeville this time, but Los Angeles). We would then return via a southern route, covering nearly twenty states and the country of Mexico once the dust had settled. I had no driver's license and would be excluded from the driving rotation. Everyone took their turn except Mama. Fine by me. I'd not be accountable for any mishaps along the way; well at least not from behind the steering wheel. While back country two lane roads can be challenging when in boondocks America, the more challenging portions of the trip are when rural Americans find themselves on interstates and superhighways. These were not the best-case scenarios for T.J.

One such episode stands out far and above all the rest. On the return trip we arrived in Houston, Texas for a couple of night's stay. We had timed our stop to attend a baseball game. Our team, the visiting Atlanta Braves, would be battling the home Astros. At this snapshot in time the Astrodome was the only existing domed sports stadium. It was dubbed a virtual eighth wonder of the world. I was excited. We were going to see our Braves play there. I can still visualize the namesake players of that era; Hank Aaron, Rico Carty, Felipe Alou, Eddie Mathews, Joe Torre, Phil Niekro, Felix Millan, Pat Jarvis, Ron Reed, Cecil Upshaw, Tony Cloninger, Clay Carrol. Oh yeah, Tony Cloninger became the first National League player that year and the only pitcher to hit two grand slams in one game. So, we had arrived in Houston, one of the last significant legs of our trip. Another memory flash while I still have it, Daddy, Billy Joe and I bowled in a bowling alley that must have had nearly a hundred lanes. I recall walking down the midway with lanes spread out on both sides. We were the only three bowling in the alley that morning. They must have gotten wind we were in town.

Now it was game time. We could see the Houston Astrodome looming in the skyline from our motel. I could hardly wait, in awe of what was to come. Hindsight, awe wouldn't nearly describe the experience ahead. We exited our motel parking lot and soon were on one of those six lane new fangled interstate roadways. The dome inched nearer as we approached. Odd, after a while it was to our left and then to our rear as we continued to travel the roadway that was supposed to carry us there. For well over an hour we found ourselves circling the Astrodome. It was almost within our grasp, but Daddy couldn't find a way to get there. We were on what they called the perimeter or loop road. It was indeed living up to its name. We continued to loop around the dome. It was almost game time. Real men think they will eventually overcome driving woes, but the passengers were on the verge of a mutiny. Daddy had to finally take an exit and ask for help. As chance would have it, the gas station attendant pointed us down the very road we had exited onto. Like magic we had arrived. That night we witnessed Hank Aaron hit a solo homer into the center field bleachers in a losing cause. The two teams also broke out into several bench clearing brawls during the game. I can't recall what prompted the melee.

There must be something about baseball stadiums or big cities that challenged Daddy's driving abilities. Every time we attended an Atlanta Braves ballgame at Atlanta's Fulton County Stadium with Daddy at the wheel, we always got lost on the streets of Atlanta. He struggled to find his way back to interstate 85 North. Like in Columbia we'd pass the gold domed capitol building from every possible direction before finally locating 85. I'm not sure if a GPS would have helped him or not. Guess we'll never know for sure as that technology didn't come along until after he had earned his wings, becoming the Lord's next challenge.

Funny thing though. Daddy never became frustrated or befuddled, not that we could tell. Being lost didn't seem to rattle his cage at all. Not to worry, the passengers more than made up for his lack of concern. God only made one T.J. Ask anyone. Years later a young starting pitcher for the Atlanta Braves would miss his rotation one night. Pascual Perez had just received his license and earned the nicknames 'Perimeter Pascual' and 'Wrong-Way Perez' after missing a start on August 19, 1982. Like Daddy, he circled on Atlanta's Interstate 285 (a ring road/beltway) 3 times looking for Atlanta-Fulton County Stadium. He eventually ran out of gas and arrived at the ballpark 10 minutes late. Daddy was the trail blazer but at least he never ran out of gas.

One other side story happened in Daytona, Florida. He should have been familiar with Daytona since we went there for two-week vacations almost every year around July 4th to attend the races. I recall we had just had seafood at one of the local mom and pop spots, one we always visited. We were returning to our beach front cottage motel. Guess he took a wrong turn and we suddenly found ourselves airborne, like the Dukes of Hazzard's General Lee. With no seat belts back then, our heads slammed the ceiling before our butts slammed the seats and floorboard. All I remember seeing was the ocean directly ahead in our headlights as we came crashing down on the beach. Daddy had driven into a beach access road launching us no telling how many feet into the air. It could have been fun if I had known to prepare. Daddy caught hell that time too. Mama could dish it out and I guess he deserved it.

Driving had always been a challenge for him. I've seen Daddy thrown off riding lawn mowers, the Snapper motoring along the yard with him chasing after it. After he retired, he and Mama took up bike riding, the one speed kind, not a Harley. Theirs sped only as fast as they peddled. They often biked from Marshall Avenue to South Main to Granny and Papa's house. Other times they would take short trips around the neighborhood. No, he didn't get lost but that doesn't mean there weren't adventurous trips just the same. Daddy had a basket mounted on the front of his bike, perfect for taking Poppy, the brown Chihuahua along. Poppy loved being a passenger, the wind blowing in his face, better than hanging his head out of a car window. That was until daddy somehow wrecked his bike, tossing poor Poppy into the air and onto the ground. Luckily the duo landed on the grass. Neither sustained serious injuries. Just the same, Poppy would no longer ride in that basket. He leapt out of it as fast as Daddy would situate him in it. The thrill of the ride was gone forever in a pup's eyes.

All kidding aside, I miss Daddy and especially his antics. Well maybe a little friendly humor doesn't hurt in this case. The Lord only made one T.J. The Lord now has him back to sort through his little creation and make sure it doesn't happen again. I just hope He keeps any keys or motorized heavenly vehicles out of Daddy's hands. I sure hope daddy quickly got the hang of those new-fangled wings without causing an eight-angel pile up. Stay off the perimeter clouds, Daddy. They'll only lead you in circles. We certainly don't need you whipping up a funnel cloud. I guess I shouldn't worry with Mama still as his copilot, whispering *stop for directions. I mean it this time.*

This is a Weather Alert…Really?

Date: January 7, 2014

During my weekday morning commute at the beach I was tuned in to the local talk radio station, WRNN, listening to the hosts, Dave Priest and Liz Callaway, jabber about this and that. Their weather alert announcement spurred the following, opening another portal, causing me to digress in time down life's nostalgic highway. It's funny how one statement can launch a flood of memories. The statement was simple, not earth shattering or life threatening. There was no mention of fear of a government shutdown or talks of how our country was flushing us down the toilet due to the stupidity of self-righteous politicians. There was no imminent terrorist attack, not even a whisper of some local catastrophic event. It was but one brief announcement that triggered my flashback.

Horry county schools were on their regular schedule while Georgetown and Marion Counties were on a two-hour delay…really? Allow me to set the stage for my annoyance and utter disbelief. I presently live at the beach, Myrtle Beach to be more specific. We had been here for nine years at the time. It's the beach, get it! Yesterday the daybreak temperature was 66 degrees on my ride just before seven. Granted, an arctic blast was heading our way and temperatures did plummet 20 degrees by the time I headed back home. Much of the nation was being bombarded with frigid temperatures and blizzard conditions. I get that and my heart goes out to those dealing with it. My point, here AT THE BEACH, nothing frozen was falling from the skies, or was forecasted to fall from the skies. Sure, 18 to 20 degrees is cold but so is 100 degrees hot. School delays, really? Have we gotten soft or what?

Now it is time to venture to way back when. No, I am not going quite that far back in history when parents or grandparents spun their tales of trekking miles in the snow to school barefooted. My school years spanned from 1959 to 1971. While snowstorms were rare in my neck of the woods in Abbeville, they did happen. When snow, sleet or freezing rain was in the forecast, regardless of the percentage chance or accumulation predictions, we clung to our televisions and local radio, anticipating a cancellation, a reprieve from attending school. If nothing frozen was falling from the skies, no matter what the thermometer read, we had no escape plan to avoid the learning process. School, as did life, moved forward.

Sitting in those classrooms with nothing but a wall of windows between us and the outdoors didn't seem to be too concerning to kids used to a seasonal winter. Sure, it could be quite frosty if the temperatures outside had deep dived to frigid conditions, but that's why our parents dressed us appropriately. I cannot remember anyone suffering from frostbite in class. If it was cold, you kept your coat on, not that complicated even for a kid. Same went for summer conditions. The oppressive heat was regulated by how many windows the teacher allowed us to open. If we were lucky the room was equipped with one of those large stand-alone fans. Either way, we sucked it up and bided our time until the last bell rang granting us permission to go home. School was never dismissed early for something as silly as global warming or cold temperatures.

I remember one time when weather conditions drastically changed before day's end. I must have been in second or third grade. We lived one block from Langley Milliken grammar school. The principal decided to get the jump on worsening conditions and dismissed school early. I didn't ride a bus, not for the short distance I had to travel. Most days my parents allowed me to walk, unless it was raining. There was no fear of someone kidnapping us back then. When the announcement was made over the loudspeaker, cheers irrupted. I grabbed my coat, readying for the signal to leave. I retrieved my backpack and prepared for the official dismissal from our teacher. We were anxious, set on ready and go. Boys and girls start your engines; the green flag was moments away.

Count down, 5, 4, 3, 2, 1, we have lift-off. Whooping and hollering sounded down the hallway. We were heading home early. Bidding farewell to my fellow inmates I ventured out the gate just as it began to sleet. Frozen stuff of any kind is supposed to be fun, right? Sleet coming down in sheets isn't quite as fun as those huge wet fluffy snowflakes. My one block walk became my personal survival story. Sleet was blowing sideways and seemingly coming from the direction I was headed. I had not worn gloves nor had the zip on hood for my coat. Now I was being plummeted by what felt like a zillion bee stings. I buried my chin against my chest with my eyes closed except for the occasional squinting. I even attempted covering my face with my bare hands, but the sleet ricocheted off my skin nearly bringing me to tears.

My walk, including all the required horsing around, usually took me less than ten minutes. I was moving at a snail's pace in worsening conditions. Running only made it hurt more. Sadly, my parents didn't know school had been let out early so there would be no rescue in my future. Horror scenes infiltrated my little naïve brain. I could die out here and no one would ever know it until they found my body frozen and crumbled alongside the street. I had somehow made it to the turn at Hunter Street, right into the teeth of hell itself. I didn't know it was possible for sleet to fall horizontally. My house was the fourth house on the right just up the street. My brain convinced me that I would never make it alive. The punishment was too severe. It was taking its toll on my fragile little body. Can't you feel the suspense building? Obviously, I did survive.

Today would require no search and rescue from Abbeville responders. A neighborhood dweller driving by observed my dilemma and prevented a disastrous outcome by picking me up and driving me the rest of the way home. The pelting was a learning experience and apparently one still etched in my old brain. Most kids are drawn to snow like magnets, but sleet and ice don't make for much fun and frolic. Venturing down the snow globe memory trail, I recall other wintry events tickling the brain cells. I can't remember the exact date, but it would have been in 1990's while I was employed at Flexible Technologies. Snow began falling before the first shift folks began reporting to work. Many had opted out in the early going. Fact, in the deep South, once snow or any frozen precipitation begins sticking to the roadways, the snow bunnies are out in it and shouldn't be. People begin braking going up hill as well as down. Those behind them end up in ditches and never make it to the store to stock up on bread and milk.

It was almost white out conditions for our area with the snow accumulating much too fast. Many third shift employees had volunteered to stay over and work awhile because the first shift folks were calling in left and right saying they couldn't make it. I recall only one other time it was nearly as bad and that would have been in the mid 70's. Our plant manager, a Sasquatch size man, showed up that morning with two of those black outdoor trash bags strapped to his feet. Apparently, this was his version of redneck snowshoes. Odd, I don't think he originated from the southern hemisphere. Bless Mr. Charley Hodge's heart. Anyway, back to where I was headed, the snow storm of the 90's. I think it was falling inches an hour and by mid morning it was time to send folks home while they still had a fighting chance of getting there safely. I think they had waited just a tad too late to make that call.

I was the Quality Control supervisor. I followed up by phoning to make sure my third shift Q.C. inspector had made it home. To my shock her husband had not seen her. Betty had been gone for nearly three hours. She didn't have a cell phone. Most folks didn't back then. I informed my boss, Kirk Husser. There was nothing for us to do but follow her route to Lake Secession in hopes we'd locate her. We expected to find her stranded somewhere in a ditch. Kirk had a front wheel three-cylinder Sprint dubbed the Jap Trap because it was one of those made in Japan vehicles. Don't go all politically correct on me. I didn't nickname it that and I won't snitch on the one who did. To this day I have never driven or ridden in snow coming down like it was that morning. We were virtually the only idiots on the highway. We literally had to navigate by keeping it between the ditches. You couldn't see either lane of the roadways, no white lines, yellow line, nothing. Then again no one would be passing us or us passing anyone.

To make matters worse the windshield wipers became absolutely worthless. They were unable to keep the frozen stuff dislodged from the windshield. The defroster was in overdrive and not up to the job either. We'd have to stop frequently and shovel it off with our hands just so we could see where we would potentially be wrecking. There were some steep drop offs on either side of the roads on our route. The three-cylinder vehicle chugged right along hardly slipping or fish tailing at all. What should have been a thirty-minute ride transformed into Gillian's three-hour tour. Perhaps we should have renamed the Sprint the S.S. Minnow. Fortunately, we didn't become stranded. Bless our hearts. We never located our missing employee. When we returned to the plant, we called her house again. Betty answered the phone, explaining she had stopped on the way home to check on her mother. It had failed to register with her the importance of letting somebody know where she was. I had no front wheel drive and barely made it home in my Chevy Luv pickup. There must have been ten inches of snow on the ground by the time it ended.

As a kid it wasn't unusual for my folks to decide to take a daytrip up to Cherokee, Gatlinburg or Pigeon Forge. We'd leave in the early morning hours and arrive around noon. Once we ventured to Cherokee and Daddy apparently failed to verify weather conditions. We didn't have the Weather Channel or cable television back in those days. While we were there the weather conditions began to deteriorate. Snow began to fall to beat the band. Luckily Daddy had snow chains in the trunk of the car. He and our cousin mounted them on all four tires, our version of four-wheel drive back then. The snow covered the roadways very quickly. You've already read this part of the story in a previous chapter. We stopped by an old country store on the winding hairpin roads and purchased a one-man sled. We then pulled off on one of those secondary deserted roads with a steep hill and put the sled to use, having a blast. There were five of us. We took turns or stacked bodies three high and down the hill we would go.

As mentioned previously, we had to call it a day and headed home. Conditions worsened, even too much for the snow chains. That Sunday we ended up spending the night in a motel with nothing but the clothes on our backs. As Paul Harvey might say, and now we have the rest of the story. The next morning, we still had to wait before heading back to allow the roads to thaw. I remember Daddy going out for coffee and biscuits before we did and slipping on the sloped driveway. He was quickly down for the count, our breakfast fairing worse than he. I missed going to school that Monday, an extra vacation day for me. The family memories made it worthwhile. I can recall other times standing out on the frozen lake in Walhalla with people ice skating. Seldom does that lake ever freeze over anymore though.

Missing the good old days can be filled with good stuff, those days when family bonding was a way of life. As an adult I have had a history of working in these little excursions. We have traveled to Boone, N.C. or Maggie Valley for Thanksgiving and even Orlando. I prefer the mountains though. There's just something special about being in cold crisp air for Thanksgiving. Both in Boone and Maggie Valley it snowed and helped set up the arrival of Christmas. Even in Orlando they had a skate rink with fake snow.

Judy, her sisters Charlotte, Norma and hubby Jerry once spent turkey day in Helen, Georgia. While there we noticed on a flyer that there would be a Christmas parade. On the afternoon of the scheduled parade we arrived hours ahead of time to secure our spot on a hill in the town Gazebo. We fended off cold blustery conditions for this annual extravaganza. The entire parade was over in a blink of an eye, one horse drawn carriage, a blind dog and flatbed truck with Santa in the back. I have it on video, time lapse less than two minutes. Once you visit the handful of tourist trap shops in Helen, there is nothing else to do. We would have gladly welcomed a snowstorm. We soon realized four days in Helen was way too long and decided to check out on day three. Norma spotted a large K sign during our backroad's commute. She was quite excited thinking we had stumbled into civilization and had found a K-Mart. It turned out to be a Kangaroo quick stop station. We did stop and shop after gassing up.

I began this story yesterday and this morning we had a heat wave at the beach with the temperature four degrees warmer than yesterday at 22 degrees. Still, the radio host announced a two-hour school delay for surrounding counties. It is Wednesday and I don't get it today either. I sure didn't get a two-hour workday delay. Saturday and Sunday, it will hit the seventies again. Keep the kids inside for the weekend. We wouldn't want them to get heat stroke or sunburned, now would we? Are we just getting too soft or what? I have earned the right to rant. That's my story and I'm sticking to it; sitting here as I hum *Frosty the Snowman* in my little world.

We're Not in Kansas, Toto

Sadly, some memories of our past are not those we wish to dwell on, but I think this one is worth the return trip. Growing up I never thought much about local weather conditions. Those afternoon thunder boomers would pop up bringing with them awesome lightning, cracking thunder, and torrential rains. Big deal. We would just stay inside until they passed. Snow of any significant accumulation was rare. We enjoyed it the day it fell because typically it would be melted that same day or at least by the next day. As mentioned, we would get a good snow once in a blue moon but more likely we were prone to have one of those ice storms. They would topple trees, snap pine tree limbs, and bring down the power lines. My dad removed every pine tree from our front and back yard after a severe ice storm made our Marshall Avenue home site resemble a disaster movie set. I can remember a couple of times being without power for several days due to the freezing rain.

I for one had never given tornados much thought one way or the other. Same thing goes for hurricanes, until now living in Myrtle Beach where we are more in the bull's eye. The Grand Strand has not had a significant landfall since Hugo in 1989. We are overdue for the big one. In the past ten years, living here, a couple of them have skirted the coast but none have been much of a threat. At least with hurricanes you have plenty of warning. Only the stupid fail to heed them and get the heck out of Dodge when advised. Hurricane parties, not a chance, I'm just saying. Doppler Radar has certainly hedged the bet where tornadoes are concerned. Back in my day the warning basically consisted of that familiar freight train approaching sound, so say those who have lived to share their experiences.

I pause here to update this hurricane segment. Nearly two years after I wrote the above, we indeed experienced our first hurricane. Hurricane Matthew struck the Grand Strand, making landfall on Oct. 8, 2016 southeast of McClellanville, South Carolina. It made landfall as a Category 1 hurricane with 75 mph winds. We reside off highway 544 in Evacuation Zone II, between business and bypass 17's. We were not asked to evacuate. The front side of the storm was just rain with some wind. The back side of the storm was just plain scary. Trees were toppling all around us. Fortunately, we sustained no direct hits but were without power for about three days. I have never seen so many downed trees in my life up and down the coast and nearly all the way to Columbia. Some golf courses lost as many as 150 trees. No hurricane party for us, I promise. They order us to leave. We leave. I'm not sure why they didn't send us packing for this one. What a mess?

And in September of 2018, Hurricane Florence made land fall. We were ordered to evacuate then, and we did. Some neighbors stayed. We didn't lose power or suffer any damages. Lucky for us we do not reside in a flood zone. Florence stalled and pumped in the moisture for days. Many locations in the Carolina's received over 35 inches of rain. It was catastrophic. Okay, now resume reading my thoughts from two years previously before Mathew and Florence…back to tornadoes.

I do vaguely recall Papa talking about the big tornado that stuck on the lower end of South Main. I seem to remember something about a couple of sisters being killed. The details are fuzzy. I did recently try to Google this but came up empty. As a kid I couldn't really comprehend the power of a tornado. My only references were from the Wizard of Oz. My first up close and personal experience occurred in 1973 as it did for many in Abbeville. I had married in January of 1972. I was a mere nineteen-year-old. We lived in a rental house on the north side of Abbeville. We paid fifty dollars a month for the four-room abode on McGowan Avenue just across the street from the entrance to Spring Valley Mobile Home Court. Trailer parks are usually tornado magnets. There was nothing abnormal about the start of that April 31st Saturday morning in 1973. If memory serves me, we had experienced one of those significant snowfalls not too many days prior to that date. That April day started with a sunny spring like morning.

My wife, Beverly and I decided to go bowling that night in Anderson, about thirty minutes westward and up highway 28. We picked up two of her cousins on the way. We arrived at our destination around 7:30. While attempting to bowl that perfect game, I noticed thunderstorms had nosily moved into the area. Flashes of lightning followed by cracks of thunder often caused the bowling center's lights to flicker. Undaunted, we continued tossing the balls down the lanes. Anderson is named the Electric City and it seemed to be living up to its namesake that night. Finally giving into the fact that no one would have their breakout 300 we headed home somewhere close to 9:30. The lightning was quite impressive as we headed toward Abbeville. The spectacular flashes would briefly make it appear almost daylight. It was sort of scary in a cool way, but I never felt threatened by the stormy weather. Thunderstorms were frequent in the south and had never concerned me. That was about to change. We dropped off our riders and headed on down 28. I am not even sure if I had seen the local weather forecast on television that day. I certainly had never been one to watch the news segments with any frequency.

We passed Culbreth's Garage just a couple of minutes away from McGowan Avenue. This was before Sky City or Ingles had been built on the wooded hillside. As we approached the end of the cemetery where the Lowndesville Highway intersects with the beginning of North Main we found ourselves staring at an array of flashing lights. Police cars blocked our way. We needed to go another couple of blocks to make our right-hand turn towards our rental house, but they were not going to allow us passage. First thoughts, there must have been a bad wreck or possibly a house fire. It was eerily pitch black except for the blue and red emergency vehicle lights. The police motioned for me to turn around. When I did my jaw dropped as my headlights aimed in the general direction of the McKenzie Acres subdivision. The field and wooded area was a twisted mass of sheet metal and trees. I thought the end of the world had happened.

Panicked now, we made the trek towards McGowan via the bypass. We expected to find our rental house leveled. As previously mentioned, tornados are said to be attracted to trailer parks. Spring Valley was unscathed, as was our home. We were eventually able to contact and meet with our parents, mine, and hers. They filled us in on just what had bulldozed its way through Abbeville while we were bowling. While shocking to hear, morning would tell the real story. These vivid images are still embedded in my mind all these years later. Six or more people died. It had wiped a motel off the face of the earth in Calhoun Falls. McKenzie Acres and other neighborhoods in its path were disaster areas.

The National Guard was keeping people out except for those who lived there. The next day we managed to breach the check point while taking food to some friends. I had brought my Super 8 MM movie camera along but could hardly hold the camera still as I filmed our journey into a world I no longer recognized. I struggled to fathom the power and force it had taken to do this and the almost uncanny selective process of the twister. Houses were swept off their foundations, gone, while one next door appeared untouched. The next might have just the bathroom still standing while the next was a pile of splinters, almost looking as if it had exploded. Fear had a new meaning. While I had not experienced its wrath, I had now witnessed its fury. I was almost twenty years old and forever changed.

The people of Abbeville as did those in other towns devastated by these storms, pulled together and helped family and friends get beyond it and rebuild their lives. I didn't know anything about shingling or repairing a roof but helping Daddy and other volunteers, I climbed on top of Sally Tribbles roof and learned how. After that day in '73 I began paying attention to the weather forecast. It mattered. And when those tornado rashes break out in other towns across the country my heart goes out to the survivors and those families who didn't. I cannot even begin to understand how those who live through one cope with it and hope I never will. As I write this, April is just two months away, but I feel like it was just yesterday. Nostalgia doesn't always have to be funny, warm and fuzzy. Sometimes it just needs to teach us life lessons. The Abbeville tornado of '73 is one of those lessons learned and will never be forgotten. December of 2003 is another and you who lived in Abbeville then will forever remember its impact. A storm of another kind, in ways even worse than that funnel cloud, struck the town of Abbeville with pure evilness. We will forever remember the two fallen officers and an even darker time in Abbeville's history. Transplants from northern regions committed cold blooded murder. December's Darkest Day is available on Amazon. That was a tough one for me to write. Below is an excerpt from local newspaper.

Abbeville, Calhoun Falls, SC Tornado Damage, April 1973

Posted January 30th, 2009 by Stu Beitler

TORNADO KILLS 6, INJURES 35 - 3 MISSING IN NORTHWESTERN S.C.

Abbeville, S.C. (AP) -- At least six persons were killed, three missing, 35 injured, and an estimated 165 homes damaged when a tornado slashed through a section of northwestern South Carolina, leaving behind a scene Gov. JOHN C. WEST called, "a terrible catastrophe." The governor said he would do everything possible, knock on all doors, to have the federal government declare the section of Abbeville County, a disaster area.

Ironically, this morning, April 13, 2020, we were briefly under a tornado warning in Myrtle Beach as a tornado moved through Georgetown and skirted just a couple of miles east of us along the Grand Strand's coast.

The Wild, Wild World of Cow Pasture Sports

Backyard shenanigans are nothing new for most of us back in the good old days. For me, a ball of some type played into the scenario. For the record, I am not athletic. Please don't confuse me with a jock or have high expectations for where this tale may eventually take you. Don't get me wrong, I loved playing sports and still do. Excelling is where I fall sadly short. Don't break out the crying tissue just yet. I was not necessarily the last draft pick for any of our antics. I was good enough to get by and better at some sports than others. Expectations are considerably lower when it comes to competing on the backyard level. That played well into my strengths, what few I had.

Keep in mind I am relating to my experiences, not those of Joe Namath. Sure, Broadway Joe, aka Joe Willy burst into the spotlight back in my day, 1965 with the New York Jets. He is possibly best known for boldly guaranteeing a Jets' victory over Don Shula's NFL Baltimore Colts in Super Bowl III (1969). He then made good on his prediction with a 16-7 win. Trust me. There was no predicting the outcome of any of our football games, even though many were quite memorable and not necessarily for all the best reasons.

One of my more memorable movie moments of Joe Namath was in C.C. and Company released in1970. Joe starred as biker C.C. Ryder with Ann-Margaret and William Smith co-starring. In the opening scene C.C. Ryder is walking through a grocery store making a sandwich as he goes, washing it down, etc. It's basically his version of a drive through with a shopping cart. He didn't pay for anything. We thought that was the coolest back then. Joe had the swagger to pull it off flawlessly, no serious acting stretch for him. Every boy had a crush on the red headed vixen, Ann-Margaret. I could use those tissues now to wipe the drool from my chin.

See. I'm sort of babbling football, so I may as well begin with the pigskin sport. We usually didn't play tackle and not because we didn't love tackling one another because we surely did. One must remember that a thin layer of clothing separated our skin and bones from being annihilated. We wore no pads or helmet to soften the blows. We opted for touch football, two hands required, supposedly much safer. How did that go you ask. Bruised, bloodied, and battered, two handed touch didn't prevent us from feeling our oats and delivering the pain and punishment. An aggressive two-handed push and a well-placed two-handed grab could serve the same purpose as an awesome tackle. We usually played on Sunday afternoons, setting the stage for the battle worn, hobbling and limping warriors of Monday mornings at school.

Any given Sunday usually offered up the same bunch of combatants; The Hall brothers, Speedy, Jody and Eddie, the Price brothers, Stanley and Butch and their cousin Pete Price, Larry Harrison, Glenn Cannon and yours truly rounding out the crowd. Hopefully, we would have even numbers but when we didn't, we handicapped the sides as best we could. Most games were played in the Hall's front yard, the length of our battle ground probably less than fifty yards long. The house, various trees and shrubs served as the out of bounds markers. Fairness depended on honesty. Conflicts and controversy were not uncommon. We didn't have the luxury of referees or replay. Majority ruled, like it or not.

Football yard style was supposed to be for fun, but fun is not for losers. The setup was the same most every play. The center hiked the ball to the designated quarterback. Everyone else went out for a pass, including the center. Anyone rushing the passer had to count to five first. No quick counts were allowed. The defense rarely rushed the passer. If you did rush, the quarterback had the option of running with the ball. Finding an open receiver wasn't easy but eventually the passer had to throw to somebody.

There were no first downs. You had four tries to score or punt it on fourth down. None of us were accomplished punters. Mostly it was four and out if we didn't score. One thing guaranteed in an afternoon of two-handed touch; someone was going to lose their shirt. Let me clarify lose for you. No, you couldn't reclaim it in the lost and found. And no, we weren't playing shirts and skins in football. The winner didn't get to pick the shirt off an opponents' back, not that the eventual shirt wouldn't be considered a trophy. It was a given. One unlucky individual would have their shirt ripped from their body. That wasn't necessarily a good thing on one of those cold February afternoons. We operated from the same playbook. A successful game was gauged by the condition of the shredded shirt. And there would be more than one pair of jeans with holes ripped in the green stained knees. We were warriors. Snatching hold of a shirt tail slowed down your opponent until others arrived.

Someone came up with this harebrained idea to take on the Mennonite boys one Sunday. For reasons defying explanation, we figured they couldn't know that much about football. Up until now it had been our afternoon pastime. Now we were opening it up to strangers, outsiders, and our version of playing an exhibition game with another league. It was extreme for us to do this in football. We did have cross county rivalries with other boys in softball but had never opened it up to football. We should have learned our lesson based on those softball outcomes, but we hadn't, so we tossed out the invite. They accepted. We stuck to our original rules of touch football. There was no home field advantage.

And, yes, someone did get their shirt torn to shreds during the butt kicking we received from our Mennonite brothers. Wesley, a classmate and Mennonite, lost his shirt. We learned a valuable lesson that day. Mennonites are not ones to dismiss what we take for granted. Their parents don't take kindly to the destruction of personal property, including clothing. He sincerely feared going home. The winner ended up being the loser this time. To this day we have no idea what sort of punishment he faced when arriving shirtless. He never talked about it, nor did they ever play football with us again. Their record stands undefeated over us, 1–0.

Moving on to softball, we opted for the larger ball to its smaller cousin. We didn't have a large enough stadium to contain a baseball being whacked. Softball didn't require a talented pitcher either. Our field was the Hall's cow pasture. Back then we had no sponsor beating down the fence gate to have it named after them. A fertilizer company or possibly a slaughterhouse would have been appropriate or maybe something catchier; Cow Patty Memorial Field, *where **utter** sports are appreciated.* We should have had a seasonal cow chip tossing event or an annual cow tipping marathon. Guess we didn't really think outside the box, focusing too much on the national pastime instead. Well, softball wasn't baseball, but it was close enough for us.

Our usual likely suspects participated in the Sunday afternoon slugfests. Let me tell you, it's tough to field two teams with only eight or nine players. Softball requires ten. Scenario, let's say we had our usual nine. We were faced with our first dilemma. Options, the odd man out pitched to both teams. That usually didn't set well because everyone wants to swing a bat. Option two, we often recruited the Hall brothers' little sister, Robbie. She didn't exactly even things up so whoever was lucky enough to get her, we gave that side at least one extra out at bat. That settled. How do you field ten positions with five people? For sure, we needed a pitcher and a catcher. That left three. Each team developed their own strategy. Some opted to use the three as outfielders with the pitcher and catcher covering all the infield positions as best, they could. Others used two outfielders and one roving infielder. Whatever, we somehow made it work and had fun. Heck, we were in a cow pasture; we had other things to worry about like where we stepped.

Picture the layout. We located home plate, pacing off yardage from the fence line near the roadway. We had learned another valuable lesson to not have the roadway to our back and must chase missed pitches and foul balls over the barbed wire. While not geometric, the fence line served as our right and left field boundaries, deep center was where they angled and met. We had no backstop, scoreboard, dugouts or restrooms. Boys can improvise I assure you. We couldn't help Robbie improvise though. We had enough gloves to go around, three or four bats and a couple of softballs. We were set. No one threw the ceremonial first pitch. We weren't much on game protocol. The only statistic we maintained was how many long balls were smacked by each player. Some of us were sluggers. Others were just happy to get on base and not make that last out. Most scores were of epic proportions, double digits more like a basketball game than softball. We did keep an accurate out count but maybe not so good on innings. We usually just played until we got tired or the score became too lopsided. Then we would either call it quits or choose sides again for the double header.

I was more comfortable playing the outfield, mostly the right side of the pasture. There was too much responsibility and extra positions to play in the infield. At least in the out-pasture I had time to think about catching the ball or chasing down the grounders. The grass was not closely cropped and there were those familiar patty mounds present, some hard and dry, others way too fresh. Bad hops and ricochets were common occurrences, further testing one's athleticism. Fortunately, the cows were herded into an adjacent field during our games, so we didn't have them as an additional handicap.

The power line passed over right field, paralleling the roadway. Rule, if you hit it, you got a ground rule double. One of my fellow combatants creamed a long fly ball. I positioned myself for the catch, but those power lines were coming into play. I misjudged, thinking the ball was coming underneath the power lines, but instead it just cleared them. The ball caught me square between the eyes, knocking me whacky and into next week, sending me to my knees, dazed and seeing stars. My day was done. I was in pain and placed on the injured reserve list. We didn't rush off to the emergency room when we got hurt. We just sucked it up and managed.

My face was hurting and badly swollen. My buddies had a field day, giving me crap about my misfortune. Giving crap is what we did, hurting or not. It was expected. In a twisted way I enjoyed the extra attention. The next morning, I sported the raccoon look to school. Both eyes were black as could be. Of course, there I caught more crap from classmates. Kidding just seems more acceptable when being dished out by friends. In my day, as in the present, bullying and the levels of cruelty existed as well. The difference, I didn't fear being shot or stabbed; beat up, bruised and bloodied, yes. I already had the jump on that with the raccoon look. I did receive my fair share of pity from the girls. There are a few perks of being a pasture jock.

One more note on softball; we did have our across town rivals, the boys from the Sharon Community. This became an annual tradition to take them on in softball. At least we could field a full team of ten counting Robbie the girl. I think those boys played ball professionally though. They ate our lunch. Our record was zero to something against them. It was always ugly, the Sharon boys scoring a lot of runs while holding us to very few. Thank goodness they always brought extra balls. Seems I spent a lot of time crawling through that barbed wire fence to retrieve homeruns. I should have delegated myself to the infield when playing them, but their hard infield liners were nothing to be taken lightly. None of them seemed fazed by the uneven playing field or abundance of cow patties. Country boys will survive.

That brings me to basketball. I'll keep this one short. We picked sides or played HORSE. I preferred playing HORSE. I couldn't dribble worth a crap, but I did have height to my advantage, towering over most of the little munchkins. Jody thought he was Pistol Pete Marivich. He even had his hair cut in the same style. He was also a diehard Clemson Tiger fan. I think all Clemson fans are wired like that. His bedroom would almost make you puck with the orange shag carpet and purple walls. He had a hot temper too if things didn't go his way. He was second oldest of the Hall clan and a year or so younger than most of us. Whining just put us into a feeding frenzy, quite merciless with our kidding. Back to the game of HORSE though. I had one patented shot that no one could match. I could toss the ball under my leg and into the basket. Eventually they banded it from play. I cast the only vote to keep it. HORSE didn't seem so fun afterwards, at least not to me.

Regardless of the sport, we'd usually work in a drink and snack run to a *close by* rural store. Hot and bothered, we'd often double up on the bottle drinks and assortment of chips or candy bars. We only knew one way to do things, wide open. Someone puking later was almost guaranteed. You can not get too hot and fatigued and then expect to successfully stuff your face with too much sweet liquid and goodies. The body doesn't' always appreciate the sugar overload. We called it renting junk food. Oh yeah, expect the friendly abuse and crap for certain to be dished out on the unlucky one who did literally spill his guts.

Eventually I found my calling, a sport where I excelled. Bowling was my game. I owned the green machine, an oddly colored lime green bowling ball. I also had my own bowling shoes and bag. I was the king pin on the alleys. Seldom did anyone beat me or at least take the night series. Most of the time we opted for the drive to Anderson, about thirty minutes away, mainly because everyone but me lived on the that side of Abbeville. I resided in L.A. (Lower Abbeville), on Hunter Street, at the end of South Main. The other boys lived just off what we called the old or the regular Anderson highways. Most of the time I would drive to the Hall's house, off the old Anderson highway, and then Speedy, Jody and I would go pick up Stanley and Pete, both just off the regular Anderson highway.

This time Speedy opted to drive. His folks owned a yellow two door Toyota Corolla. Toyota was a new species to most of us, having mostly grown up with Chevys and Fords. Speedy took the dirt road off the Shrine Club Road, a short cut to Pete's house. We were shooting the bull as always, darkness having already fallen in the middle of winter, not a care in the world. The dirt road takes one hair pin right, somewhat of a blind turn. As Speedy negotiated it, suddenly headlights flashed on out of nowhere. The head on collision sent us as little projectiles slamming into the dashboard and back of the front seat. Wearing a seatbelt had yet to become lawful. Optional, who really wore them? The black man had parked there, binge drinking. He had only switched on his lights when he had seen ours. The Buick fared much better than the Toyota. The driver said he'd go for help, never to be seen again. Cell phones had not been invented.

We were stranded in the dark in a wrecked car. At least none of us were seriously injured. I couldn't say the same for the car. Jody volunteered to go for help. We never envisioned he'd run all the way home instead of opting to stop at the first house he came to. In a panicked state he wasn't thinking. Furthermore, we had no way to communicate to Pete or Stanley as to why we hadn't shown up to pick them up. We never made it to bowling that night. The other driver was eventually located. He had no license nor insurance of course.

The Toyota was deemed totaled and parked in the back forty, never to be driven on the roadway again. Speedy would be caught speeding on his Triumph motorcycle over the course of the next week. I would also be stopped for speeding and ticketed a warning in my Monte Carlo while heading to Greenwood. Highway Patrolman Vassey, the same state trooper would be the officer of record for the Toyota, the Triumph and Monte Carlo situations. One other common denominator, Speedy was present at all the crime scenes. Vassey pointed this out during the last one, the Monte Carlo speeding incident, after recognizing him in the backseat. He suspected that Speedy probably had asked me to see how fast my car would go.

We had our times with cow pasture sports when kids embraced the outdoors. Amazingly, all the participants are still alive and well or at least were at the time I scribbled this little journey down memory lane. We certainly had plenty of incredible close calls, too many to mention I must add. Anything we say can and will be used against us, so I think I'll leave well enough alone, at least for the time being. I can't promise I won't or haven't used some of these in my novels. I do try to change the names to protect the not so innocent. If you could see the smile on my face right now…guilty as charged…

Lounge Lizards and Gigolos

I know what you are thinking and no, this is not a selfie spotlight. First, I couldn't carry a tune if my life depended on it. Well, maybe I could muster up a song just to prove my life wasn't worth that much. As for the last American Gigolo, I was never in the running. That one time spin the bottle event does not count. Sorry. That episode was documented in my first memoir. Now that we've gotten that out of the way, just ponder where do lounge lizards and gigolos originate. I've never heard of a training camp for either. Does one just venture into the life of lizards or gigs by mere chance or could it be inherited? I'm thinking it's more a gift, something that oozes from the pores at an early age. *By the way I used to be married to Morgan Fairchild. Yeah, that's the ticket.* That's just a line tossed out for the Jon Lovitz fans, those who remember his SNL character, Tommy Flanagan, the pathological liar. By now you should know that I ramble my way towards my point.

Let us begin with the legit, the certifiable lounge lizard, Duncan Singleton. No, not necessarily the Duncan many of you know as the shoot it straight, responsible college graduate. This is the four-year-old version. He commanded the stage at a very early age. His stage was the brick hearth at their home. We were his captive audience. All he was missing at the time was the iconic fishbowl to collect tips. He would stand on that hearth and croon with a spoon or anything else that could he could use for a microphone. Your undivided attention was demanded. Choosing to talk during a performance met with dangerous consequences. I should know. I was the heckler in the crowd. The headliner didn't take too kindly to hecklers. He would unleash his anger on those, like me, for being disrespectable. I've been put in my place more times than I can count by the kid crooner.

A lounge lizard must have a fallback though, just in case his other career goes down the tubes. Introduce the master magician. Young Duncan would have fit in well on Vaudeville, forever versatile. Card tricks were his specialty. As when belting out a tune he didn't tolerate inattentiveness. Never underestimate the wrath of a four-year-old; been there. We even gave him a magic kit for Christmas, a means to step up his act. Jokingly I introduced a collection device for tips, bad idea on my part. The freebies were over. He became a headliner, requiring pay for his performances. Lounge lizard acts aren't cheap. Seasoned performers can empty your wallet in a mere performance.

It would go to figure that the young hearth performer would eventually make it to the big show. He soon wowed us in his roles on the school stage as a napkin in Beauty and the Beast, an orphan in Annie and a munchkin in Wizard of Oz. He would go on to command many larger rolls in Carolina Forest high school productions like Grey Garden. Song and dance would become part of his routine, performing with the show choir and later for several seasons in the beach amphitheater as part of the high energy show, High Stepping Country. He even transformed into theme-based characters at Hard Rock and Freestyle amusement parks as an Ogre and various Country Bears.

Opening Act and Mic Improvising

Duncan with Microphone Upgrade

The elder grandson, the lounge lizard had indeed found his calling. He is as comfortable on the stage as he is behind the scenes running the lights and sound for various show productions. We knew that great things were in store for the adult version of the elder grand boy. I fear the tipping jar will soon no longer guarantee a seat at one of his performances. My only wish is to be his agent when he hits the big time. An update since I originally penned this piece. Duncan graduated Winthrop with a music degree and the University of Florida with a lighting degree. He is now employed by Disney World in Orlando.

While Duncan had the market cornered as the lizard of the lounge, little brother followed on his heels. Winn ventured down an entirely different path. When he was merely three or four, I dubbed him the blue-eyed gigolo. He could wrap any age female around his little finger. All were fair game. Flashing those baby blues complemented by perfect dimples, he'd have them eating out of his hands. He could parley his little gift into all sorts of extra freebies from toys to good eats.

One of my fondest memories is Winn, the gigolo wonder, working his magic on me while I cooked. One of his favorite places to be was perched on a stool at the kitchen bar while I cooked bacon on the electric griddle. He resembled a baby bird in the nest, mouth open, waiting for the next worm. In this case it was bacon. He'd look at me, bat those blue eyes and sport those dimples, prompting me to pop a bite of bacon into his mouth. I always followed through, fearful that his gaze might equate to that of Medusa and turn me to stone if I refused. Yeah, he could work the males too, especially me.

The Griddle Charmer

At Christmas Mimi had to put the reins on me. Boy how I enjoyed buying goodies for them. Winn was easy. His Christmases were themed with cars, balls, flashlights, and ropes. At a young age he'd have every pocket stuffed with Match Box vehicles. Give him any sort of ball and a flashlight and then forget about him. He would entertain himself for hours. Brother Duncan commanded your attention and would not tolerate deserters. The flashlight and rope became sort of a running joke. Winn's adult neighbor, Rusty, tended to use both as part of any backyard chore. Rusty, a big kid at heart, was caught in Winn's web too, their version of Little Rascals or Our Gang. Google them.

We eventually moved to the beach where the boys lived. Duncan soon became my very first cheap golf date. The summer heat eventually did him in; a 113-heat index was not fun for golfing. Duncan tossed his clubs and decided to take up the sousaphone instead with the school band. It looked like a tuba to me. A few years later Winn stepped into the spot as my cheap golf date. He loved it. He was my Mini-Me. We dressed like Payne Stewart in golf knickers, hat and vest, accessorized with knee high argyle socks. Our saying was Look Good, Feel Good and Play Good. He added and Smell Good. Winn hung in there until eventually he outgrew me, the curse of the young teenager, tossing ole grandpa to the curb.

Me and Mini Me

As mentioned, the younger Singleton followed somewhat in older brother's footsteps, enjoying a good magic trick and taking center ring. His stage performances included Billy Duck in Honk, an Elvis Impersonator in the church program, a Shepard in a Nativity Scene, a bodiless old man in the Halloween haunted house in his garage and Snoopy in Charlie Brown. He even played magician Houdini in Ragtime. He sang and danced his way across the Carolina Forest stage also as a member of the acclaimed show choir. When just a young tike he would often profess to be Duncan's twin, one suffering from extreme dwarfism. To me he'll always be little Payne, or royal pain as I sometimes called him.

For more years than I can remember Winn and I have always had our unique way of greeting one another. It begins with a chest bump, then banging our fists and ending with a thunderous head butt. It's something special just between him and me. We still enjoy our little ritual to this very day. Probably one of the greatest memories was Winn, at a young age, giving me a Father's Day card, referring to me as his granddad. I have no children and that's about the best thing I've ever received. I framed it. I had never received a card for Father's Day before then. Now I get cards from both. I'm proud as banana pudding, seeing what fine young men they are becoming. Both of my cheap golf dates have far surpassed lounge lizard and blue-eyed gigolo status. The sky is the limit for where these two will go. They are destined for wonderful futures. I'm glad to have been their cheap grandpa date along the way; priceless to say the least.

The Good Old Garnet and Gold

For most of my school life I was much like a chameleon, possessing the ability to blend into my surroundings. I flew below the clique radar, obscure and unknown to those marching to a greater beat and higher calling. I was just another one of those not so special kids stumbling and navigating through a world that had engulfed me. I didn't really dwell on the premise of being liked. I held true to my conviction. I am who I am, like it or leave it, your choice, not mine. I had nothing to prove to anyone. I did what I liked to do regardless of whether it complied with form, fit or function. Those with vivid imaginations can easily escape the world designed and ruled by others. I was nothing unique, just another face in the school yard or classroom. I did what I had to do to maneuver through another day dominated by those who valued their specialized lives within the social network. I've always been happy with who I am. I have never yearned to be anyone else.

To further prove my foothold on obscurity, I attended my fortieth-class reunion, the class of '71, somewhat kicking and screaming I must admit. My arm had been twisted behind my back by Judy Cannon, after skipping all the others except our very first one. Reunions never held any special place in my heart. I didn't really miss school. I never ran with the *in crowd* so any memories I had were mere blurs on life's grand scale. Most would have pegged me an introvert, possibly awkward and even geeky through my high school years, if they even noticed me at all. Again, this doesn't bother me, never really did. This is no pity party, far from it. I got away with my share of stuff because of this social stigma, perks of the trade. Being a wild child when no one but close friends knows it has its advantages. My friends knew better than to dare me to do anything. I was a master instigator to boot; traits most of my classmates never knew existed. No, I was not a member of a secret society but that would have been a hoot. Dang, wish I would have thought of it back then.

Back to that reunion thing…I am nothing like most remembered me in high school, those who remembered that Tommy. Oh, I am Tom now, but that transformation from Tommy to Tom only happened in my thirties. The owner of the company I worked for dubbed me with my new grown-up sounding name when he hired me. Evolution and writing led to a newer persona, my author name, T. Allen Winn. I'm a far cry from that introvert some remember. I am quite social, a wild card, the joker, fast at wit, the master of sarcasm, often the main attraction when I want to be. No, I haven't really changed that much. I was a smart butt back then but only those who really knew me experienced my wrath. At the reunion, classmates were asking, who is this guy and where did he come from? Some hadn't even remembered me graduating with them. I never was the social clique type, but I bet I had a lot more fun than many of them did. Again, there are perks in not really giving a rat's butt about most everything, my mantra back in the day, *born for fun, loyal to none*. I even had a black tee shirt with this printed on it.

I guess I could have been a jock and gained notoriety from being a sports icon. I did have quite an extensive sports history at the ole alma mater. You gasp, not remembering this I bet. Allow me to clarify my version of history for those of you who don't remember me lettering and dressing out for those various sports. Let's see. There was B Team Basketball. I really liked basketball and was a descent shooter. I had a height advantage, tall and lanky. Sadly, I couldn't dribble. That's okay. Just toss me the ball and let me shoot. Unfortunately, they don't call it basketball practice for the heck of it. Running those drills up and down the court, my tongue lolling about, me on the verge of puking, legs and lungs hurting. None of that seemed anywhere close to backyard basketball. I think I lasted a week. Basketball didn't seem so fun anymore.

I am quick to sign up, but not so eager to commit for the long haul, especially if I don't enjoy the experience. I did the same thing for junior varsity football, an uncle encouraging me to go out. I wanted to be a wide receiver. My uncle encouraged me to be a quarterback. The coach didn't have me pegged as either. Those drills up and down, up and down that long hill in Hite Stadium quickly stifled my enthusiasm. Plus, I had my driver's license and was missing out on too much cruising time. I think I lasted about a week there too, an obvious theme developing. Puking wasn't my favorite thing to do. Those drills in the heat of summer led one to emptying one's guts.

During gym class I had found my greater calling. I could high jump with the best of them. Lurch, the appropriately nicknamed Mr. Harrington, history teacher during the school day, track coach in the afternoons, caught wind of my talent. He approached me during history class and encouraged me to come out for track. Why not, I knew, as did he, that I was as good as anyone he had on the team clearing that high bar. Lessons learned hard. Coach had me running all these relays, sprints, and hurtles and such. I only signed up for the jumping. I should have stipulated this in a contract. All this exertion prompted more puking. I was seasoned at it for sure. Is there no sport that I can do just what I want to do? Why does it always require all this extra stuff? You got it. After about a week I quit. I still had to face a very pissed off Lurch in history class every day. Try as he might, I never came back out for track. I was history for refusing. The big man treated me quite badly that year. He was the teacher. I was the kid. Back then we had no rights. His revenge and abuse of me went unchecked. It was nothing physical. He just made it tough on me in class. I'm quite good a being stubborn even when being bullied by a teacher.

Even before high school, in sixth grade, I hankered to be in the newly formed junior marching band. I wanted to play the drums but so did every other boy. I settled for the Coronet, the music director's choice, not mine. I was quite awful, and that disciplined practice thing came into play. I did march in the Christmas parade that year and pretended to play. My stint at being the next greatest Coronet player lasted one school year. The neighbors were cutting cartwheels at my decision, having heard my attempted practice secessions. My parents weren't too happy though with a perfectly good horn and no one to play it. I blame them for my failures, sort of. They never made me finish one of those commitments. As parents they could have made me play but they didn't. Who knows, I might be raking in the bucks in some sort of sport right now. Fantasy scene, Wayne's world…

Here's a quiz for my classmates. Just how many of you knew I had tried out for all three sports? Then there were all those clubs one could be part of if one chose to be a participant. Let's see; science club, nope, beta club, I don't think so, chorus, trust me you don't want to hear me attempt to sing, special interest, I had none, and on and on. I don't remember joining any. I wasn't much of a joiner, too much the loner and enjoyer of my freedom. Traveling in a pack didn't really appeal to me. Someone would probably just tell me what to do and have greater expectations than I was willing to fulfill. I saved the teachers yet more disappointment.

I should receive some sort of medal or recognition for that. Being the class clown better suited me, but that position was taken by way too many more talented and outgoing kids than me. I wasn't quite that willing to be the center of attention. It would have blown my cover forever. No, let others enjoy the spotlight and take the heat. I picked my opportunities, keeping it close to the vest and among an even closer bunch of friends. Ours wasn't really a clique because only we knew it existed. We liked keeping it that way. Like a shark, I swam just below the Garnet and Gold surface.

Becoming a senior apparently emboldened me. Most didn't notice but I realized the transformation. The rebel within me yearned to emerge. Like James Dean, I really had no defined cause. In the twelfth grade I was forced to take two extra classes that I didn't need to graduate. This positioned me for six classes and no study hall, unconstitutional, don't you think? Try as I might, requesting to drop one or both, the powers that be would not see it my way. This just fueled my rebellious juices. It gave me purpose, an actual cause. Creativity, innovation and an active imagination, a few of my strong traits, would not go untapped. Physics and trigonometry were my foes on this battlefield, commanded by Mr. Fowler and Mrs. Marshall. Defiant, a strategy developed. Slowly but surely, I would emerge from my armored shell with reckless abandon. Everyone must be good at something. The butterfly was ready to spread its wings. Crashing and burning was of little consequences. The simmering pot had been placed on the burner. Watchful I waited for the right time to serve up my stew.

Mrs. Marshall, dedicated and determined to mold our young impressionable minds, had never encountered one as stubborn and self destructive as me. Trig, I had just the right angle in my arsenal to challenge a teacher's fortitude. I possessed the determination to disrupt the higher learning process. During class I never participated. There was no hand raising, no real interest in understanding the significance of a right-angled triangle. I had struck a nerve. She had never encountered someone as pig headed as me. When given tests I would merely sign them and hand them back in, placing the paper back on her desk before she had given out all of them. I know. This was cruel and quite self destructive, but I had to make my point. I didn't need this credit, didn't want to be there, end of story.

We muddled along for most of the semester. I held my ground. She questioned my ethics. Then came that defining moment when I completed all the questions on a test, those referring to Sine, Cosine and Tangent, the most common fundamentals in Trig. I aced the test. She was simply ecstatic with this breakthrough, on the verge of cutting cartwheels and shouting **Hallelujah** at the top of her lungs. Timing is everything. The next test I reverted to my old ways, signing it and placing the blank copy back on her desk. She made me stay after class and asked me why I had done that because it seemed I understood the curriculum. Ah, but there lay the method to my madness I assured her. I never said I couldn't do the work or pass the class. I told her I shouldn't be there in the first place, nothing personal. I upped the ante after that incident. I began covertly mimicking animals while class was in session. Frog and monkey calls were my specialty. Eventually she busted me and sent me to the front office.

Sending one to front office is the ultimate price in playing the game; that is if one reports there. I didn't. I roamed the halls the final semester, often blending in with one of those classes reporting to the library, my version of the study hall that had been robbed from me in my senior year. The system doesn't always work like a well-oiled machine. She never knew I wasn't spending my hour in the front office and apparently the front office hadn't known I was supposed to report there. Assumptions never work. She never followed up on me. Possibly I was now out of sight and out of mind. Yes, I flunked Trig royally, mission accomplished.

Then there was my other dilemma, Physics with Mr. Fowler, a funny fellow according to Robert Fossett. I had taken chemistry previously under Fowler, so I knew the drill. I intentionally flunked the first semester. To prove I wasn't a complete idiot, or maybe not, I got out of my physics exam the second half of the year. Of course, I failed it for the year. That was of little consequences to one who didn't really care. Mission again accomplished. I had a knack for self destruction. Do I regret now that I should have tried instead? I really don't dwell on it one way or the other. I had to follow my path my way. I have no do-overs.

Was I an 'A' student? Of course not. I was a 'B' at best. Could I have been an 'A' student? Possibly, but I was too busy having fun to focus on that. I had my priorities, as wrong as they were. Too bad I couldn't have been as committed to basketball, football, track or band as I had been in flunking those two classes. My life may have taken a different path if I would have. Then again, I'm happy with my life as it is, having survived many more perilous and self-destructive incidents on the road to arriving here. Rebelling in school would just be the tip of my melting iceberg. The worst was yet to come, bless my now deceased parents' hearts. The rogue elephant still had much trampling and stampeding to do. I'm lucky I survived life in mostly one piece. Let's hear it for the good old Garnet and Gold. Confessions are good for the soul, right?

One is an Only Number

Born May 25th, 1953 to Thomas Jefferson and Mary Elizabeth Bowie Winn, I was so perfect, them having just one of me was enough blessings to fulfill a lifetime. That's my story, being the skewed imagination spinner that I am. Mama always painted a different picture though; one that possibly makes me seem not so special. Shortly after their marriage Daddy was shipped off to Korea, serving his country coming first. I'm not sure how long his tour lasted. I wasn't around then yet, but when he returned from the ravages of war, he was a changed man, so said Mama. He refused to talk about his experience building bridges during his tour. Daddy wasn't much of a talker anyway but what happened over yonder must have traumatized him because he stayed hush mouth, even if anyone pushed for details. Even someone as pigheaded as her couldn't make him budge on the subject. All she would say was that he was forever changed, different, and let it go at that. War does that to so many.

I'm not sure why she ever shared this with me or others. I am not sure what even prompted her to explain it, but being Mama, she did. The specifics are vague at best. Maybe I just mentally blocked out any graphic details, if ever there were any. She basically said he must have missed her a lot because he was obsessed in catching up after he returned. His aggressiveness was almost a turn off to her. It's not easy treading down some memory lanes but the means produced an end…me. I wasn't too sure how to take this tale at first. It sounded like I was the ultimate accident and not the result of well thought out planned parenthood. Of course, in only a way she could explain it, she was blessed with my birth. She loved me and I loved her, end of that story.

Proud Parents

Not to worry, don't turn the page just yet or give up hope. This isn't going to be one of those dirty little confessions of being abused as a child. I have no memories of being anything but forever loved. With both working in the textile mill for forty something years I can never remember going without anything. I wasn't spoiled, at least not in my mind but I lived the good life. I did not have to wear hand-me-downs. Being an only child has its perks. I wore new stuff. This was before consignment shops. I do still have my very first tiny little shoes, another slightly larger pair of tiny shoes, my very first pair of tiny little cowboy boots and what looks like a miniature Payne Stewart cap. Oh yeah, and I still have my very first rocking horse, original springs and still functioning like new. I used to have my very first highchair, but I think I failed to retrieve it from the attic before a divorce. In my possession also is hand-crafted doll furniture, built by Papa for Mama. There is a bed, chairs and table. I tend to cling to old memories by keeping those old items.

Being an only, as was Mama, I was blessed to inherit belongings she and Granny treasured. Those black cast-iron cornbread making skillets were passed down from generations before me, seasoned with love. I am not a packrat, but I like holding onto history, my past, even though I have no children of my own to pass it along to. As you might recall, I have that hand crank grinder that Papa and Granny used for processing the meat for their home-made hash. Homemade was just that. Granny canned many vegetables using her pressure cooker and Mason jars. I never mastered the pressure cooker technique but did pickle many peppers, dill pickles and okra in Mason jars. Granny had a little corner what-not shelf in the living room. Named appropriately so I suppose because various little items graced the tiny triangular shelves, each having its significance to Granny and Papa. I sadly regret that I didn't keep that what-not shelf, but you just can't hold onto everything or you would indeed be labeled a hoarder. I did keep some of the what-nots though. Nostalgia, when you get right down to it, is a combination of memories and possessions; those hand-me-downs often being what spur the memories in the first place. Some folks can't wait to get rid of the old stuff that belonged to their parents or grandparents. I like latching on to them. I guess I don't have brothers and sisters to trade stories with, so this serves as my memory library, my connection to my roots, my past, and my heritage. I realize when I'm gone that they'll most likely hold no place in the heart of anyone else but that's okay too.

I should probably take time to catalog them, write why they were important to me, just in case. I have this old storage or travel trunk, metal and black and it belonged to my grandparents. The trunk is in excellent condition and I'm sure it would be worth a pretty penny to a collector. It's filled to the brim with more stuff, odds and ends, anything I could squirrel away inside for safe keeping. I have Mama's old cedar chest too. We use it as an accent piece in the bonus room. It has a few goodies stored away in it as well. I grew up on Hunter Street with my very first bedroom suit being the one that Mama had grown up with, a mahogany one. It had a four-spindle post bed, dressing table, matching seat, an upright chest, and end tables. Granny had the exact a bedroom suit like this as well on South Main except with it they also had a matching wardrobe. We ended up picking the best from the combo after my folks and grandmother passed away. We presently use it in an extra bedroom.

Sorry, this bedroom suit is part of my upbringing and will most likely remain so until I am gone. Blue Boy and Pink Girl pictures and curio pieces are also part of the décor in what we call Granny's room. I still have an assortment of quilts made by the hands of Granny and friends, and Mama. This is sort of the Granny shrine I suppose. I used to have a pair of Papa's red camel overalls and a fedora hat, but I think I also left them at my house in a previous life. Maybe someday I will get them back. If I don't, I have my memories.

Speaking of Papa, I do have that old original coal bucket and his personally hand-crafted fire poker. Papa hauled many loads of coal into their mill house in that bucket. I totted the kindling in it. As I got older, he allowed me to two fist the coal bucket up the back-porch steps and into the house. I was better at carrying the kindling. Papa's twisted and handcrafted poker has poked its share of hot embers in the old pot-bellied stove and in my fireplaces. I have used it to poke and arrange the logs. Both predate me so they are older than sixty-seven years old.

Does anyone remember or know what a slop bucket was or is? You got it. I have their original one, heavy, durable and with a lid. It's about the size of a regular bucket but instead of plastic it is metal. Granny used it to collect table scraps, the old timey version of a garbage disposal. Have you not heard the term, slopping the pigs? Well, they didn't have any pigs or at least I don't remember them having any during my lifetime. I do think Papa might have fed the chickens from it. Chickens, like pigs, will eat just about anything. Sometimes I remember him dumping it in the back alley, a smorgasbord for the neighborhood dogs and cats or a passing possum. By the next day it was usually gone.

Some folks used the slop bucket or slop jar as a collection vessel for bathroom waste, mostly because they didn't have indoor plumping. A trip to the outhouse during the middle of the night wasn't always practical. Granny and Papa had an inside bathroom just outside the kitchen and off the back porch, so they never had to use it for that reason. I don't think that's something I would have forgotten. I have the old upright metal medicine cabinet from that very bathroom. I use it as a storage cabinet in the garage.

Papa was a jack of all trades. You had to be back in his day. You couldn't hire someone to do every little job or project. He was a painter, a builder, a plumber, whatever was necessary to meet their needs. His daddy before him was cut from the same cloth. Survival meant you had to know how to do this stuff. Out in what used to be the old chicken house (later a converted storage building for Papa's stuff), was stored a long metal toolbox. It was heavy and pert near three feet long. It had latches and a huge handle, so it was meant to be portable if you were *Paul Bunyan*. This was the carpenter's version of *Felix the Cats* bag of tricks.

The toolbox originally belonged to Papa's daddy, Daddy Bill Bowie. The tools were his daddy's tools for the most part with a few he had added along the way when they needed to be replaced. There was an assortment of hand saws. The workmanship and handcrafted handles left little to the imagination that these were special. There was an old level, a hand cranked drill, hammers, a hatchet, and other assorted items. After Papa passed away Granny wanted me to have them. I still do of course. I am an only, so if I do not hang on to this stuff, who would?

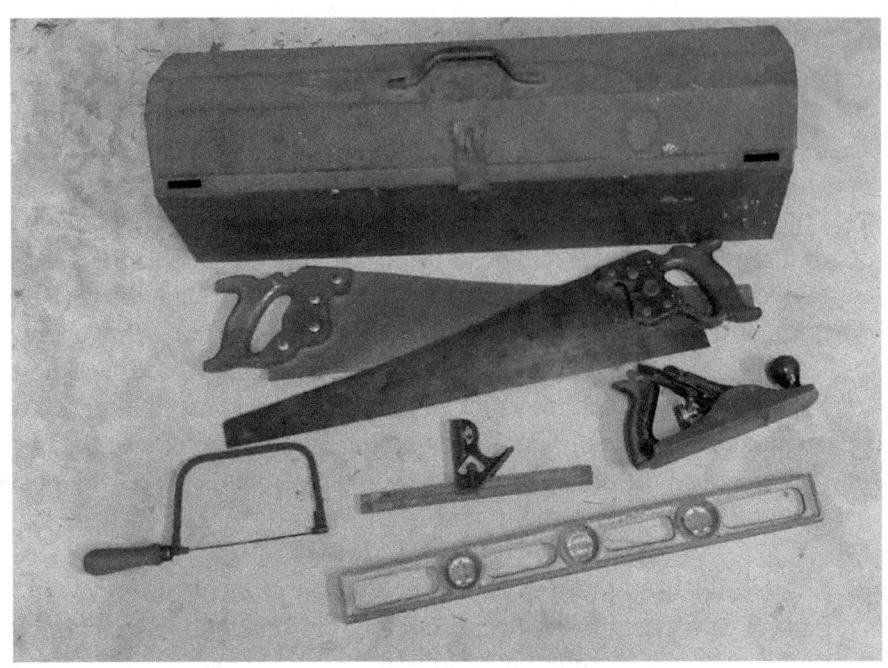

Toolbox and Some of the Vintage Tools

Old photos or photos of any kind are typically cherished. With the passing of my parents and grandparents I have, of course, inherited all their photographs and portraits. Talking about taking a trip down the nostalgic dirt roads, it's all there. Many of the folks I recognize but only because I have looked at them with my folks numerous times over the years. Others have dates and names on the back of them. Some of the dates inscribed were part of the photo processing back in the day. Sadly, there are those others, some long-lost friends of my folks or maybe relatives that I never knew or met. It saddens me that those faces, and memories will forever be lost because those who could identify them are no longer here.

There are a lot of photographs from Daddy's Korean War, something that he would never recap for us. There are those of me as a newborn, bare butt on the bed or being bathed in Granny's kitchen sink. Today you would be accused of being a pervert or sexual predator by just possessing them. Back then they were staged and thought to be precious, a rite of passage so to speak. Daddy and Mama and all my grannies took turns posing with me like I was some sort of prize. Being a first and only grandchild for Papa and Granny Bowie was special I suppose.

Thomas Jefferson Winn in Korea

I don't have mementos from Daddy's side of the family. He was not an only child like Mama. Granny Winn had a bunch of grandkids to compete for the leftovers. Papa's only sister, Aunt Shug Blanchard was quite artistic. She painted portraits and made handcrafted what-nots and painted them too. I have many examples of her talent, including a painting of the old home place where they lived as kids. It hangs in granny's room of course. There are vases and platters and an assortment of other items. Aunt Shugg didn't sound like the rest of the Bowies. She had one of those low country brogues. I am guessing she moved to Summerville, South Carolina as a young girl and it just sort of grew on her. I liked to hear her talk. My cousins from Adams Run, near Charleston, sound much like her. Daddy's sister Sarah had also moved to the low country at an early age and no longer sounded like her Winn siblings.

Aunt Shug Blanchard

I probably took my quest to hold onto the past a little further than most. When I realized Granny was no longer going to be able to live in her old mill house due to health reasons and had to move in with my folks, I decided I must latch onto some of the natural history. Granny had two green thumbs and could root almost any plant from its parent plant. She had thrift bordering her flower beds in the front yard. The flowing groundcover with purple flowers was older than me. She had a unique story to go along with its origin. She and another lady had swapped plants so to speak. She had gotten transplants of the thrift to start in her yard. In exchange she had swapped onion bulbs, the original onion plants having a heritage too. Granny said the history of the thrift and onion bulbs went back about fifty years. I made sure I got some of both and transplanted them in our yard in Greenwood.

Granny had an old fig bush that originated from ancient roots too. Even though I don't like figs, I did dig up several offshoots and transplanted them. I did something similar when Mister Joe's old farm place was sold. Mr. Joe Sanders was Judy's dad. I transplanted one of her fondest memories, a pear tree. I even gathered about ten bricks from where her childhood house once stood. These were remnants of the front porch. I spray painted them gold and etched the date on them. These were later given to her sisters as Christmas presents. I am a sucker for doing this sort of stuff. We still have one of the last surviving milk transport cans from

Mr. Joe's dairy farm. It anchors our front porch. We also have his porch swing in Myrtle Beach now. I no longer have any of the thrift, the fig bush, or pear tree now. They are part of our Greenwood home.

You can sometimes hold onto too much stuff. I should know. I have been accused of it but how else do you keep those nostalgic memories alive. Each tells a unique story and pieces together part of the puzzle. I held onto to Papa's 1961 Chevy Apache 10 truck from 1988 after his death until 2005 when we moved to the beach. I fretted something awful about letting it go but we would have no place to keep it when we completed our move. Luckily, Judy's son-in-law took it off my hands, so it remains in the family and resides at his dad's old home place in Conway, a stone's throw from us. He and his brother, Danny, have worked on it from time to time. I have not laid eyes on it since we moved to the beach and not because I couldn't go see it. I am glad it's in the family but going out there to look at it holds too many memories, all good. I will forever regret letting it go. For now, not seeing it, but knowing where it is, is therapy for the soul but not the heart. It's a connection to my Papa. It was passed on to me and it's hard for me to explain the connection just like I had with his double barrel L.C. Smith shotgun. That gun was stolen six weeks after we moved to the beach. My heart still aches when I think about it.

The 1961 Chevy Apache 10

Keep things that mean something to you is what I am saying. If the item pulls at your heartstrings don't let anyone talk you into getting rid of it. Sometimes you must draw that line. I have had to pick and choose my battles over the years. Sometimes you finally must let some things go and that's all right too, once you've worked through it. Passing them along to those who cherish them as much as you do is always a better option, if given that option. I go back to my old rocking horse. Who can possibly make a connection with it when I am gone? The answer is nobody unless I take time to share those stories with someone. The grandboys might just be the perfect candidates. Perhaps during one of the family gatherings I should drag some of these items out and give the history lesson. That might minimize the chances of them being tossed or sold. It is only nostalgic if it can be shared with those who love you and care about it. Writing this now makes me want to go dig out some of the old stuff and venture down the path just one more time.

Just for a hoot, I included this bit of poetic creativity from 1991, a Father's Day card I had written for T. J. Winn.

DADDY

You always help everyone
And never do you complain!
You always push foward
Despite any aches or pains!

Everyone gives you a hard time
For doing things without thinking.
You're criticized for your actions
Because you do them without blinking!

You're gentle and kind
And seldom ever get mad.
You're a golfer, a bowler
And an all around great Dad!

ONE THING IMPORTANT TO YOUR SON
IS YOU'RE MY WONDERFUL DADDY.
FOR ME, YOU GET THE JOB DONE!

The Perfect Square

Never ever say what you will never do or try. And this coming from the lips of the ultimate daredevil is indeed a mouthful. Dare me, right? I will usually consider it. Double dare me and the challenge is on. I am not fearless, and I really have no phobias or fears. I cannot recall a single event, incident or even a food I have ever shied away from at least trying once. I was like this as a kid and it remains my mantra. Older and wiser though, I do take precautions in weighing the outcome now. I have no death wishes nor am I going to attempt anything suicidal. Within reason I am always game.

I am guessing I was in my mid forties and living in Greenwood when my wife posed the following scenario. A couple, more friends, and acquaintances of hers than mine at the time, asked her if we'd join them at the open house of their square dancing group. Sometimes you just say yes without completing any research. What harm could there be in going and seeing what they did, so I figured. We arrived early at the church parking lot where the group met in the building's basement. She hadn't spotted the friends, Don and Carolyn Rochelle yet, so we decided to wait in the car until they arrived. Soon vehicles began pulling into the parking lot and what emerged from them made me shutter.

The guys were wearing gosh-awful looking green shirts with bright yellow scarves around their necks and black polyester pants. The ladies wore the same color green, except in hoop dresses with frilly under garments that extended what looked like three feet in any direction. I glanced over at Judy and announced that I was not going in there. She thought I was kidding. I wasn't. I asked her if we had to dress like that to square dance. She shrugged. Not taking any chances I repeated I was not going inside. She could but I wasn't. Not happy about my decision, she was not going in without me, so we drove home. She was not a happy camper. There is no honor in reneging on a commitment.

A few days later her friends, not mine yet, asked her why we hadn't come to their open house. She informed them that we had. Seeing the puzzled look on their faces she told them how I had refused to get out of the car after seeing them dressed in their square dance attire. They informed her that they always dressed out in the Merry Mixer club colors for open house nights. Club colors, they certainly were not making me feel any better when she recapped that story. Somehow, and I'm still not sure how, she talked me into going back the next week. This time the friends met us in the parking lot. Against my better judgment I ventured inside where an entire herd of these funny dressed people greeted us. What had I been thinking? I hadn't but I figured I'd muddle through it and then we'd be done with this little idea.

The caller, Don Franks, explained the basic setup and premise of square dancing. He then asked us to form a square. What the heck did I know about forming a square? Soon I realized that a square is made of four couples, four men and four women, boy, girl, boy, girl, etc. There were maybe eight or nine more of these squares of eight in the room. We newbies stood out like sore thumbs. We were not dressed in the tacky Grand Ole Opry garb. Holding hands, we began walking in a circle until the caller prompted us to stop. Well, I could do that part easy enough. He then began explaining our positions and responsibilities within the square, stuff like corners, heads, sides, centers, and ends. Don and Carolyne, Roy and Mary Whitt and Al and Debra Dansby were our square mentors. Don and Carolyne were the friends that got us into this mess. Jury was out as to whether I would call them friends. For now, I was a round peg stuck inside this square.

Don Franks, the head Don, began explaining calls; the basic instructions that would make us do different stuff inside the square. Allemande left with your left and back to the partner for a right and left hand grand. Ace of diamonds, Jack of spades, meet your partner and promenade. I resembled a fish floundering on the riverbank. Guilt or some other unknown force prompted me to agree to take beginner lessons with the Merry Mixers. This would last for countless weeks and eventually we would graduate as certified square dancers, new members of the Merry Mixers. Really? Me, wearing one of those gaudy outfits, I don't think so.

Somehow, I survived the weeks of intense training, and yes, we graduated. Now we could purchase and flaunt the club colors. Well, allowed wasn't exactly the correct term. We were supposed to dress like them to represent the club. I had become what I had feared, wearing those green shirts and polyester pants. I found out just what a big deal square dancing was with clubs located state and nationwide. You can virtually dance somewhere different every night of the week within driving distance. We became obsessed with our newfound club and friends, squaring them up every chance we got. The host club always provided vittles for any visiting squares and offered up friendly fellowship.

Soon we reached new levels of advancement. We were introduced to calls such as the Acey Deucey, Crossfire, Explode the Wave, Fan the Top, Grand Swing Thru, Peel Off and Load the Boat. This was just the tip of the iceberg, keeping all these calls straight in your head. If you missed one or misunderstood it, you could break down the entire square. Real square dancers did not take kindly to this. You could quickly be banned from their squares if you were dubbed reckless repeat offenders. While this is a friendly environment most of the time, like in anything, some take it much too seriously. You quickly learn to pick and choose your poison. But this is not about the protocol of the dance. It is culture and history. It's more nostalgic nonsense and in this case, an assortment of memorable tales from inside and outside the square.

For the record square dancers are made primarily of let's just say, those well outside and beyond their teen years. I'll just leave it at that. One of our elderly gents, Mister Joe, could always come up with some ditties. While sitting on the deck of his Lake Greenwood home he once said, 'I wonder what the poor people are doing.' Another time the conversation centered on the topic of banks and Mister Joe quipped, 'The only banks I trust are the riverbanks and the piggy banks'. Shorty was another one of our whimsical mixers. Once we had an ice cream themed dance where each member was supposed to bring ice cream. Shorty shows up with a churn of homemade ice cream. The churn was packed in ice and its contents were inside. In the serving line many were drawn to the homemade variety. Inside was Neapolitan, a perfect blend of strawberry, chocolate and vanilla. You don't suppose Shorty was yanking our chain, do you?

Gathering at the local Shoney's after a home turf dance was an extended social event. Most weren't hungry but this was another fellowship opportunity to gather, have coffee or sweet tea, maybe desert. Plus, it was always a hoot watching those gawking at us, the funny dressed folks we were. One of our mix of merry ones was somewhat of a tightwad. He was way beyond thrifty, possibly on a fixed income. Instead of coffee or tea he'd order only ice water. He would then utilize the plate of sliced lemons meant for the entire table, squeezing them in his glass, adding a little sugar and making lemonade. When it came time to tip his wife placed fifty cents on the table. He discretely retrieved one quarter, leaving only a quarter tip. It must have been the going rate for a glass of free water and plate of lemons.

I got into the theme dances. The Halloween parties were my favorites, but then again, I have always been drawn to Halloween. I came dressed as Elvis once, thank you very much. There is always the element of surprise though. I was not your typical hunka, hunka burning love. Elvis sort of left the building. I slipped to the bathroom, one that had a door accessible to the outside nearby. I retrieved my clown outfit then completed my transformation and re-entered by the main entrance. I am talking full face mask, colorful wig, big clown feet and gloved hands. It was an outrageous wardrobe. I showed up just as they were line dancing and I joined right in. I don't line dance. It proved to be great cover for my ruse though. No one had a clue as to the identity of this intrusive carnival sideshow. I eventually exited and reappeared as the King, leaving them all guessing. Another time at Lake Junaluska, N.C, I appeared as a vampire, fanged and accessorizing with a Dracula cap. I made a fine blood sucker corner.

At our Christmas square dance, we were all tasked with helping deck the halls of our basement gathering place. I brought a bubble blowing Santa, already having gained fame in the art of bubble blowing, but I'll get to that next. The night of the dance I noticed one of our elderly patrons standing in front of Santa, moving about wildly and then clapping her hands. I asked Evelyn what she was doing. She said she was trying to get Santa to blow bubbles and wasn't sure if he was sound or motion activated. I placed my hands on her shoulders, looked her in the eyes and told her to give it a few seconds. It was on a timer. I get a lot of mileage retelling that tale and mimicking her antics. When we had overnight stays, I never left home without a bottle of bubbles. Blowing bubbles from balconies became my trademark.

We traveled to many club dances all over South Carolina, attended State and National Square Dance Conventions, as far away as Orlando. We maintained our perfect square as much as possible, consisting of Don and Carolyn, Al and Debra, Roy and Mary. If any of us broke down the square, we just laughed it off. Perfection isn't always perfect. Friendship is what's important. We eventually burned out after a few years, dropping from the square and round dance circuit. We sold or gave away most of our attire. Some has even shown up from time to time on the Abbeville Opera House stage in plays.

As for that perfect square, it is no more. Shortly after our friend Don retired as a banker, he and Carolyn bought a home in Greenwood. They had planned to move there from Calhoun Falls and enjoy retirement. Don had tied off a tree in the yard and was using a chain saw to bring it down when somehow the tree twisted and fell on him, killing him instantly. Carolyn witnessed this from their porch. We were all devastated by the loss. Al and Debra eventually divorced. Roy and Mary, the eldest of our perfect square carried on the tradition without us. Both have incurred health issues. We've seen none of our friends in many years, losing touch after moving to the beach.

Ironically, Judy was at the Dollar General not far from our home and who of all people did she see, Don Franks and his wife Jan. They were attending a square dance event at Springmaid hotel. Years ago, we attended that very same event as proud Merry Mixers. Those funny looking dressed people made a lasting and positive impression on me. I'll never regret giving it that second chance. Square dancers make good friends. Dressing up in funny looking attire isn't half bad. 'Allemande left with your left and back to the partner for a right and left hand grand.'

A couple of updates since originally penning the above: In 2014 we ironically and accidentally ended up on a seven-day cruise with Debra and new hubby Rocky, the Carnival ship leaving out of Jacksonville, Florida. Tragically her new husband, Rocky passed in 2016. We have crossed paths with Al in Abbeville at Cherokee Trail. We have not seen Roy or Mary in recent years. Carolyn did drop by one of my book signings in Abbeville in 2018. It was wonderful reminiscing.

Merry Mixers We Were

Sock Hoppers

Twas the Four Days of Dickens
a not so Christmassy Story

Local authors at the beach organized BAN, Beach Author Network as a network to promote our work and to support one another. We met in various libraries at the beach and attended events when we could. We had decided to reserve at booth at the local Dickens Festival just prior to Thanksgiving. It seemed like a great idea. We anticipated that we would have an abundance of opportunities to sell our vast selection of published masterpieces. From children's books to Who Done It's and everything in between, there was something for every shopper, perfect Christmas gifts for those special people in your lives. The festival had been extended to four days this year offering shoppers an extra day to take advantage of the bountiful stuff down every aisle. Conceptually the premise appeared to be a sound and solid investment, each author paying their share of the reservation slot. The Dickens extravaganza had always been a major draw at the Myrtle Beach Convention Center. Expectations were high. The venue seemed perfect for nearly a dozen hopeful and hungry local authors, ole T. Allen included.

Beach Author Network, brainchild of our faithful to be eventual leader, Mary Anne Benedetto, had got its start at the Tupelo Bay Golf Club House as the site of the very first meeting. There we came up with the name and scope of the authors' group. We wanted to be more than just a bunch of authors meeting monthly to critique one another's work. We decided then and there that our mission statement would be to promote our work and network ways to sell our greatest accomplishments. Most were self publishers. Some had sold some work while others had paid dearly to traditional publishers to see their work in print. One common thread bound us. None of us had landed that million best seller nor were our doors being beaten down to own a piece of our crafty goods. We had our work cut out for us. Force in numbers, we forged ahead, optimistic that we would overcome these obstacles and leap over every hurdle tossed in our path. A learning process often trial and error, but we were in this together. WE ARE BAN.

Gimmicks, not specifically of our own doing, but participants in the festival were required to dress in Dickens attire. Each author was responsible for meeting this criterion. I researched *Dickens* to find out how the people dressed back then. Examples were plentiful. Compliance might pose problems for some. For me, it paid to have connections in all the right places. I had access to clothing used for Carolina Forest school plays and the singers of Vocal Edition, a local choral group. Vocal Edition dressed in Dickens style attire when performing during the Christmas holidays at such venues as Brookgreen Gardens in Georgetown County. I had a start, a top hat and full-length tail style coat. All that was missing was a scarf or ascot, shoes, an appropriate ruffled style shirt and pants. Challenges, undaunted, I pressed onward.

Innovation, imagination, and persistence prevailed. Scarf dilemma overcome by converting and forming a conventional necktie to mimic an ascot. Shoes…had long clunky black loafers that would pass the glimpse test. I had an assortment of golf knickers and knee length socks, styling and profiling during the cooler months at the beach on the links. I am Payne Stewart in appearance only. You can pick me out amongst the woods and bushes while searching for that errant hook or slice. Pat, one of our authors, solved the shirt problem, offering up what I could only describe as a puffy shirt of her husband's, once used for a Dickens event. I bought a wood walking cane to accessorize my wardrobe. I looked quite spiffy and Dickens like, game on. Let's sell some books.

I couldn't join my fellow authors until after 4 PM on Thursday and Friday of the event, curse of the working man when the others were basically retired. Within my first hour of my first day I had sold one copy each of my two books. I was off and rolling right out of the chute, so it appeared. Foot traffic was steady, more lookers that buyers so it seemed as the night wore on. I had played this game already, déjà vu, reliving two days in Columbia, S.C. for the State Book Convention. I only sold two books at that two-day event. Let's do the math. Drive to and back from Myrtle Beach and Columbia, one night in a hotel, food and then twelve hours manning the booth with a handful of other author hopefuls; not very profitable. Oh yeah, let's add the blown right front tire traveling 70 MPH on the return trip to the beach and being stranded on the side of the highway for over four hours. You ask, why I didn't change the tire, use the spare. I tried but my jack would not give me enough height to replace the deflated tire. Ford provided oversized rims for my F150 truck but didn't think to provide me with a jack that would match. I eventually dialed Star HP and the highway patrol sent a rollback wrecker to assist. My rescue ranger quickly assessed and solved the problem, placing the jack atop a cinder block, providing enough clearance to change the tire. He even left me the cinder block saying I should keep it in the back of my truck.

One memory takes me to another, the Rock Hill festival. Fellow author, Bob Freeland and I attended this festival. May he rest in peace, taken away from us way too early. We were inside the visiting center and what seemed to be a perfect place to flaunt our books. Seven hours later, I hadn't sold a single book. Bob gave free copies of his war saga, *Balance*, to veterans and didn't sell any either. Okay, so I got off the Dickens story.

Sometimes you just must go where the nostalgic moments take you, one memory triggering a different one. Trust me. I will make the correlation to those I've just mentioned and the wonderful world of Dickens.

Twas the end of day one of the Dickens event and my sales stood firmly at two books, a copy of *Road Rage* and a copy of *Dark Thirty*. We had over two dozen books up for grabs, each author proudly flaunting theirs to passersbys with very few nibbles. Tomorrow would be a new day filled with new opportunities and challenges. Did I mention that you must pay to park, even venders? Four days of parking fees tacked onto my cost to rent the booth was not balancing out with the two books sold. Not to worry, we had three more days to go and the weekend mother lode of visitors waiting in the wings.

Twas the beginning of day two and I joined my fellow band of authors after work for more fun, fellowship, and salesmanship. There were plenty of visitors, all looking for that special something. Unfortunately, books didn't seem to fit the scenario of that special something. My pals and I kept a stiff upper lip, not quite yet ready to scream uncle and toss in the towel. Some were close. I tried a new approach. I took my walking cane on the road or down the aisleways to be more specific. My fellow patrons, decked out in their assortment of Dickens attire, tossed praises and kudos my way for the authenticity of my costume. I tried the pied piper approach hoping shoppers would follow me back to our booth. Like a beached whale, my ploy failed. Twas the end of Day two of the Dickens debacle and my book sales stood firmly at two. Other members of the supporting cast didn't fair much better.

Saturday and Sunday I had signed up for daylong duty, about twelve hours worth each day. What had I been thinking? This time I brought my ace in the hole, a personal gimmick, an old man Halloween mask, white stringy hair with a white goatee. It was Scrooge like, an image that only a mother could love. I figured it might just be the perfect method to my ever-growing madness, a way to reel in potential customers. I developed a character and launched into action. Foot traffic abundant, many stopped and asked could they take a photograph of me with them. Hindsight, I should have charged for the photo opts. Others thought I wasn't real, a dummy, until I moved. I was beginning to agree with them. I was a dummy for participating in this fiasco. My alter ego took on a new persona. I transformed unto Little Tommy Dickens, the prankster, reaching new lows to try reeling in potential buyers. Gloria, one of our authors, specifically enjoyed one of my tricks. Scrooge mask in place I would hold nuts close to the mask's mouth and lizard like tongue pluck them from my fingers. It was a showstopper. At least Gloria liked it. One can eat just so many nuts though. Day three of the Dickens doomed event came to an end. My book sales had skyrocketed to two and still standing. It had been two and done that first day.

Twas the last day of the Dickens festival and a fourth day of dressing in the gosh-awful hot costume. Sore feet, aching back, I now used the cane for more than just a window dressing prop. I needed to graduate to a walker. I had become just a tad too punchy and totally over this event. Silliness prevailed. Nothing was out of bounds. One of my fellow authors and I waltzed to the music playing in our heads in the aisle in front of our booth. We received cheers and claps but generated no book sales from our efforts. Wearing Scrooge, I stood manikin still, waiting for a victim to approach and examine me more closely before scaring the you know what out of them. One must draw from the little pleasures in life, revenge of the authors so to speak. That will teach the gawkers and drifters. I might have mooned them if it wouldn't have been such an effort to do so wearing the Little Tommy Dickens outfit. Fun and games were getting a lot less fun. The experience accomplished one thing though. It solidified our love for one another as BAN members. Misery certainly thrives on company suffering the same ill affects. Day four of Dickens Hell came to an end. My book sales total stood firmly at two with one book swap with Mary Anne. Some twenty-two plus hours of the nightmare know as Dickens and I can only say 'Bah Humbug, nevermore in my lifetime.'

**The Dickens Merry 'BAN'
from left, Danny Kuhn, Pat David, T. Allen Winn,
Goffinet McLaren, Mary Ann Benedetto and Gloria Flecker**

Tailgating for Dummies and In-laws

Growing up in Abbeville, I attended my fair share of Clemson Tiger football games. I didn't exactly pick them as my favorite collegial team, nor did I attend Clemson. I reckon it just happened. Various cousins attended the upstate rival to the South Carolina Gamecocks, so possibly that indirectly steered me in their direction. I do vaguely recall attending Cousin Stan Newton's graduation there. Granny Winn, Aunt Cornelia and Uncle Jerry became devoted IPTAY members. Being one of a tiny handful of grandkids in proximity, I drew the winning lottery ticket by default and ended up accompanying them to many games. I had nothing against the Gamecocks and to this day I don't get caught up in the inner state rivalry, Tigers verses the Cocks. I pull for both, almost taboo living in the Palmetto State. People expect you to pick one or the other. When the big game arrives at the end of the season between the two, I tend to lean towards the one having the better record, unless I'm just in the mood to pull for the underdog. I really have a method to my madness when it comes to picking one over the other. That does make me an anomaly.

I have never attended an actual Gamecock game at William Bryce Stadium in Columbia. Clemson games at Death Valley were free if I attended with my kinfolks. Free tends to trump paying the price of admission any given day. As an adult I did once attend an exhibition NFL pre-season football game at William Bryce. It was between the Bears and Bills. I don't remember who won. If memory serves me correctly the tickets were free, explaining why I went in the first place. As for professional football, I have attended two regular season games in my life, both being Atlanta Falcon games. One was at Fulton County Stadium and the other at the dome in Atlanta. Like the pre-season one, I don't remember who was playing the Falcons or who won, not very impressed apparently.

Talk about creatures of habit, my IPTAY supporting family had a specific routine for attending ALL Clemson games. We pulled out of Abbeville at 8 AM to arrive in plenty of time to secure the best parking spot for tailgating before the game. It didn't matter whether the game was a noon start or a night game; we still left at 8 AM sharp. There was no wiggle room. It had always been that way and that way it would remain. Deviating was not going to happen. It obviously left plenty of time for tailgating and roaming the campus, especially when it was a night game. You had eight or more hours to kill. Good food was to be had but there would be no alcohol. I was too young to drink adult beverages back then, so it was never ever a consideration. Ripping and romping better fit my wheelhouse until kick off time.

I've witnessed my fair share of barn burners, nail biters and blow outs. Like my attending Atlanta Braves baseball games, I think I've seen the favorite team come up on the short end of the stick more times than in the win column. Diehard fans don't get caught up in this, cherishing the wins instead. While I always preferred seeing a Tiger win, a loss didn't devastate me or ruin my life. Those who thought otherwise could be cheap entertainment. Sore losers can always lay blame on something else, the refs, the coaches, the cheerleaders or water boys. That's why I focused on the tailgating. There were no losers when it came to stuffing your face with your favorites. Between grazing the buffet we'd toss the old pigskin or Frisbee around to kill time. Sometimes a noon start was changed to a nighttime start due to being televised. Television games were long, commercials interrupting the natural flow.

Tailgate food somehow seems tastier when served in the great outdoors. Fried chicken would always be on the menu. I think that is a 'must have' in the tailgate bible. Deviled eggs, byproduct of the yard bird was likely to be part of the food being consumed. Potato salad or slaw would make up the menu. Potato chips and some assortment of dips were a given. Let's not forget pimento cheese or egg salad sandwiches. Fire up the grill and cook wieners and beef patties. You can never go wrong having hotdogs and hamburgers. My kin rarely did that though, not that we didn't have plenty of time to cook from scratch. Hauling a grill, charcoal and lighter fluid required too much effort and room in the trunk. The 57 Chevy four door or 66 two door Chevy Caprice weren't suited for hauling too much cooking equipment. The '57 was referred to as the five-seven. You could have probably hauled a Pit Master smoker in the trunk of the classic.

With my dear relatives long departed, Jerry and Norma Solomon, my wife's sister and her husband, were given four free tickets to attend a Clemson game. It was homecoming with Tiger-rama ongoing. They asked if I'd like to go, Norma having already invited a coworker but had the one ticket left. Sure, I hadn't been to a Clemson game in ages. We left about 7:30 for the 1 PM start, tailgating goodies plentiful. It was late summer and still plenty hot for attending a day game. Cloudless skies, the weather was perfect. The heat didn't really bother me anyway. It was just a little over an hour drive from Abbeville to Clemson, perfect timing to tailgate before attending the game, right? We had plenty of food and beverages. It felt like old times, driving on campus. I soon spotted Clemson Memorial Stadium, popularly known as Death Valley, Frank Howard Field.

I thought about Clemson tradition and the rubbing of Howard's Rock by players entering the stadium. Howard's Rock is a large piece of white flint. The rock is the center of a longstanding tradition where players touch it before running down the hill in the east end zone. The rock was brought to football coach Frank Howard in the early 1960s as a gift from Samuel C. Jones. Jones found the rock while driving through Death Valley, California and gave it to Howard as a reference to "Death Valley," the name Howard used to refer to Memorial Stadium. The coach used the rock as a doorstop until 1966. He was cleaning out his office when he told Gene Willimon, a Clemson booster, to take this rock and throw it over the fence or out in the ditch. Do something with it but get it out of my office. Willimon placed the rock on a pedestal in the east end zone, where it remains today.

Everything has a starting point, an origin, that moment when it just falls into place. Thus, was the case for Howard's Rock. So, the story goes, the rock showed up on the scene September 24, 1966. The tigers were losing to Virginia by 18 points with seventeen minutes left in the game. Clemson made up the deficit and won the game 40-35. From there sprung tradition. The next season rubbing the rock upon entering the stadium began. Howard reportedly said to his players, 'If you're going to give me 110 percent, you can rub that rock. If you're not, keep your filthy hands off it.' Fact or fiction, maybe there was just something lucky about that rock. The Tigers have always continued this tradition since 1967, except for two-and-a-half seasons between 1970 and 1972. This was due to new head coach Hootie Ingram's changing the team's entrance to the west end zone after Frank Howard's retirement. During those seasons, Clemson held a bad record at home of 6-9. Before the South Carolina rivalry game in 1972 the team voted to enter via the east end zone and run down the hill. They later won the game 7-6.

Sorry, sometimes trivia is part of nostalgia. Clemson is rich in both. Getting back on track, let's talk tailgating, an American tradition. This is a sensitive and painfully upsetting memory personally. No, not from those long-ago times with Granny, Aunt Cornelia, and Uncle Jerry. Those are wonderfully nostalgic. I was so looking forward to an afternoon of football with the in-laws plus one and making new memories at one of the classical Tiger homecoming extravaganzas. Home games are a circus like atmosphere. Anyone who has ever attended a college football game knows that the first thing you must absolutely do once parked is set-up the tailgate party. This is like going camping. You first set up the campsite. It's a no brainer, right? The Solomon's insisted on walking around first, not realizing that everything on the Clemson campus is up and down hills. I tried to convince them otherwise. First, we tailgate and do a little grazing then there is plenty of time to explore before game time. Nope, they had to walk about first. I gave up and went along. Cousin Louie would call them greenhorns.

The first 'I told you so' came into play quite quickly. Huffing and puffing, sweating bullets, the in-laws and their friend realized there was little flatland to be found. Suddenly ambling about, partaking in the collegial spiritual ambiance didn't seem too appealing to those not accustomed to attending sporting events. I suggested that we should go back to the SUV and tailgate. I convinced them to head back in that direction. We still had several hours before game time. My mouth was watering just thinking about it, having worked up an appetite venturing up and down the campus hills. Of course, heading back and getting there came with its challenges. The trio alternated between shade and breather stops. Summer in the south was taking its toll on them. We paused in the entranceway, in the shadow of Death Valley. Norma suggested that we go inside the stadium instead. I thought she just wanted to peek inside. I then realized she meant go inside instead of back to the car.

I insisted we should go tailgate first. She said it was too hot and a long way back. I countered that it was way too early to go inside. She held firm to her stance. Now I was getting a tad bit perturbed to say the least, telling her this isn't how it goes. People tailgate before attending the game. She suggested we could tailgate at half time. What, I screamed. You've got to be kidding. I informed her that once we went inside, they would not allow us to leave the stadium. Either she didn't believe me or didn't care. Either way I was having no luck convincing her or her supporters otherwise. I should have asked for my ticket and the keys to the car right then and there. Hindsight isn't worth a flying flip.

What had I been thinking? They had invited me, so I was sort of afraid to leave them alone. Well that's the only logical answer I could come up with, as lame as it sounds. Highly aggravated now, I followed them inside. We easily located our seats. It wasn't difficult. We were the only ones inside the stadium. The vendors hadn't even opened shop yet. They were good seats, not too far up on the fifty-yard line. The second 'I told you so'…it was too hot in the sun, she said let's go to the car. Sorry, no dice. Once in, you can't go back out. An attendant confirmed what I had already told them before we entered. Game time was nearly three hours away and now we couldn't go tailgate. I was fuming. I tried to calm down and make the best of it; free game, homecoming, and I hadn't been here in years. It wasn't easy though, trapped in this Twilight Zone episode with people I couldn't reason with.

Finally, after a couple of hours, people began filing in and eventually the game started. They had bought food and beverage from the concession stand once they had finally opened. Pigheaded, I had refused, knowing we had brought all that tailgating food and drinks. I'd hold out until after the game and grab something then. For the next two quarters those I shared the bleachers with complained about the sun, the heat, the hard seats, the noisy crowds, etc. I just tried to mentally block out my anguish, frustration and their whining. The game was close, still anyone's for the taking. As halftime approached, I told them that they would thoroughly enjoy the Tiger band and halftime proceedings. Just as halftime approached Norma announced she was ready to go. In shock, I asked, 'ready to go where?' Unbelievable, they were ready to go home. I asked didn't they to want to watch halftime. Nope, she was ready to go, too hot, blah…blah…blah. I exploded.

I recap the scenario. I had gotten up at 6 AM to come to a Clemson homecoming game and now she was insistent on us going home at halftime. Nobody does this. Nobody comes inside the stadium three hours before the game begins. Nobody puts off tailgating before the game. This was absolutely beyond the craziest notion I had ever heard or experienced. There was no talking her or them out of it. We were leaving. I was livid. We left the stadium. I couldn't begin to fathom it, but we did. When we got to the car, a deserted parking lot I must add, she had the audacity to mention tailgating. Not going to happen I assured them, and I meant what I said. We drove from the parking lot and down a car-less highway, not even a state trooper in sight. The comment was made about how nice it was without any traffic to contend with. Duh, everyone is inside at the game. We were the only morons pulling a stunt like this. I dared anyone to turn on the radio and listen to the game on the ride back. I didn't even know the final score of the game until the 11 PM news segment.

Unbelievable…totally insane…something I vowed I would never do again…attend any sort of sporting event with the Solomon's. Many years have passed but every time Clemson comes up in conversation in the company of my precious in-laws, I recant and relive the most awful sports memory of my life. Lot of it is now done in fun but it remains a painful and unprecedented event etched in my recall cells. Those with whom I have shared the tale, share my sentiment and find it difficult to rationalize. In contrast, when we attend a Coastal Carolina Football game with the Singletons, we traditionally tailgate, milking it to the very last moment before going to our seats. Following Rhonda's lead, we remain in our seats until the last second ticks off the game clock, regardless of how close or lopsided the game might be me. Now that's the way it is supposed to be. Upon occasion, the Singletons have suggested maybe the Solomon would like to attend a CCU game. Not going to happen I tell them. Sports and Solomon's don't mix, at least not on my watch. Nostalgia, it's not for the weakest of hearts but often worth recapping. Love you Jerry and Norma but sports and you and I are not in the cards, unless on television, and then tailgating not required, only optional. Burn me once, shame on you. Burn me twice…not going there.

Sometimes you eat your words. Norma and Jerry did attend a Coastal Carolina game with us many years later. Nope. I didn't invite them. They were fascinated by the experience of tailgating. We stayed in our seats until the game was over. The tailgating for dummies and in-laws box has been checked.

Going Coastal

I know what you are probably thinking. He meant postal. Not necessarily. Just possibly this is going to be a twisted tongue and cheek version of the cliché associated with postal workers off the rail in an episode of craziness and rage. Sometimes I might walk the straight and narrow when it comes to spinning a story but not often. For one reason or the other, in 2005 we relocated to Horry County, South Carolina. It has its perks, fun, sun and beaches included. Ah, now you think you have this one figured out, don't you? Be forewarned. Never try to outguess a knuckle ball thrower. Location, location, location can be quite deceiving. Yes, we did move to the coastal community. Doing so after living in Abbeville and Greenwood all my life did take considerable adjustments.

While the Myrtle Beach community isn't exactly big city living, it's a lot worse on many levels. It's a tourist town with challenges a plenty. You learn quickly how to navigate the roadways often flooded and bottlenecked with those who are just here to visit and potentially ruin your life if you let them. Adapting as quickly as possible is the key to living here year-round. In the early going it did inspire the plot for my fictional novel, Road Rage. Some of my coastal friends still think I might be the serial killer depicted in the book. They thought I might be burying bodies to cover my trail.

Growing up in Abbeville and sort of midway between the state capitol and Tiger Town, you were expected to pick a team and defend it with honor. You had only two choices. You either pulled for the Clemson Tigers or South Carolina Gamecocks. You never pulled for both. That was un-American and strictly against the Palmetto State's codes and ethics, downright unlawful in most folks' eyes. It was marginally tolerated if you pulled for either when they played against the Georgia Bulldogs. Tiger and Gamecock football is serious business, hallowed ground to many. I royally upended that applecart and premise.

I didn't like or dislike one team than the other; something best kept to one's self I learned. I pulled for both to have winning seasons and when it came down to them playing at the end of the year, I usually pulled for the one that had the best winning record or opportunity to advance to a bowl game. Call me a flip flopper if you wish but that was just the way I saw it. I never attended a Clemson vs South Carolina game. Obviously, I ended up pulling for the Tigers at home all the time and it didn't matter who they were playing. Several of my cousins graduated from Clemson and I attended their graduations. I even saw legendary Bob Hope perform once at Little John Coliseum.

Let's go back to that 2005 move to Murrells Inlet in Horry County. Conway is home to CCU, Coastal Carolina University, and at the time, a Division II School. Judy's daughter, Rhonda and son-in-law Gene Singleton had season tickets on the fifty-yard line in the Teal seats. They asked us to attend a game. The hook had been set. We began attending the home games with them. Guess you can say we adopted them as our team. Not to worry. No diehard Clemson or Carolina fans were cringing at our selection. The Chanticleers were in the minor league, far from the big show and real football teams. David Bennett was the head couch and our designated seats were directly behind the Bennett family. We got to know them well, including Ma Bennett, his mother. Now she was a hoot. She'd turn and make us standup when the defense was tying to hold the opposing team on 3rd downs. Not standing was not an option. We stood a lot and knew the drill.

The Singletons lived a couple of blocks from the campus and stadium. It was an easy walk, but you never really want to walk to a tailgate party. There is just too much stuff to carry and then where would you store the stuff while you were inside watching the game. Unlike Jerry and Norma, we did know when and how to tailgate. We embraced the experience. Instead, we rode to the stadium in style. A '57 four door Chevy was our tailgating ride for many years. The Singletons had a reserved parking place located almost within the shadows of Brooks Stadium. We could stack passengers in that old Chevy like cordwood. It wasn't unusual to have eight to ten people inside. We resembled one of those clown cars disembarking the teal colored vehicle. The trunk was huge. We could have packed a month's supplies inside and still had room. We were quite the draw, rubber-neckers gawking with envy. And like any tailgates, the food and fixings were plentiful.

When it was announced in the late 1990s that CCU would establish a football squad in the coming years, Rhonda, a football fanatic, and diehard Clemson fan, knew then and there that they would be season ticket owners. The Coastal Carolina Chanticleers football program played its inaugural season in 2003 on campus at Brooks Stadium. The team's first coach as mentioned was David Bennett. He held the position until December 9, 2011. The university named Joe Moglia, former CEO of TD Ameritrade, as its new head coach on December 20, 2011. My gut told me that he bought his way into this position. One man's opinion, what can I say. Moglia didn't like facing the sun from the home side of the field so he moved the team to the visitor's side. You do realize that the team then began playing all their game as if they were the away team. The bulk of the Coastal fans sitting in the nice seats were now looking at the opposition assembled below them.

This eccentric maneuver rubbed me the wrong even though I was not a season ticket holder. I began researching the opposition prior to the scheduled home games. No. I wasn't brushing up on the stats to better prepare me for the game. I wished to know the opposition's team colors. I figured if I was going to be sitting on the side of the team playing against CCU, I may as well dress the part. My protest, my way, for the first season under his leadership, I dressed as close as I could to the team now positioned on my side of the field. I really hoped this might be a fluke, but it wasn't. He continued this tradition of idiotic behavior for the next seven years. I did eventually go back to the teal colors, but I never warmed up to the new coach. I didn't like him or his demeanor on the field. Thank goodness he has stepped down for the 2019 season and Jamey Chadwell will be at the helm in 2019. Rumor has it the team will return to its traditional side of the field, the side where the home fans reside.

Coastal, little known in the state, has defeated such traditional Football Championship Subdivision (FCS) powers as James Madison University (ranked No. 1 at the time), Furman University, Wofford College, and the University of Montana. They won seven Big South Conference championships and have had several former players enter professional NFL careers. CCU's primary football rivals while in the FCS were Liberty and Charleston Southern. In 2006, the Chanticleers made school history when the team received its first FCS playoff berth, also the first playoff berth for the Big South Conference, losing a first-round contest to Appalachian State. Appalachian State would go on to win the FCS national championship that season. The team is now in the big league, moving to division 1 ball in 2016 and into the Sunbelt Conference. Times have been tough during this transition. They had success in the Big South, winning five conference championships and being co-winner in two others. In the Sunbelt they have struggled to win games and haven't had a winning season yet.

I have so many memories I could share of games and friends tailgating with us, but it would take way too many more pages. Amon and Faith Wilson joined us a couple of times. Rest in peace dear Faith. Sammy (Cuz) Cannon and his bride Judy also joined us. Miss and love that man, dedicated my book to him, 'Cuz, My Brother, Life is Good, God is Good.' Going Coastal has been one of the wonderful experiences of beach life, thanks to Gene and Rhonda for making us part of the family tradition.

Me with Faith Wilson

Cuz, Judy 2, Judy1 and Me

Grandsons Winn and Duncan Singleton Bookends

Stephen King Doppelganger Guy Dozer

Judy 2 and Cuz Chowing Down on Wings

The Ultimate Tailgate Vehicle 'The Teal '57

Better Be Glad You're Not My Young'un

In today's times parents are criticized for being abusive parents when they spank a child. It is depicted as an unlawful event. Don't get me wrong. I'm not advocating beating your children, but let's face it; this timeout junk is a lost cause. Scare me by making me go to my room or sit in a corner, right. If my parents had used those tactics on me, I would have been in hog heaven for sure. Let me count the ways I can entertain myself and not have my butt or legs red and stinging. Here I go again, deep diving into the world of that which children today have no clue once existed. It's time for one of those little history lessons kiddies.

I grew up in a time when we feared our parents. We did what they said or faced the consequences. I must confess. I received very few whippings in my life. Back in the day before unruly kids thought they had rights, it was called getting whippings, not beatings or child abuse or inhumane brutality. You did something bad; you most likely were going to get a whipping for it. Behaving was expected, not an option. Misbehaving warranted something you weren't going to like. Sometimes you must whip your kids to let them know just how much you love them. Proverbs 13.24 from King James Version of the Bible: "He that spareth his rod hateth his son: but he that loveth him chasteneth him betimes." Perhaps better translated; *He who spares the rod hates his son, but he who loves him is careful to discipline him.* In a 17th century poem by Samuel Butler called "Hudibras" a love affair is likened to a child, and spanking is commended to make the love grow stronger.

> "What medicine else can cure the fits
> Of lovers when they lose their wits?
> Love is a boy by poets styled
> Then spare the rod and spoil the child."

Back in my day, we knew the difference between right and wrong and picked our battles wisely, fully comprehending what would happen if we got caught doing what we weren't supposed to do. Back talk, I don't think so. Parents and teachers were the rulers of our humble universe. School teachers and especially those dreaded principals and vice principals had the authority and permission to paddle our tails if deemed justified for the crime we had perpetrated or allegedly perpetrated. Forget a trial and jury of your peers. Peers could be as guilty as you. You didn't argue with adults, period. If they said you did it, then you did it, whether you did it or not. Kids of my day did not live in a democracy. Parents seldom rushed to our defense. They sided with the teachers. Boy, how that has changed for all the wrong reasons. I could never be a teacher in today's world of *political correctiveness*. I would be locked up for sure for not putting up with their behavior. Parents please grow up. Take some responsibility and own proper parenting. Teachers are not to blame for your kids' arrogance, disrespectful attitudes, and misbehavior. Raise them right and they do right.

There was a low tolerance level for disrespectfulness in the day before kids thought they were above punishment. Don't get me wrong, kids of my era were not prim and proper Stepford children. We had our fair share of rebels without a cause. As a teenager I became one of those smart mouth little rebels, but for every action taken, there is an uglier reaction waiting in the wings. Rebels got spanked too or at school it was called being paddled. No one laid a hand on you, but a wood paddle served as the best attitude adjuster; batter up. I always think of that scene in Animal House with Kevin Bacon in his tidy whities, bent over and holding his ankles while being paddled as part of his initiation saying, 'Thank you, I'll have another', each time he was whacked.

Some teachers governed by the ruler. If you disrupted their class or crossed a line you knew better than crossing, palms up or palms down, the twelve-inch wood ruler worked the same. You never forget that noise or the end result. I received my most memorable ruler incident while in the first grade but if you read my other memoir, *Cornbread and Buttermilk, Good Ole Fashion Home Cooked Nostalgic Nonsense*, then you probably remember that one from my first year at Langley Milliken Grammar School in L.A. (Lower Abbeville). Then there were those belts and switches. Daddy's leather belt, ouch, dare I say more. The worst possible scenario in a kid's mind after they have completed a wrongful deed plays out something like this when confronted by their parent.

"I want you to go outside and pick a switch off that tree and bring it back to me. If you pick something tiny and flimsy it will only make things worse."

How can things be any worse? Tasked with choosing the disciplinary weapon your parent is going to use on you and warning you not to pick something that will not work, just adds insult to injury yet to come. By the way, for those of you only privy to timeout tactics or punishment by taking away your phone, video games or car, a switch is a small limb plucked from a tree or a bush with all the leaves stripped from it. Liken it to one of those little thingamajigs that jockeys use to swat their horses to make them run faster. The infamous switch could be directed at your hinny or even worse, at your bare legs, if you were wearing shorts or you were forced to drop your pants. What I hated even more was them telling me I better stop crying or they would continue swatting me. How does that really work? It makes absolutely no sense. Sometimes what parents say defies logic in a kid's mind.

Speaking of swatting, some parents preferred utilizing the trusty fly swatter. Ironically, one could miss a fly with it, but it was dead on when the kid was the target. Parents land themselves in jail for using any of these tools of discipline now. Political correctness continues to derail this country. I am older and wiser and understand the value of those whippings now. Tough lessons learned. Parents didn't whip us because they hated us. They didn't whip us because they enjoyed it. It was necessary in the learning process. Right from wrong, we realized that respect was expected. My mama would often cry when she had to pop my legs. The message had to be delivered by her or Daddy to teach me that I should know better. Hindsight and hurt hinnies weren't the same.

Each parent had their preferred tools of trade, whether it was hands, belts, switches, fly swatters, paddles or just good ole leather straps. All of them got our undivided attention and filled our lungs with whimpering bouts of 'I'm sorry. I won't do it again. I mean it.' Not that our parents didn't believe or trust our sincerity, but break the rules, suffer the consequences, not up for negotiation. Very few pardons were ever granted. Do the crime, face the fine. Look around you. Is today's society and crop of kids better off because parents can no longer be parents and do what they think is right to raise their children? Back in the day, given the choices, if I would have had a choice, I would have opted for being the whistle blower and avoided whippings. Tattling on others was not cool but diverted attention elsewhere, until the CSI team completed their investigation. Lying was a much larger crime. Best not get caught fibbing, just saying.

Today, however, I have no patience for unruly children. Parents please don't cop out and say I can't make them behave or we can't have anything because of them. Who's the grownup and who's the kid? There's nothing worse than to be in a nice restaurant seated next to a screaming or crying kid. Just as bad are those bouncing off the floor and ceilings doing whatever they want to do while the parents tune them out. I am for those kid free restaurants or better still, seat all of them in a designated family section. Enclose them in the cone of silence away from child free adults just wanting to have a peaceful meal. See how you like that, grazing in a wild herd. And no, I don't want to hear you cursing your children or witness you slapping them on the face or head. And please don't ask them for the zillionth time to stop doing whatever annoying thing they are doing. It's not working. The kid knows it. We know it. Once you can escape the world of denial, you'll know it too. Possibly I give you too much credit sometimes. Your kids learn from you. If you think you are the center of the universe, so will they. Rotten apples tend to not fall too far from the tree.

Screaming or talkative children in a movie, play, or show is totally unacceptable. I paid for the entertainment, not disruptive behavior. Take it outside and settle it before returning. Who cares if you miss what you paid for? You should have gotten a babysitter. Simple, don't ruin it for everyone else. After about the third *stop it*, it sort of grows old. Same goes for church; you should be teaching them to have better manners. Having wild little banshees running amok in the aisles of stores and screaming at the top of their lungs will not get you nominated for parent of the year either. Show a little class and do not yell at them like you're the only ones occupying space in the world. We grow tired quickly of your yelling. In my day, one *shush* or that dreaded *Mama Look* would have been all it took to transform me into the perfect child. One more thing, keep the itty biddies away from the buffet. Grimy little hands and sneezing and coughing just does not set well. Serve their plates please.

I must confess. I'm not a parent but I did stay at the Holiday Inn Express once. But you don't have to be a parent to recognize terrible parenting. I don't really blame the children. After all, who raised them? Maybe you're the one I should send outside to pick a switch. No, then I would be accused of assault. Parents, act responsible and teach them right from wrong. Teach them how to whisper and that when you say *No*, you really do mean *No*. **Stop** actually is the opposite of **Go**. Lay out the ground rules and the consequences for breaking those rules. Stop being a talking, meaningless head. All I can say is when faced with one of these screaming unruly terrors, you better be glad you're not my young'un. Spare the rod and spoil the kid. Sometimes you really do have to beat them to show them just how much you love them. Man, just how would I have turned out if today's philosophy had been applied back in the time when parents and teachers ruled the world?

Thank your lucky stars I am not a teacher or your daddy. No, I would never abuse you, but I would promise you one thing; you'd learn from your misjudgments and think twice before crossing that line again. Eventually you would even appreciate the fact that I love you and only did it because I do. It is time parents begun acting like parents, setting the example and, if you do, just maybe your kids will look to you as responsible role models. Neglecting or passing the baton off to teachers is simply wrong. Blaming them for doing their job is even worse. To quote *Mad Max* from the *John Boy and Billy* radio show, '*quit ruining my life.*' And in this case, the lives of your kids and those around you caught in the aftermath. I'm blessed to have been raised in that 'once upon a time' world that taught me better. Am I perfect? No, a far cry from it but I thank my parents for doing what they were supposed to do. Parents, please behave like parents.

Skating, Surfing and Skiing

Abbeville is not exactly a mega for surfing or skiing. The Banzai Pipeline or even Squaw Valley is a far piece from South Carolina. Little (Parson's) Mountain didn't exactly offer skiing opportunities even if we did so happen to get a record snowfall. You would have to get there first and people in Abbeville are not known for their ability to negotiate snowy roadways even when a dusting is involved. Icy conditions and a foot riding the brake can quickly take out a slew of cars landing them into ditches and telephone poles. The snow bunny is to be feared on the highways and byways when a wintry mix is in the forecast. Southern tradition, brake first, doesn't matter whether you're going up or down a slippery slope. Not to worry that every vehicle behind you is taking evasive actions for your ill-fated maneuver, most ending up stranded while you drive away unscathed. It would be better for them and for us if they remained focused on empting the local grocery stores of bread and milk at the mere mention of snowflakes on the nightly news and not venture out after it arrives. One never knows when you might have to hunker down for a day or two in the Deep South frozen tundra. I'm not exactly sure why people do that, but many families would buy 2 loaves of bread and 3 gallons of milk when the weather called for snow.

So, you are wondering what the rambling and psycho babbling man is up to this time, aren't you? Just when you thought it was safe to sponge in the next nostalgic snapshot, he ventures into a hodgepodge world of flashbacks. Maybe they are connected. Maybe they aren't. Fear not. The paths will cross sooner or later if you have the patience and fortitude to hang in here with me. The three 'S's of recreation were part of my life, even without an ocean and a ski resort to link two of them to skating. No, we are not talking ice skating. That would require a frozen lake. Little Mountain lake doesn't freeze over and offer a venue for Abbeville on Ice. For the record, we had no ice-skating rinks back then either. Sure, if temperatures reached below freezing, strategically squirted water from the hose pipe onto the drive did make for slips and slides from those of us hankering to test our skills. It was still a far cry from the Greenville Memorial Auditorium Ice Capades. An icy capade is an icy capade I reckon in the imagination of those yearning to be the next famous ice figure skater.

Can the ice skating. Back in my day we were better suited for Roller Derby duty. My peers and I were taking out unsuspecting skaters before we knew it was a sport. Well, I'm not so sure I would categorize the Roller Derby as a sport. It was more like the wild world of wrestling with wheels. Pulling for the good guys against the bad guys was our version of a soap opera. Roller Derby and Saturday morning wrestling had its heroes and villains and fair share of underdogs. Good, bad or in between you pulled for your favorite. Enough on the professionals though, let's talk the amateur division. Who remembers those roller skates with a key? One size fit all foot or shoe sizes. The skates were metal, four wheels with a toe expander and ankle strap. The body of the skate moved like a slide rule to adjust to your foot size. You used the funky shaped key to tighten it and lock it in place. Many of us wore the key around our necks on a string so that we wouldn't lose it. You didn't want to have to wear your skates permanently, shoes affixed to them. Skating back then required balance, coordination, and plenty of luck. We were stuntmen in those early years or possibly just mere crash dummies ahead of our time.

Paved driveways and cement sidewalks were our playgrounds. If you learn to navigate the imperfect surfaces with minimal skinned elbows and knees and bruised butts, you were ahead of the game. We learned quickly how best to fall. Legs moving awkwardly while swinging your arms back and forth somehow prompted perpetual motion. If lucky you moved forward. Gaining speed and coasting mimicked grasping that golden ring. Eventual crashing and burning were almost guaranteed until you got the hang of it. Stopping techniques varied. Face forward onto a grassy spot at minimum speeds or snatching hold of a passing pole or other stationary objects were optional methods. None of these were graceful maneuvers. They were survival techniques. With practice came perfection. We wore our battle scars until then, our newly discovered blood sport. I don't think elbow and knee pads, or helmets had been invented. We were daredevils without safety nets. Parents didn't seem too concerned. They bought us this stuff and then let us have at it. I can't really remember any of my friends ever breaking any bones. Maybe we were a tougher breed back then, not the wussies of today.

We did have a few venues for skating. Greenwood, 13 miles away, was the closest skating rink. It may as well have been a hundred miles away though. Getting there wasn't easy unless our parents, relatives or friends were willing to spend their time to take us, and of course pay for it. If we were lucky, we knew an adult who loved to skate too. We were in the big-time arena when we got to skate on wood floors with those ankle high shoe skates. Too often we were poorly prepared for the speed and centrifugal force encountered in the one-way oblong circular raceway. Holding hands was permitted until you got into the swing of it. Sort of like those snow bunnies and flooring the brake pedal on the slick highway, it took but one person to fall to create a chain reaction of crashes behind them. I had perfected the forward fall, breaking it with my hands and knees. Rarely did my feet ever zip out from underneath me causing me to fall unceremoniously on my butt. I had some friends whose butts took a battering though.

Sometimes we just waited, impatiently of course, for the skate rink to come to us so to speak. It was a common sight to see a traveling skate rink set up on the outskirts of town. This was roller skating under the big top. It more resembled one of those revival tents used by the roving evangelist spreading the gospel. Only difference, ours had a portable wood floor and those seeking the Holy Ghost were on natural turf. Obviously, these traveling rinks were small in comparison to the permanent ones, but they sure beat sidewalks and driveways. We could hardly wait for our chance to go. If profitable these rinks would remain in one location for weeks, possibly even months. One price, you skated if you wanted. The parking lot never lied. Plenty of cars parked at the rink worked better than a billboard to reel in the paying customers. Oh yeah, did I mention they sold drinks and snacks on the side, a kid's perfect storm.

I seem to recall one the favorite locations for them to set up camp was located beyond the four way stop and flashing lights on highway 72 towards Calhoun Falls. There was a huge vacant lot just perfect with plenty of parking spots. Of course, it still took us kids begging, whining, pouting or by whatever means necessary to get someone to drive us out there. It was the perfect babysitter of sorts. Out parents would drop us off and come back and pick us up later; much later if we were lucky. Most of these places played the oldies, except back then they were new songs, not yet in oldie status like we remember them today. They would even have sweetheart times when the boys were supposed to invite a girl partner. Switch and bait, the girls would have a turn to pick their favorite boys too. These would be awkward for some of us, no matter who was the designated picker. If you had a hidden crush, then was the time to exercise your draft pick. That is if you didn't suffer from cold feet. Depending on whom you selected or who selected you, it could result in a feeding frenzy among your pals. We ate up opportunities to raze one another.

I mentioned at the first of this stroll down my forgotten past that there was no surfing or skiing in Abbeville. That was partly truthful. Somewhere along the way the art of skateboarding became popular in our little neck of the woods. This would be in the 1960's when the craze caught fire in Abbeville. Kids of my era were quite innovative. Most of us were unable to afford one of these new-fangled surfboards on wheels. What did we do? We found a new purpose for those discarded roller skates. We utilized scrap wood planks, sawing them off to a desired approximant length. We then took one of our roller skates apart, loosening and separating the two sections and then nailed each to the forward and back sections of our newly fashioned piece of wood. Like magic we were soon sidewalk surfing, the envy of those who no longer had their old roller skates to covert. Our creations weren't much too look at in their crudely constructed fashion and were not the smooth rides of a store bought one, but they served our purpose. If we messed up this one, we always had that second roller skate for the new and improved version.

I think I eventually owned only one store bought skateboard in my life. It was no frills but was still a step above those homemade ones. We had an asphalt circular drive around the backside of our house. It made the perfect skate track since we didn't have an actual sidewalk on our street or any of the nearby streets. Welcome to rural America. The closest sidewalk from Hunter Street where I lived was in front of the Langley Milliken grammar school. There you had to jockey for position with other surfers, skaters, bike riders and walkers. Otherwise you had to venture up South Main to find the next greatest sidewalk. And I do mean uphill from my neck of the woods. This made for spills and thrills on the way back. You still had to be prepared to avoid foot traffic. Nothing came easy. We had no surfboard parks back then. Equipped with our vivid imaginations we did construct a few crude jumps and obstacle courses.

Skiing, as mentioned, no snow slopes existed, thusly none of us owned the equipment custom made for the Alps. We had to rely on the water sport kind. I didn't grow up with family or friends that water skied. My parents and adult cousins did camp at Elijah Clark State Park on Clark Hill Lake but any activities involving boats were limited to fishing, putting out bottles or running trot lines. Well it was known as Clark Hill until 1988. It had been named this most of my young life, after the nearby South Carolina town of Clarks Hill and the Revolutionary War hero Elijah Clarke, whose was buried at Georgia's Elijah Clark State Park. In 1987 our Representative Butler Derrick introduced a bill before Congress to rename the lake after Strom Thurmond, the Palmetto State's long-time Senator. This riled the local folks, having it renamed after a segregationist politician. To this day most in these parts still refuse to call it Lake Thurman. I reckon to me it will always be Clarks Hill too. Nostalgia often causes you to ramble off point, but you learn stuff when we do.

I think I was a high school senior when I had my first opportunity to water ski. One of my pals had a boat, so we headed off to Lake Secession located in Abbeville County. The lake had always been sort of a gathering place for us, the dam's spillway, a double dare and done it venue. Death defining stunts for those thought to be supper human and bullet proof were commonplace inside our tiny clique. Yes, we both dove and jumped from the spillway, lake side of course. We were dare devils but not stupid. Well stupid is debatable. One favorite spot to test the dares, adjacent to the dam was an outcrop bank a couple of stories high. It was ideal for running and plunging into the depths of the watery hell below. The first time I completed the dare and sailed feet first into the great beyond, it scared *the you know what* out of me. After I experienced the splash down, I seemed to sink forever into the water abyss. I was suspended in the watery underworld. There didn't seem to be bottom and I wasn't sure I'd ever reach the surface again. When I finally did, I yelled in triumph and never disclosed the fear I had felt. It's easier to not show that you're sweating when immersed in water. And no, I didn't spot any of those legendary six-foot-long catfish while down there. Some claimed they existed and were large as a Volkswagen bug.

Okay, I think I got off the skiing episode, didn't I? With every success story comes the agony of defeat so it seems. The jubilation of success is often followed by the trials and tribulations of failure. Well, so goes my interpretation, life's experiences to support my spin on it. Picture this. A tall, lanky, one hundred fifty pound seventeen-year-old sitting on the dock, legs suspended over the water, skis dangling at the surface, both hands firmly planted on the reins of the ski's bar at the end of a rope. Slack now but I'm waiting for the boat's captain to ease the throttle forward for my very first lift off. Roll the dice. This might or might not work. It could be a total disaster, me crashing face first or forgetting to let go if I do. The possibilities seemed endless on the cheap entertainment scale. There was no ceremonial countdown. Slack gone, boat captain giving it throttle and Houston, we have a lift off. The eagle is in the air or in this case on the water surface. The naysayers, those yearning to see the ultimate crash and burn had been foiled. Of course, getting up and staying up pose different challenges.

First hurdle to overcome, I had absolutely no technique. Tug of war best described me being yanked about behind a speeding boat. I ebbed between falling face forward or butt backwards, anyone's guess which way this might end. Meanwhile my cohorts safely out of the water did everything they could to hedge the bet from the speeding boat. Wide turns and faster speeds had me, the human projectile, bouncing along with the inevitable a certainty. Somehow, I continued to defy the odds. I just hoped there were none of those acrobatic jumps on the lake to further challenge my untested skills. I am not sure how long they pulled their catch about, flaunting me shamelessly for anyone to see. It felt like an eternity, but I think it was more like ten or fifteen minutes. Fact, this boy never fell no matter how hard they tried to knock him off the hill. I remained king, Neptune, rooster tailing my way into the record books. A tad bit theatrical… maybe.

Finally, they waved about in some sort of hand signals that they were apparently heading back to our disembark territory, the dock. I refrained from hand responding back, double fist death gripping the reins still being my best option. Land, the shoreline looming larger in my sight, I prepared for what might be an ugly dismount. I counted on one of those blooper moments, me head over heels and then cartwheeling my way towards the shallows. My face had almost begun to anticipate the stinging impact surely to come, a skier's version of a belly flop. On unsteady wobbly legs I released the rope, freewheeling now and most certain to end up crashing and burning. The Lord apparently had one last miracle up his sleeve. I glided like a swan, skimming the surface until I gradually sunk into the lake's calm waters. I had somehow survived and avoided the worst-case scenario. I had skied. I had not fallen and had arrived back where I had begun my quest, sore but not battered or bruised. Thank goodness for life vests. I remained afloat.

Smiling and weakly waving to my pals, I then began the short swim back to the dock. Dog paddling is swimming, right? I had no choice really. My feet clung to the surface behind me, the skies still attached. I hadn't been instructed to remove them. Every muscle ached, but the water masked the pain, buoyancy my present friend. In a slow-motion sequence, I snailed my way in the direction of home base. Finally arriving, I rested my elbows and chin on the dock, taking a little breather before I hoisted myself from the lake. One of my buds swam up and thankfully removed my skies; not that he wanted to be helpful, he just needed the skies for his turn. I'd settle for anything, even a not so sincere helpful hand. Okay, time to climb onto the dock; not so easily accomplished I soon realized. My arms and legs were Jell-o like, unwilling to make this an easy task. Floating there a few more minutes, I figured it would pass. The wait didn't work. I still couldn't pull myself onto the dock.

Friends sometimes, not all times, react to a comrade in distress and despair. A hand was extended, and more him than me, I was pulled onto the dock. Reality check, I hadn't retained my land legs. Gravity and lack of muscle control double teamed me, keeping me firmly planted butt down on the dock. I could not stand. This was the price I had apparently paid for my unorthodox fifteen minute follow the leader ordeal behind that speeding boat. I would try and then collapse and laugh. My pals finally got their most funny moment, Mister Spaghetti Legs down for the count. Thankfully, this was before home videos were the rage or my not so fame like moment might have been cashed in for a fortune as the ultimate blooper footage. I don't know; thirty minutes, maybe an hour passed before I was able to make the leap from crawling about to actually standing. I did try several more times to ski that day, but I was one and done, too many spills, no more thrills. And that to this day has been the only time I ever water skied. Once you've done it, you have nothing else to prove, right?

I have been to the ski slopes of North Carolina and Tennessee several times over the years. I looked the part, a male ski bunny, sitting around the lodge, styling and profiling while sipping hot chocolate. No, I never attempted to master the slopes. Mountains, trees, and potentially hurtful falls! Why push my luck and sport some sort of cast to flaunt my escapades? Nope, I never attempted ice skating or ocean surfing either. Balancing on that sliver of ice-skating blade or venturing to depths of Davey Jones's locker as shark bait has never interested me. Fortunately, no one ever dared me to do either. Of youth comes bruised and battered. Adults tend to break things. Still a dare devil by heart, older and wiser, I am more selective in taking on the double dares. Don't test me though. I still have game. The days of have done and could have remain wonderfully nostalgic. In our minds we are still that person we so fondly remember. The mirror makes a compelling argument otherwise. Above dirt, the quest continues. The bar has been lowered just a tad. Don't try this at home has never loomed larger than the present. We have become them. Ours parents for the most part didn't raise fools for a reason or at least they gave it their best shot.

Songs do come to mind.

I got a brand new pair of roller skates,
You got a brand new key.
I think that we should get together and try them out, to see...

Brand New Key was a pop song written and sung by folk music singer Melanie

Or who could forget Roger Miller's **You Can't Roller Skate in A Buffalo Herd**

You can't rollerskate in a buffalo herd
You can't rollerskate in a buffalo herd
You can't rollerskate in a buffalo herd
But you can be happy if you've a mind to

The American Car

It was 1969, my junior year in high school, I drove a 1963 white VW Bug to school. I learned to drive and obtained my driver's licenses in a 1959 grey Bug. It was easy to parallel park but tough to stop and go on a hill. At age seventeen just driving anything to school and not being chauffeured by parents or riding the bus had its perks, Believe me. I'm not complaining about the ride. I loved that Bug. This was a time before the Love Bug craze of Disney film fame. Wheels of any kind were good because many of my peers had none. Sadly, a Bug was not exactly a chick magnet. That four in the floor complimented by an equally impressive hand brake didn't lend to very many cuddling opportunities in the rare event I snagged a date. The small back seat didn't help the cause either but gas for pennies kept money in my pockets. One must live with sacrifices.

My parents continued to work the second shift four to midnight, so that opened more options for an innovative unsupervised teenager. My house became the ultimate party house providing my buddies scrammed before midnight. We could optimize the phone for calling girls or gather around the concrete picnic table in the backyard with a bottle of Mogen David or Boone's Farm Apple wine. Four to six of us could easily get silly and loop legged off one bottle of the sweet nectar. This is my confession. We were not angels. We were typical teenagers. Living on the edge and right recklessly at times, we survived those wild times.

Sometimes you envision upping the ante. These decisions are not often meant to be the wisest of decisions. I soon schemed that I could occasionally park the Bug and opt for the Mercury Marquis parked in the garage. I knew where my parents kept the keys. I gambled that they would always leave work at midnight. Riding in style improved my image and reputation. I would cruise and cut the square. That's what we called downtown Abbeville. Basically, what we did was circle the square, exit out South Main towards the Bantam Chef and then up to Cream Land and back. We honked horns and greeted our friends following the same route over and over, unless we parked on the square and allowed the cruisers to come to us.

My parents drove the 1959 Bug to work so my plan worked flawlessly. I always filled the tank back up, but it never dawned on me that they could check to odometer. Fortunately, they never did. They must have thought I was trustworthy. Often, I wheeled back in the garage just minutes before midnight with the engine hot and pinging loudly as it cooled down. I just hoped it would quiet down before they arrived home. Apparently, it did because I never got caught and they never suspected me possible of something so devious. Devious was my middle name. I was pretty good at it. Not something I should be proud, but it just happened.

Let's fast forward to 1970. My Daddy returned to his roots and got rid of the VWs and purchased a brand-new Chevrolet, America's car. Daddy had always been a Chevy man but in back to back years, 1964 and 1965, he had brand new Chevy Impalas stolen from the Milliken Mill parking lot while he and Mama pulled their nightly shift. After the second theft, a car ring from Georgia was busted and Daddy even met the man responsible for stealing our two cars before he went on trial. Under police supervision the perpetrator demonstrated just how quickly he could access a vehicle and hot wire the engine. That's what prompted Daddy to buy the first Bug to drive to work, figuring no one would be interested in stealing it. We did own a 1966 Chevy Caprice for a few years, but he never drove it to work. He eventually sold it to Aunt Cornelia Winn. That is when he purchased the Grand Marquis.

This new 1970 Chevy looked nothing like any Chevy previously manufactured. Daddy had proudly purchased the very first one in Abbeville, right off Buddy Reid's showroom floor. Better still, it being my senior year, he told me it was my car to drive. He and Mama must have still been eaten up with guilt from that Christmas two years prior when I asked for a red Camaro. They had wrapped up a plastic red one, sick humor even for parents. To this day, I still have not bought myself a red Camaro thanks to the trauma inflicted by my parents. Well that's my story. Makes it sound more dramatic and a good read, fiction optional.

I stood there and admired this cream colored two door streamline and sleek coupe design. It was like nothing I had ever seen before and a far cry from the odd shaped Bug. The Chevy Monte Carlo resembled no Chevy to have ever hit the roadways. It was fitted with the longest hood ever on a Chevrolet. The 350 cubic inch V8 was a far cry from the rubber band driven Bug's puttering rear engine. The bucket seats sported a unique stick shift but guess what, it was a 3-speed automatic. I had no more fear of stopping on hills in traffic. I never imagined my devious ways could be rewarded so nicely. Of course, they didn't know I had a dark side. I couldn't wait to drive it to school and wow my friends and other peers.

It was indeed a hit. I now drove an instant chick magnet if I would have been macho enough to play that card. I wasn't though. At over six feet tall weighing one hundred fifty pounds wet my nickname, Tommy Toothpick suited me to a tee. In my small clique of friends, I was quite wild and crazy. To others I hardly existed. My pals knew better than to ever dare me to do anything, but outside that small circle, my introverted tendencies oozed to the surface. In the eyes of the general public I remained in the shadows. I suppose I could have been depicted as Jekyll and Hyde, the early years, except I had no murderous urges. Staying out of the spotlight allowed me to get away with murder, no pun intended. I worked that to my advantage. A mere nobody lived a life taking it to the limit.

One Friday night, Speed Hall, Larry Harrison, and I headed from Abbeville to Greenwood on highway 72, less than a fifteen-mile drive. This was before it became a four-lane roadway. On this open stretch just before reaching the Greenwood County Line, for no particular reason other than just feeling my oats, I decided to open that V8. Nothing crazy, I clocked in just over seventy mph. Luck would have it a state trooper pulled from a side road and met us, not nearly as impressed by my antics. Smokey whipped around and followed us toward the county line. Hitting the brakes is like waving a red flag at a policeman, an admission of guilt. In a panicked state I did it anyway; bad choice indeed. The blue light special ensued. He pulled me over just as I crossed the county line.

Highway Patrolman Vassey emerged from his patrol car and swaggered up to my window. He asked for my license. I nervously fumbled for it inside my wallet. Larry sat across from me avoiding eye contact with the trooper. Speed occupied the backseat, none of us uttering a sound. Vassey leaned in the window to check out the occupants. His attention quickly diverted to Speed and he remarked, '*Is that Speed Hall in that back seat? I know Mister Hall very well. I bet he was encouraging you to see what this baby could do, now weren't you? Yeah, I bet you said open it up.*' He smiled proudly of his discovery. We remained quiet as little church mice. Back then, right or wrong, you showed the police the utmost respect, just like you did teachers. Fear can instill the best behavior.

Vassey and my pal Speed had unfortunately encountered one another twice within the prior week. You remember one of these encounters from a previous chapter. Speed was pulled for speeding on his Triumph 650 motorcycle and the second when he collided head on in his Toyota Corolla with the drunk driver parked on a short cut dirt road. Vassey had been the officer on the scene for both incidences. Thank goodness Vassey didn't remember me but he sure recognized Speed. He directed his attention back to me and requested the registration and asked me, '*What make car is this?*'

I answered, '*Chevrolet*,' as I fumbled in the glove compartment for the registration.

In a heavy southern drawl, he responded, *'Boy, this ain't no Chev-er-lay.'* The Smokey then proceeded in circling the Monte Carlo, taking in every curve bumper to bumper. He removed his hat and rubbed his hand through his hair as he made his way back to the driver's side window where he snatched the registration from my shaking fingers. He took his time perusing the registration. After a pause of what felt like endless silence he finally replied, *'I reckon this is a Chev-er-lay. Now tell you what. I know you had to be clocking seventy or better but I'm going to let you off with a warning this time. Just don't let that Hall boy in the backseat there talk you into doing something foolish again. You keep it under the posted speed limit, you hear?'*

I smothered him with yes sirs. He scratched his head as he gave the Monte Carlo one last look, still disbelieving the make. That traffic stop plum took the wind out of our Friday night sails. We cut the night short. Next, I had to face the music with Daddy. Devious would not get me out this one.

I think that Monte Carlo had been cursed or something. Driving up South Main toward town, a guy on a motorcycle made a left turn in front of me as he attempted to cut me off and pull into the Seven-Eleven. I creamed him. Fortunately, neither he nor I were going very fast, but he still ended up on my hood with his face pressed against the windshield like a bug. His motorcycle was lodged underneath the car. No obvious damages could be detected on my car, but I couldn't say the same for his motorcycle. He gave me all his pocket cash, about twenty-five bucks and asked me not to file a report. No cop arrived on the scene and the devious me agreed. We kept the accident between us and a few onlookers. What happens on Penny Hill stayed on Penny Hill this time.

The hits just kept on coming with this new Chevy. All the likely suspects, Speed Hall, Pete and Stanley Price passengers on another Friday night many hours after a football game, were headed to Greenwood much later than we had any business doing. We did have an alibi though. We were supposed to be camping out at the river but got hungry and figured we'd find something open in Greenwood. Back then you didn't have an abundance of chain style burger places to choose from and what slim pickings were out there, weren't in Abbeville where they rolled up the streets after dark. Somewhere around 1 AM we headed back toward Abbeville and to the river to retrieve Stanley's old station wagon parked in the Winn Dixie lot. Sadly, we were still hungry because Greenwood apparently rolled their streets up too. We managed bottled drinks and crackers from vending machines.

My passengers had all nodded off to sleep leaving me the only one still awake, but not for long. Climbing the last long hill on Hwy 72 inside the Abbeville City Limits, Mr. Sandman struck, and I drifted into slumber land. As my head tilted to the left and against the driver's side window, my right hand clutching the steering wheel followed suit. Speed, riding shotgun in the front seat, for whatever reason, woke up and watched as the Monte Carlo drifted across the double yellow line. He thought I was pulling some sort of a stunt, but if I had been, it was surely wasted on my sleeping audience. He glanced over and saw me asleep at the wheel, not to be confused with the Texas swing band with the same name. He grabbed the steering wheel, jerking it back to the right preventing me from veering off the road and saving the day or night in this case.

I suddenly woke up and would have none of that. I instinctively jerked the wheel back to the left sending us off road in a non-off the road vehicle and up a steep embankment. I hit the brakes and brought us to an abrupt stop. The passenger side door rested mere inches away from the ground as I had successfully parked the car in the ditch and in nearly a ninety-degree angle. Neither Stanley nor Pet was wearing seat belts, not required by law back then. Stanley ended up piled on top of Pete on the passenger side. Everyone had awakened from their slumber in a most precarious situation.

We had only one escape path. We managed to push the driver's side door open and climbed out. Assessing the situation, we decided to attempt to rock and push the Monte Carlo. I got back under the wheel while the others did just that. We hoped to dislodge it from its perch and then back it off the embankment. After several attempts our worse fears surfaced. We were not going to be able to free the Chevy. As we circled the wagons and contemplated our next move, the blue light special alerted us that our hopes were surely dashed. This was no longer a covert operation. The city cop pulled to a stop directly in front of the stranded Monte Carlo. Luckily for us, this wasn't another encounter with Patrolman Vassey. The policeman assessed us and our suspect condition. We made sure to speak clearly and exhale our every breath in his direction so he would realize without a doubt that none of us had been drinking. I explained to him what had actually happened and his first comment, '*I'm sure glad you boys didn't try to dislodge this vehicle yourselves. You'd surely have flipped this vehicle over.*' We decided best not to tell him we had unsuccessfully attempted that maneuver.

He called a wrecker and had my ride towed away. He then gave us a ride to Stanley's car. No way was I going home at 2:30 in the morning and explaining this to my folks. We did the only thing we could do. We headed to the river and waited until dawn. None of us slept a wink, especially me. Stanley, playing the Neil Diamond song *Cracklin' Rosie* over and over from the 8-track player nearly drove Pete over the edge. I had Stanley wait until about 10 Saturday morning before taking me home. Daddy usually worked a few hours at the mill on weekends. I figured it would buy me some time and I could deal with Mama instead. Daddy met me at the door and his first question was where my car was. I was busted and grounded. The A frame had been bent on the Monte Carlo and it, as was I, was out of commission for a while.

1972, I married, and my folks allowed me to keep the Monte Carlo, saying it looked like me. I wasn't sure how to take that comment, but I accepted the gift graciously. In 1973 I traded the '70 for a new Monte Carlo and my next greatest adventure started. The tales I could share about the '73 would really ruin my reputation, so best leave them alone for now. I'm not ready for a full confession just yet. After I got rid of the '73 I never purchased another Monte Carlo, however, I did eventually own a couple of Chevy trucks. With those my luck improved. I can't say the same thing for the Plymouth, the Honda and Ford; never a dull moment in the life and times of me. Wild and crazy can be extremely dangerous and hazardous to one's health. It's a miracle that I am here to put any of this to print. I suppose the Man up above pulled the strings. Possibly He had something special in mind for me. Time will tell I suppose.

Here are a few Chevrolet Slogans over the years.

Chevrolet, an American Revolution

See the USA in your Chevrolet

The Heartbeat of America

The road isn't built that can make it breathe hard!

Eye it - try it - buy it!

Little Tommy and First Chevy in 1954

Cousin Ann Winn with my 1970 Monte Carlo

Around a Table, Just Not a Knight's Tale

The dinner table is almost obsolete in many homes today. I'll be the first to confess, unless we have company, we eat our supper (dinner to some) at a coffee table in the sunroom while watching television. We have had this table since 1995 and it unfolds with hinges to the perfect eating height. We have plenty of other eating options, a round glass top table in the kitchen, bar stools and a dining room table, but we choose the sunroom setting. Families today are always on the run, heading in opposite directions and following their own agendas. Texting has replaced actual sit-down face to face conversations. Social media has instilled anti-social behavior. Conversing and having real conversations are an ancient activity, what we, the older generation, refer to as the way we used to do things. Yep. It's time for another one of those 'way back when' nostalgic snapshots, a time when families acted like family and enjoyed being around one another. Buckle up, the reality check is here. Put away those cell phones please. Surely you won't suffer withdrawal symptoms just for a few precious moments.

Growing up in the 50's through 70's, tradition stood its ground in my life. Family ate all meals together and we sat at the kitchen table weekdays for breakfast, lunch and supper. Sure, there was that snapshot in time when families used those folding TV trays, but my parents didn't abuse these newfangled workarounds for family meals. My folks worked the second shift in a textile mill (Milliken) for most of my adolescent life. It was important to them that we have breakfast together every morning before school and always enjoy a family summer vacation. On Saturdays we ate our other meals together at that same kitchen table. The dinning room was reserved for larger family gatherings or when we had invited guests. Most Sundays we headed over to Papa and Granny Bowie's for the main meal of the day, what I called dinner. Dinner was not supper. The very last meal of the day was supper. My world advanced in this order, breakfast, dinner and then supper. I don't recall lunch being a term used in our household.

Granny always served up a Sunday spread. She did her cooking on Saturday though. The Sabbath was a non-working day for God fearing bible toters like Granny. You could always count on a meat of some kind. It might be fried or barbequed chicken or a pot or pork roast or sometimes fresh caught fish. You could count on an assortment of vegetables. There would be something from the bean family, speckled butter beans, green beans, pintos, or black-eyed peas. There would usually be corn and maybe okra. Fresh sliced tomato, cucumbers and onions were a given. Cornbread or biscuits would be served dependent on the meal. There would be a couple gallons of sweet tea. Granny was the only one that drank ice water.

Oh yeah, be assured that there would be some sort of home cooked dessert. My favorites were lemon pie and banana pudding. She might have a coconut cake or chocolate icing cake. The spread was never disappointing.

Everyone gathered around their kitchen table. I was the only kid in the immediate circle of family, so I got to sit at the main table with the adults. Things were skewed much differently when they had company. Depending on how many people had been invited, I might be banished to the folding card table, usually set up at the end of the regular table. At least they allowed us kids to occupy the same airspace with them. There seemed to be assigned seating protocol most of the time. Granny sat at the head of the table on the kitchen sink side of the room nearest the stove. Papa sat to her right, Mama to her left and me next to Mama. Daddy anchored the other end of the 8-chair table. Allowances were made; seating order juggled when we had extras. But the newbies were worked in on both sides. Neither Daddy nor Granny relinquished their seats though. The Bowie household stuck to family tradition and guaranteed, there would be plenty of talking during the meals covering most any possible subject. Gathering around the table was indeed a family thing and a social function. Portable phones had not been invented. My grandparents had one black rotary dial phone located on a table in the den.

Most leftovers remained in their various pots and pans, covered of course, on or inside the oven. There they would remain until supper time when we'd once again sample the same food. A few items might be placed in the refrigerator. None of us ever succumb to food poisoning. The food was heated up in the oven or on the stove top and served up a second time. Much of it had been covered with tinfoil. There were no microwaves back in the ancient time. If there were any leftovers after the second time, samples were dished out and we took it home to have the next day. Life was simple, predictable and enjoyable. The food was always wonderful. Men folk took naps while supposedly watching some sporting event on the TV. Races weren't televised, but if they were running a race, you could usually locate it on a radio station. Outdoor listening was the typical scenario via a car radio or maybe a portable radio. Find a shady spot or just stretch out inside the car. Outside activities often included making a batch of fresh churned ice cream. Plain vanilla or banana were my favorites. Peach and strawberry were my least. Life on South Main Street in Abbeville with my grandparents was always a treat. I didn't think they were anything special back then, but boy do I miss them now.

Special occasions were indeed special. We celebrated everyone's birthday with a cake to be included of course. Holidays were a given; Thanksgiving and Christmas being the main ones. Easter and the Fourth of July were celebrated too. Giving thanks before every meal was not optional. The matriarchs usually said the blessing before serving any plates and before the first bite could be taken. Saying the blessing before every meal was part of any meal ritual; amen. We had Christmas eve with the Bowies and Christmas Day with Granny Winn. Boy howdy, how these were entirely different on every level. Granny Bowie served up good ole southern home cooked vittles. Granny Winn was not a cook. Food there was right out of the can, bland with truly little seasoning. Thankfully during Christmas other relatives brought in cooked dishes too.

Seating around the tables had its pecking order at Granny Winn's house too. The dinning room table was reserved for her and her siblings. Any extra seats might be granted to an in-law spouse. The remaining adults were seated at the kitchen table. Kids, you got it, were seated at folding card tables in the den. Kids served their plates last. Children were on the lower end of the pecking order. We knew our place and waited. Waiting could take a while with so many adults in line. I was the only kid most of the time at Granny Bowie's and there were fewer adults. This meant that all the good parts of the chicken hadn't been taken by the time it was my turn. Back then it wasn't just chicken breasts that were prepared. The whole chicken was used. There would be two legs, two wings, two thighs, two breasts pieces, one neck and one backbone with the liver and gizzard included. There were no extras beyond this serving. Snooze, you loose. Luckily Mama liked the neck and the backbone. Most times at least one breast was still left. I couldn't say the same at Granny Winn's, but then they usually didn't serve up home cooked chicken. Meats must not be too memorable there, because I can't recall any favorites. Desserts, unless someone else brought them, were nothing to flip cartwheels over at Granny Winn's.

As at the Bowie table, there would be plenty of conversation. The conversations were different though. Bowies talked about fun stuff. The Winn's tended to be more serious by nature. Or that's the way I remember it, but who am I to critique Winn dialogue? I was banished to the den card tables where we engaged in silly kid talk. At the Bowie table though, I was center stage, privy to adult topics. Well. I am sure some of it might have been censored for young ears, but not much. You learned interesting things at the Bowie table. I suspect the topics were a bit more boring at the Winn table. Current affairs were not of interest to me. Loud and uncontrolled describes the Bowie table, everyone trying to talk over everyone else with multiple conversations going on simultaneously. At the Winn main table each person took turns and you listened to that person until they passed the baton to the next. It was more organized and structured. The Bowie table could be pure unadulterated chaos. I felt like I was part of the Bowie gatherings. I was lost in the weeds at the Winn events, just another cousin in a vast sea.

Granny and Papa Bowie's house was less formal, a more intimate and family environment. Having less people allowed everyone to breathe and spread their wings. There would easily be three times as many people attending holiday festivities at Granny Winn's. There you would struggle to own an identity. You waited your turn to talk and treasured your time on the soapbox. I was one of only a handful of grandchildren that lived locally. Others traveled from Charleston, S.C., Macon, Ga. or Maryland. When everyone else had gone back home, life returned to a semblance of normalcy where I was more a standout in a little pond. Don't take this wrong. I did love and enjoy being around most of my cousins. But with them gone I had an opportunity to graduate to the kitchen table for most meals. This didn't necessarily lead to better food options, but it could mean larger portions of ho-hum fixings. Most meals at the Winn table during the weekdays were some type of sandwich and chips.

There were no simple meals at Granny Bowie's. Every meal was usually something home cooked. I loved both of my grannies, but it was a different love for each. I could be me at Granny Bowie's house. I could ramble through the cabinets and refrigerator at will. I didn't do that at Granny Winn's. You waited until mealtimes or designated snack times. Deviation from the schedule was unheard of. Snacks were served at the same time every night, a tiny cup of Pepsi and two cheese crackers. Coca-cola was not allowed in the Winn household. Pepsi was the preferred soft drink. Granny Bowie seldom had any soft drinks; maybe an Orange Crush or Nehi Grape in the bottle if you were lucky. Your choices were usually sweet tea, water or milk (sweet or buttermilk variety.) I usually chose sweet tea. There was never unsweetened tea inside the frig. There was only one kind, sweet. Drinking and eating healthy had not been discovered back then, not as far as I can recall. The Bowie table catered to hearty and hungry appetites. Portions were the norm at the Winn table, everyone served up equally. Seconds and thirds could be had at Granny Bowie's but portions at Granny Winn's didn't lend to additional helpings or leftovers. No to go boxes were featured there. We always took something home from Granny Bowie's though.

As mentioned, at Granny Bowie's fresh churned ice cream was served many Sundays, especially during the summer months. Occasionally churned ice cream might be on the Winn dessert menu. These were hand cranked churns using crushed ice and Morton Ice Cream Salt. Churning was hard work, the men swapping turns until the process was completed.

Granny Winn's house did have one perk. Uncle Dolph was a big wig at Borden's in Savannah and eventually Macon, Ga. Most trips he would bring an assortment of Borden's ice cream. Granny's freezer was a treasure-trove of frozen Borden goodies. Again, you just didn't venture out to the utility building and freelance inside the freezer. Borden's ice cream was a social activity served up at a designated time chosen by Granny. That made it special I suppose, cherishing those times when we got it.

Life around the family table is almost a thing of the past now. Families and their schedules are so fragmented that rarely does everyone eat at the same time. Many eat on the run or just grab something at a fast food chain later. Sunday dinners rarely exist. Going to Granny's house has almost become obsolete. Everyone has some other place to be, more important than visiting with parents or grandparents. Keep it up if you think the universe revolves around you, but some day, and possibly too late, you will realize differently. When the grandparents are gone, they are gone. There aren't any do-overs to capture and lay claim to that lost time. Same goes for your parents. I pity those who have never had the opportunity to have experienced time around the dinner or supper table with family. It was a special time in my life. It was expected and anticipated, no dread involved, a time before the distractions of cell phones, computers, video games and social media. They talked. We listened. We even had chances to toss our two cents in. Heads were held up and focused on those around us instead of being buried head down focusing on their phones and the latest and greatest tweets.

My folks would have probably prohibited phones being brought to the table. It was a time for reverence and family, no ifs, ands or buts. It was our way of life, a life less cluttered or distracted with turmoil and drama, forever embraced and enjoyed around the table. I vote for phone free zones at any meal table. I say they should be confiscated or turned off until after the meals. Try it. You might just recapture those family feelings or discover a world that you never knew existed…around the family table at mealtime. Dust off those placemats and place settings and enjoy each other before it is too late. The real social media still exists, and it is right under your nose. Lift your heads from your phones and open your eyes. Talk to those around you before you forget how. I miss those times, but then again, I experienced what many have never experienced. The bar was set high back in my day though, when families behaved like families. Love and discipline went hand in hand. We knew the actual meaning of respect. Family, forever love, and food existed around the table.

**Vintage Photo Around Bowie Table
Pictured left to right (Jerry Winn, Robert Winn,
Thomas (Daddy) Winn, Jean Winn and Papa John Bowie)**

**Bowie Kitchen Table: Mary (Mama) Winn, Merry Mite
and Papa John Bowie**

Clockwise: Billy Joe and Leila Campbell, Daddy, Bill Siegler, Mama, Papa, Granny and Aunt Sallie Lou Bowie – the picture taker, me, always behind the camera.

Holmes Where the Heart Belongs

In my first nostalgic memoir, Cornbread and Buttermilk, I celebrate having known my great grandmother, Granny Holmes. She was my Granny Bowie's mama. I mentioned how as a kid it amazed me that neither Granny nor Papa Bowie could read and write, yet Granny Holmes, their elder could. It was as if the ability to do so had skipped a generation. It never deterred my grandparents though. They used artwork to communicate through notes and grocery lists. A penciled critter such as a squirrel or rabbit and a clock face with the hands indicating the time would let Granny know that Papa had gone hunting and for what type of critter, and what time he should be expected home. Similar drawings of grocery goods ensured Papa picked up any special items Granny needed from the grocery store. Life explained in simple terms often speak volumes.

That brings me back to Granny Holmes, the elderly great grandparent who loved nothing better than reading the newspaper. She didn't simply read it. She read it out aloud for anyone nearby to hear the news of the day as delivered from her wise old lips. She was a squatty bell shaped little old lady, a homebody who spent her life raising her kids, never working outside the household. Granny Holmes was a Godly woman and she taught those values to her children. She lived much of her life with her youngest son and his family or nearby them wherever they resided. Junior and Jeannette Holmes and their many children, my beloved cousins, were some of my favorite kin. We visited them often. I say we because many Saturday or Sunday afternoons we would venture into the country or wherever they lived for friendly family visits. Junior was a preacher and moved around a lot.

Granny Holmes often had her own little modest place or lived with one of her children when times were hard. One of my favorite places to go when we would take that afternoon ride was when she lived between Lowndesville and Iva, near Uncle Ben and Aunt Dot Holmes. There I had more favorite cousins to play with while there. I devoted a chapter in my first nostalgic book titled Toby. It was at their country spread that I met my very first horse named Toby. In my little mind I thought all horses were Tobys. Apparently, every time I saw a horse I would point and yell Toby according to my mama. I guess I eventually learned that a horse is a horse of course. Going to Uncle Ben's and Aunt Dot's offered a city boy the opportunity to meet many farm animals that otherwise I would have never experienced up close and personal. I suppose it might have contributed to my naturally being an animal lover in general.

Granny Holmes lived at the opposite end of that dirt road in the country. We would visit her if she wasn't at Uncle Ben's homestead. Seasonally we would always leave their place with fresh vegetables and freshly churned buttermilk and homemade butter. I don't remember any names for their cow or cows, but I learned to appreciate the taste of buttermilk. This is not like store bought buttermilk that comes in a carton. This would be in quart or gallon jars. Little chucks of butter bits would be floating in it. My fondness for black skillet cornbread probably originated from these deep roots. Adding fresh cornbread to a bowl of buttermilk made it all the even better.

I remember playing with my cousins out in the county, ripping and running and begging to stay a little longer when it was time for us to leave. Our imagination and creativity were in no short supply in a world so much better than the one I live in now. We improvised and made up an assortment of games to keep us busy. In the summer we'd find an abundant supply of wild plum and blackberry bushes. Better watch for those chiggers though, little no see-ums ready to ambush us and leave their itchy bites as a reminder they saw us even if we didn't see them. Yep, it is tough to beat a fun afternoon with the Holmes young'uns. Most of them were either much older or a bit younger than me. My favorites though were Judy and Debbie, just seem to remember them more back in the day.

Uncle Junior and Aunt Jeannette had a bunch of children, mostly girls. Cousins are cousins. My girl cousins were like test tube babies, seemed each one was about a year older or younger than the next. If memory serves me there were six girls and one boy. I had my favorites. I guess because they were closer to my age. I was kind of sweet on them in a cousinly way. Like with all cousins, we played all the games of the day like hide and seek; may I, Rover Red Rover and tag and chase. What I remember most is how often they moved. It seemed like just when I was getting used to one place, they up and moved to another. I suspect this was more stressful to them having to relocate as kids. It had to be tough to make and keep friends. Maybe they appreciated me more because unlike their friends, I could find them when they moved. Maybe this was like the bigger version of hide and go seek. I guess I was mostly the seeker of the Holmes girls.

There were other Granny Bowie siblings that lived in Iva. Yep. We would venture there as well in those go visit afternoons. What I remember about those visits though is that those siblings didn't have any children my age to play with like when visiting Uncle Junior and Aunt Jeannette's or Uncle Ben's and Aunt Dot's. They did not live in the country or have any of those fun farm critters. As a kid I didn't appreciate or value those visits as much as I did the others. Remember, this is a kid's impressionable mind talking, not the adult version. Sadly, I have lost touch with most of my cousins since my grandparents and parents have passed. We moved to the beach and that added to the seldom seeing any of them. Nope. I am not making excuses. It has always been a bad trait of mine, not visiting or keeping in touch like I should. I have connected with a few on Facebook, Janet, Paulette, and Debbie.

The Holmes gals have invited me several times to family reunions in the Anderson-Iva area. For one reason or another I have never made any of them. I would probably be hard pressed to recognize some of them now after all these years. I have seen Debbie and her son in recent years at the state book convention in Columbia where several beach authors had a booth and were selling our books. I have never been the reunion type, usually passing on other family reunions, Bowie ones or those on the Winn side of the family. Heck, I have only attended two of my high school class reunions. I have no excuse or explanation for my reluctance to do so. Making connections on social media and me being older, a bit my sentimental might be the game changer. Just maybe I will surprise my cousins by attending the next one. Holmes, after all, is where the heart belongs. I certainly cherished those visits when I was a kid. I'm sure they could only be more uplifting and enjoyable now even if I struggle putting names to faces. Family is forever and forever isn't everlasting if you don't practice the option of visiting while you can. Possibly in my ripe old age I am transforming and seeing what is most important. Enjoy it while you can and as often as you can. Memories are worth revisiting. Sometimes what one has forgotten, others recall and with that, it rekindles long lost nostalgic nonsense once lost but found once again. I learned that valuable lesson with the little reunion with the Thomas boys a few years ago. It brought ole Papa Tommy to tears of joy rekindling that relationship, one that should never have taken so long to restore. It's time to visit folks I haven't visited in what seems like a lifetime. I will not squander another opportunity starting today; at least when this 2020 term of practicing social distancing due to the Coronavirus finally expires. No excuses this time just confined until the coast is clear. I'm hiding but seeking much more.

Granny Holmes with her Newspaper

Granny Holmes with Husband Charlie 1940

Granny Holmes with Daughter Ruby (Granny) Bowie 1940

Charlotte's Web

I agreed to speak at her funeral, something I had never done before. Charlotte Staggs, third of the four Sanders' sisters, Brenda, Judy, then Charlotte and Norma. Everyone who met her was instantly caught in her web. Web in this case is a good thing, wonderful to be exact. One of my fondest and first real memories of her was when Judy asked me to stage a haunted house for the Langley Milliken Halloween jamboree. I recruited a few friends, and we did just that in one of the portable buildings adjacent to the school. It was a hit, taking in more money that the rest of the event combined. I had a reputation to uphold, the superior spook house builder. Charlotte was working another room inside the main building, dressed as a gypsy, crystal ball and all, telling fortunes. We combined our resources and talents after we closed the haunted house down. I hid behind a curtain and mimicked voices from beyond when summoned by the gypsy woman. This might sound a bit familiar. I used it in the Perfect Spook House book. And no, Charlotte and I never had a love interest. That was just a fictional twist of the main characters in the book.

Julie, Charlotte's daughter had asked if I would speak at the funeral. I never hesitated, agreeing immediately. Saying you will and then executing it isn't as simple as it sounds. I loved Charlotte like a sister I never had. I was crazy about all of Judy's sisters. We had already buried Brenda, Judy's oldest. This was a double whammy in too short a time. How does one prepare for something like this, especially when you've never done anything remotely like it? Thinking of memorable events about Charlotte wasn't difficult. She provided a treasure trove of them. You could always count on her being front and center in some whimsical scene. She had a gift for doing the unbelievable. That's what made her so special.

Judy was in Abbeville when she passed, Charlotte having lost a long battle with cancer. She had licked it a couple of times but finally the dreadful disease claimed another. I was still at home in Myrtle Beach when I received the call and the request. While we knew it was inevitable, it still doesn't make it any easier to accept. Before I headed in that direction the next day, I would have time to reflect and decide how I would pay one last tribute to my dear sister. I smiled and thought wonderful thoughts as I compiled and prepared my eulogy. I took a deep breath, proud of my final cut. It had formed in my heart effortlessly, much easier than I could have ever imagined. I cherished every memory as I prepared my notes.

Funerals have always been difficult for me. I don't have any phobias about the dead. For most of my life I just didn't buy into the premise of the process. I covered these thoughts in my book, 'The Care Giver's Son, Outside the Window Looking In.' To me, funerals were supposed to be a time to be mournful of the one who had passed. Funerals and the visitations seemed anything but that to me. People standing around laughing and joking, discussing old times while a person is dead in a coffin. It has always been too much of a circus atmosphere for my taste. Plus, as my mama always said, 'If you didn't take time to visit me while I was alive, I don't want you standing over my coffin gawking at me.' I guess in recent years I had had more practice than I would have ever liked, attending too many loved one's funerals. It's a long list for sure. But that was then, and this is now, sweet Charlotte's time.

I arrived in Abbeville the next afternoon. I dropped off some items at Harris Funeral Home. The stage had been set for my last tribute to one we lost way too early. I guess we can say that about most. Dying too soon is always a concern. We know our turn will come sooner or later. We are born and we die. It's the circle of life. Still, losing a love one tends to be tough to rationalize. Charlotte was special in so many ways though. I guess this isn't the first time someone felt this way about one who had earned their wings. While this hurt, it wasn't going to be a pity party. It was a time to remember her. Boy howdy, how I had some humdinger memories to share.

People gathered in the Harris Funeral Home parlor. The time had arrived. Charlotte's daughter, Julie had asked her father-in-law to speak first at the podium, the only other speaker. This gave me a little breathing room, took some of the pressure off me, so I thought. I waited patiently in the wings, seated beside Judy, playing in my head what I had prepared. I vividly imagined what I would say and how I would present it to those attending. Preparing and executing aren't the same. Believe me when I say this. Breathe in. Breathe out. Focus. It's too late to have a panic attack. I made a promise, a commitment and now it's time to come through and pay respect to my sister. I stood and approached the podium, still feeling the moment and confident I could do this.

I nodded at those gathered and then reached underneath the podium and retrieved articles from a bag that had been stashed there yesterday. I placed an Atlanta Braves cap on my head. I then hung a Clemson Tiger shirt from one side of the podium and an Atlanta Braves shirt from the other side. I placed my notes on the podium and then lost it before I could speak the first words, choked up and tearful. It happened so quickly. Through blurry eyes and a broken voice, I tried to gather myself.

Somehow, I did. I told those assembled in the parlor how much I loved my sister, Charlotte. I explained how she loved those Braves and those Tigers. And how her dad, Mister Joe was a huge Brave's fan, may he rest in peace. I recapped the Langley Milliken jamboree episode. I shared other memories, good memories, hilarious memories that only Charlotte could inspire.

When we built our house in the Saddle Hill community in Greenwood, I had a friend at work that had sold me a weeping willow to plant in the yard. I had mentioned it to Charlotte, and she begged me not to plant it. She told me it was bad luck to have a weeping willow in the yard. She offered to buy it from me. It was that urgent to her that I didn't plant it. I asked her why. She said that if the limbs of the willow touched the ground it meant someone close to me would die. Fact or fiction, superstition or old wife's tale, the urgency and fear on her face made a convincing and compelling argument. I did as she asked and got rid of the tree.

Same house, same Charlotte accompanied me on a walk through my vegetable garden. You must remember. The Sanders sisters were raised in the country and on a farm. I shouldn't have had to point out and name the various crops to her. Just clarifying before I continue. I plucked a snow pea pod from the plant and peeled it open, popped one pea in my mouth and gave the other one to her. Snow peas are sweet and delicious. We continued the garden tour. I heard Charlotte gagging and coughing behind me. I turned to see her spitting something from her mouth. She had plucked a butterbean pod and had then plopped a speckled butterbean in her mouth. I laughed, telling her she couldn't do that to just any bean. She was the farm girl; might I remind you.

I recapped the unforgettable Savannah trip and the calamari episode. The restaurant employee had been offering samples to those passing by. Charlotte, Jerry and Norma had thought the squid was onion battered and fried rings. At least Charlotte had spat hers into her napkin, unlike Norma spewing her mouthful on the cobble stoned street of Savannah. Of course that led right into the alligator bites story when she asked me to tell her she hadn't just eaten gator and I told her what she asked me to tell her, that it wasn't alligator, even though it had been. Priceless Charlotte moments and they are too may to list. I ended my tribute retrieving a single French fry from a Ziploc, telling everyone how much that gal loved fries. We only witnessed her share them with one person, her nephew, Winn. I also told the folks gathered how much Charlotte had enjoyed those sister's trips with Brenda, Judy and Norma.

I had managed to cover everything I had prepared about dear Charlotte. Afterwards Julie came up and thanked me, saying she had never heard those stories about her mom. More memories had been made, first timers hearing a side of my adopted sister's life.

Charlotte had this uncanny spiritual connection, an uncanny supernatural awareness. She could sense evil and faithfully embraced good. There was a street located in Anderson, S.C. that she was adamant about avoiding. She absolutely would not travel down it and if riding with any of us, she prohibited us from passing it. She'd not take no for an answer. The only explanation she would offer us was that evil lived in a house on that street. She wouldn't elaborate no matter how much we pried. The expression on her face told us she meant what she said. We honored her feelings. She would sometimes sit for us with Granny Bowie after my mama had passed. Granny frequently saw people in her room. Sometimes there were children with flowers at the foot of her bed. Charlotte would go along with Granny, seeing them as well to not dishonor Granny. Granny's health was failing, and I often wondered if these people in her room might be a spiritual preview into the afterlife. She was such a Godly woman. Different folks had gifted Granny angel figurines and even an angel nightlight. When Granny passed away, we gave Charlotte the angel nightlight. She was staying at the home of Aunt Lillian, sister to Mister Joe, the Sander's girls' dad. When Aunt Lillian's time eventually came and she passed away in the hospital, Charlotte returned to the residence that night to find the angel nightlight mysteriously on. She said it was Granny welcoming her dear friend, Lillian to heaven.

Being caught in Charlotte's web guaranteed you were in for an unforgettable experience. There are countless other stories, too many to include. She left an undeniable footprint in this world while she walked among us and an incredible void when she left us behind. God must have His hands full now. One thing for sure, she will leave Him laughing and begging for more.

Charlotte and Ruby Bowie, My Granny

One childhood story that the sisters love to share is of Charlotte chasing them around the kitchen table with a butcher knife at the old home place. Of course, when their mother showed up Charlotte had lost that knife and who would believe little Charlotte would do something like that.

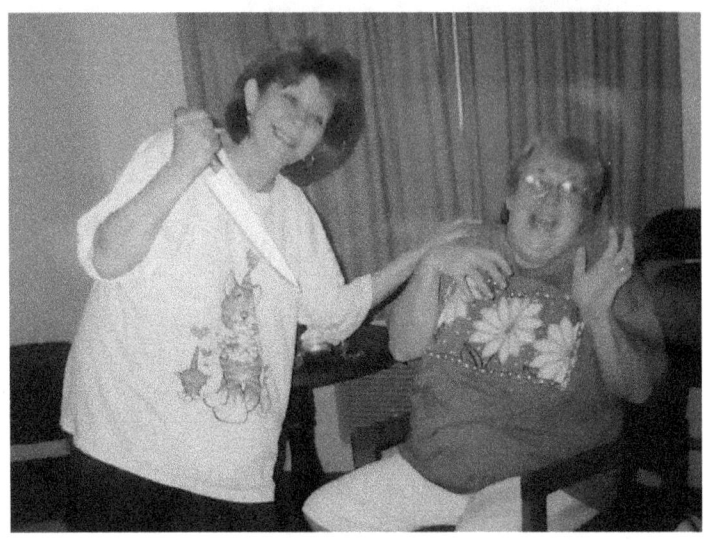

**A reenactment Charlotte with Sister Brenda Sanders
Both Gone but Not Forgotten**

Charlotte with Nephew Brian Adams

Not Your Average Duncan Donut

I penned this letter to Duncan Singleton and presented it to him when he graduated from his first college, Winthrop. I say first because he graduated a second time from The University of Florida, there earning his Masters in lighting. He had graduated Winthrop with a music degree. Now for the letter commemorating his first graduation...

To Duncan,

All graduated from Winthrop, hard to believe any way you paint it. Journeys have beginnings and beginnings have many starting points. Remembering back when to now is filled with endless possibilities. Here are a few of mine, Joseph Duncan Singleton, a virtual rewind of those you might or might now recall. I tried to influence your artsy side when you were at that impressionable age. Somewhere around the age of four if I had to guess, I bought you multicolored modeling clay and attempted to razzle-dazzle you with my hand molded creations. Seems to me I magically transformed that clay into a dog, an alligator and a dinosaur. You made some colorful cylindrical objects, abstract and ahead of your time, but they were the best ones I had ever seen. Mine didn't hold a candle to your masterpieces.

Memories, you must appreciate them for better or worse. With the arrival of Winn, you were no longer an only child. We came to the beach to welcome young Singleton to the family. Guess what, we had the pleasure of rooming with you; not just sharing a room but sharing a bed. I learned quickly just how talented you were. It was a glimpse into the future, you born to be a dancer on the stage. You tap danced up and down my back all night long. I even think I detected a tad of moon walking on my spine. But that wasn't the half of it. With the fire hearth as your grand stage and a spatula as your microphone, you owned the audience, the best crooner in the house. I realized too late that heckling was not allowed and that you demanded the undivided attention of those attending your performance. I thought you were a lounge lizard in the making, already sizing you up for a polyester suit. You had greater aspirations than working the dives though.

There were many firsts to come for me with you. I set foot inside the Myrtle Beach Pavilion for the very first time when you were five. Mimi and I took you there and watched as you rode what you wanted to ride. There were no us suggesting what you should ride. You did the picking. The Pavilion is long gone now, but I owe it to you, for me having at least visited it once. Same goes for Disney World. I had the honor of seeing you sponge in the magic of the many kingdoms for the very first time. It came with a price though. I received the double look from your mom and Mimi. You know that look they can toss at you without saying a word. Boys should be rough housed and allowed to be boys, especially when on vacation. I'm just an overgrown kid. Oh no, I got you too hyper and too close to bedtime. Moms and Grandmothers just don't get it; what we guys need. That's okay. We did ride the stick horses through the Wilderness Restaurant. Yeeha, we were cowboy partners, ride along little doggie…

I can lay claim to one thing no one can take away from me. I taught you to swim when you spent a week with us in Greenwood. We were one with the water spirits in the backyard pool, kindred. Starting slow and building your confidence, you shed those water wings and we went from angling across the pool to you eventually swimming the full width. My papa called me a tadpole in the water. Watching your transformation brought it home to me just what he had meant. From one tadpole to the next, memories are worth the making.

I had you pegged as a lounge lizard at an early age, but you threw me a few curves along the way. I watched you at a wee age as you assembled Mimi's vanity stool for the bathroom. Years later you would assemble Mimi's office furniture after we moved to the beach. I didn't teach you this trade because you didn't have any parts left over. I thought just maybe you were destined to follow in your Granddad Singleton's shoes and get into construction. Or maybe you were preparing for an elf job to help old Santa in the toy shop. Then you became a magician, still demanding my full attention and that of anyone else in your presence. Your passion to be the next famous magician prompted me to make my very first purchases on the internet, two magic kits. You didn't disappoint me, mastering every trick flawlessly. I figured then that you might still land a gig in Vegas.

Halloween is one of my most favorite holidays. You were my Mini-Me. Fangs, white face, red bloody lips, cape, we had it going. I dressed as Dracula just before dusk, had to gas up on the way from our beach condo to your house in Conway. Ironically an ambulance was filling up at the next pump. I asked if they had any spare blood to hold me over. You and I, Big and Little bloodsuckers we were, terrorized downtown Conway. At the courthouse they had numerous scarecrow displays. You were an actor before you hit the stage. We posed with the scarecrows, blending in until passing motorists were startled by things that go bump in the night. We came to life before their very eyes. We then crashed the Halloween party @ Broadway at the Beach. We were right out of the pages of the Big and Small collection in the Sears catalog. Cuz, Sammy Cannon got you and him both in trouble at the Key West restaurant, a triple dose of THE

LOOK from Judy, Judy and Rhonda. I was one happy vampire sitting on the side of the coffin for that one.

Rhonda, Mini Me, Me and Winn

Christmas was always a fun time. Spoiler alert! We'd be there at your house Christmas morning to witness the surprise on your faces as you and Winn woke to discover what Santa had left for you. Being a certified Santa's helper, it was my job to ensure the belief in Old Saint Nick breathed a life of its own. The jolly old elf, my mentor, had trained me well in the methods of smoke and mirrors. Staging the scene to perfection was important. Turning over the potted plants on the fireplace hearth supported his entry point down the chimney. Not to worry, one can not harm badly neglected plants, those limping along on their last root. Rhonda inherited this honestly, the inability to keep green plants green. Other deputized helpers made sure the milk and cookies were consumed, wrinkling up the napkin and wiping their mouths to set the stage. I focused on the outside, forming sleigh tracks in the grass (sorry no snow) leading to the concrete patio. Well placed dear tracks in the yard and dirty hoof prints on the patio made for the perfect leeway to the roof top. Remember, don't try this at home if you haven't completed the training and signed the Clauses. Don't be too distraught. Like I said, I was a certified Santa helper, keeping the magic alive.

When I got the job at Metglas I moved to the Windy Hill condo for a month before we bought a house at the beach. I had the pleasure of witnessing young Duncan in one of his first football games, a proud member of the Cowboys. I didn't quite get the plays being called though. Each play you just stood there while everyone on both teams moved about. I suppose you were in injury prevention mode, saving yourself for the college and pro ranks. Now on the sidelines you were in your element, drinking so much gator aide I thought you had gotten an endorsement deal. Football was not for you though. That's okay. You were destined for greater things than being just another jock. Roles as orphans, napkins and other pressing parts awaited you on the theatrical stage.

One memory sticks out far above all the rest. An eleven-year-old stepped up to the plate and did something most adults could never do. When my mama passed away, I asked your mom would you play Amazing Grace at her funeral. Mary Winn so enjoyed listening to you play songs on Mimi's piano. In the typical fashion of your mom she said, 'I don't know. Ask him.' So, I did. You said yes. We took you to Chandler-Jackson Funeral home where Steve Jackson introduced you to this enormous organ on site. You practiced and got the knack immediately, prompting Steve to say you were a natural. At the funeral you brought the house down, if that is possible at a funeral parlor. You did Mama and me proud. I'll never ever forget you doing that for her.

Watching you perform in the marching band, show choir, a play, at High Stepping Country or even that 'high brow' music, it always brought lumps to my throat and tears to my eyes. I'll never replace either one of your granddads and would never try, but I'm always one proud papa wantabe just the same when I watch you perform in anything. And now you're a college graduate. Where does the time go? It seems not that long ago when we were at Darlington, acting foolish at the race and now look at you. A lounge lizard-magician-assembler-exCowboy-Mini-Me vampire-performer extraordinaire now in a new segment in your life. I can hardly wait to see what the future holds in store for you. No, that's wrong; what you make of your future. The possibilities are limitless. One bit of advice though, get out of retail before you harm a helpless tourist.

Oh yeah, and how about teaching me how to play the tuba. I look stupid just holding this thing and not tooting a tune.

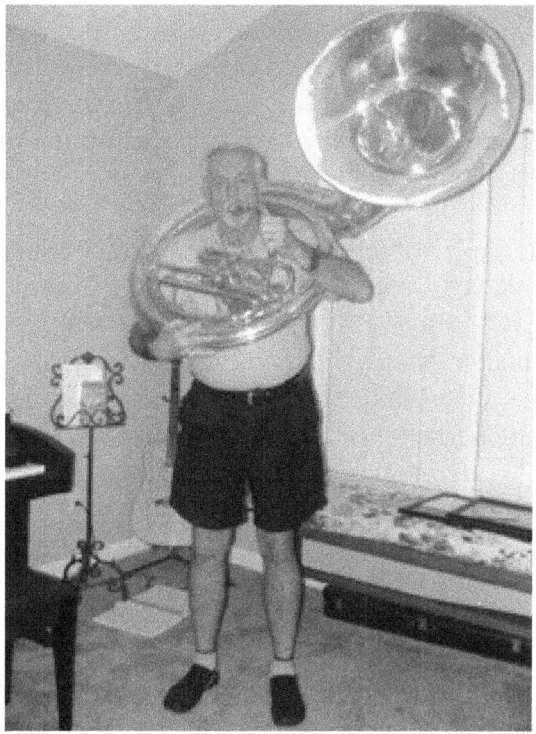

*With the greatest love and ultimate respect
To Joseph Duncan Singleton
All grown-up and graduated to boot.*

A 2019 update: Duncan, after graduating the University of Florida, is now employed at Disney World in Orlando. He followed his dreams and landed his dream job. It will be interesting to see where he soars in the Magical Kingdom, he has created for himself. It's a small world after all.

Remembering Chad

Witt, sarcasm, and my sometime twisted look on life escapes me today, so I think I will give it a rest. Instead I will reflect on my memories of Chad, my beloved nephew and the one taken away from us too soon and too sudden. For him, as a close friend put it in perspective for us, he's pain free now for the first time in too many years since that dreadful accident. I guess that's why they say rest in peace. Chad is the son of Norma Solomon, Judy's sister.

Chad for me is best described as a man child after his near fatal tragic car accident some years ago. The accident compromised his normal lifestyle, something we sadly take for granted. He was very personable and interactive one on one; however, large crowds overwhelmed him and hampered his social skills. Like anyone healthy or with debilitating issues, none of us are perfect. We all have our likes and dislikes and our buttons are pushed for an assortment of reasons, good or bad. Today is a time for remembering only the good.

Chad Rouland was present for one of the more memorable events in my life, my dad's very last golf game (my short story, The Immortal featured in my 'The Perfect Mulligan' book) at the Par Three West Golf Course in our Saddle Hill community in Greenwood. He along with an assembled cast of supporting nephews and in-laws played the nine par three holes and witnessed my dad hole a 100-yard second shot on #6 for the only birdie of the round. I expect he and ole TJ (my dad) are recapping that episode now. Chad had always embraced the game of golf and had been quite good at it. Something I can't claim for sure.

I had the pleasure of playing one other round with Chad here at the beach at The International Club. Like my dad before him, Chad struggled to complete the round due to some physical difficulties hampering his balance and walking. This round had been a cart path only day because of recent rain. The sparkle in his eyes of just being on the course was priceless though. Funny, we almost didn't get in the round. The course initially turned us away because Chad and Jerry (my bother-in-law) were wearing denim jeans. The dress code prohibited this attire. We rushed home and I tried to round up something he and Jerry could wear. Neither are my size (waist or height). I gave them pairs of my pants. We somehow managed to make them work, tightening belts and cuffing the legs. We even made it back just under the wire for our designated tee time. The waist size was too large for Chad but somehow we were able to draw them in so that they never fell around his ankles during the round.

I will never forget how Chad never missed an opportunity to thank me every time I saw him afterwards for that round of golf. Just that alone made it special for me too. Sadly, it would be the last round of golf we would ever play together. We had hoped to get in a round, Chad, Brian, me and possibly the grand, Winn but it wasn't to be. Life doesn't always stick to the script that we envision. He gained his wings and eternal body. With sure and steady legs and that old vigor, I'm sure he'll be teeing it up on God's special 18 now. He'll be in the good company of those that went before him. I can't help but smile as I envision the perfect foursome of Chad, his dad Ray, Cousin Bob and my dad TJ, having the best round of their afterlives. Y'all hit them good up there, no mulligans necessary.

Chad with Bother Brian Adams

Chad with Brother Brian

Chad, Norma Solomon (mother), Brian and Jerry Solomon

Heart of the Tiger

There is no shortage of Clemson Tiger fans, diehard and sometimes arrogant, but always devout to their beloved cats wearing the purple and orange. Some would say the same goes for the Carolina Gamecocks. Word to the wise; never get caught in the middle of these feuds. Sometimes the cream of the crop surfaces to the top. One can be a fan and not be belligerent and cocky. It's refreshing. One close to my heart was that person. Uncle Jerry Winn was born into this world in a time when society called him retarded or a mongoloid. These are harsh terms in today's world. Today we refer to these special people as gifted or having Down syndrome. Jerry was one of eight, four brothers and four sisters. He was my Daddy's youngest brother and the next to the youngest of the Winn eight. Jerry was born in the forties when times were tough even for those not strapped with challenges.

There were no special schools for his alleged kind. He attended public school making him a target of those too stupid and self centered to give him a fair shake. True friends stood by him to ensure he persevered. Love and kindness existed even in the way back time. Jerry was a manager for the Abbeville Panther's football team while in high school. He is featured in a tribute section of mine and Benji Greeson's book, 'It's All about the A'. He did graduate. The school looked after him too. He was a diehard Abbeville Panther fan too. His room was decorated in Panther memorabilia along with the familiar Tiger collectables. It was easy to buy him gifts for birthdays and Christmas, a primal cat always a winning selection. I mentioned that Jerry wasn't arrogant by nature when it came to his sports' teams but be warned, keep your negative remarks to yourself. Some learned the hard way. I was one of them. There's no such thing as friendly kidding or joking with a gifted person. Cross that line and you'll not cross it again. That is if you have a decent bone in your body. Kidding can be eyed as hurtful in their eyes.

Jerry attended most home Clemson football games along with Granny Winn, his mother and his sister, Aunt Cornelia. I've mentioned previously how they tailgated what seemed like days before the game, arriving in Clemson so many hours ahead of the game it was almost hard to stay focused until the kickoff. Then Coach Danny Ford was greeting loyal supporters at an event, people pushing, shoving, and elbowing their way for a chance to shake his hand or to get an autograph. Jerry was being pushed, shoved, and elbowed out of the way as he attempted to do the same. Ford remedied the situation calling Jerry by name and motioning him to the forefront. He shook his hand, posed for a photo and gave Jerry an autograph to the dismay of those now taking the backstage. Did Ford know Jerry? Maybe, maybe not, but he recognized him as special and brought him into the center ring, celebrity status for the moment. For those able to read lips during games, Ford could be quite vulgar and outspoken when the camera caught him on the sidelines. With Jerry though, he had expressed the kindest of hearts, one man to another, both with the heart of a Tiger.

Jerry, trapped in his world, one that he often saw differently, had a vivid imagination offering him an escape pod to better places. Normalcy is in the eyes of the beholder. Jerry had the ability to be a recording icon, singing as only he could sing. He even sang in the church choir, some wishing otherwise. You can't pretty up tone deaf. The Andy Griffith episode comes to mind. You know the one. The choir director invites Barney to join the choir before he realizes Barney can't sing. Nobody wished to hurt his feelings or be the one to step forward and tell him the truth. Barney is the closest thing to tone deaf that there is. His shrieking strikes a discordant note with all members of the choir and disrupts their rehearsals. With an important concert coming up, Andy comes up with an idea. He tells Barney he's going to be a soloist, but have him speak, rather than sing, his part. Barney likes the soloist part but insists on singing. Andy must go to plan B which involves convincing Barney that he has to adapt his voice to a newfangled "soloist's" microphone. Another tenor sings, making Barney think it's his voice. The Long Cane Church could have certainly used one of those so-called newfangled microphones for Uncle Jerry. Some questioned why Aunt Cornelia allowed him to sing in the first place. Simple, she was hard of hearing and probably didn't know he couldn't sing.

Aspiring at times to be an actor, he practiced for his time in the spotlight. The movie 'Sleeping with the Enemy' staring Julia Roberts was being partially filmed in Abbeville. If you have seen the movie then you'll remember Julia's character, Laura, living in one house and Ben played by Kevin Anderson living next door. These two houses were a mere stone's throw from Uncle Jerry's house, just two blocks away. Jerry snuck away and to go meet Julia Roberts, maybe seeking a cameo part. Did he meet her? Your guess is a good as mine. Remember what happened with Coach Ford. Anything is possible. I don't remember seeing his name in the closing credits though.

Not to worry, Jerry was quite versatile, talent wise. When not in the recording studio he might be with paint brush and canvas, stroking the next Picasso. Well, he used a pencil and notepad, sometimes colored markers, but an imagination can produce masterpieces in the eye of the beholder. Careers were in no short supply. The professional bowling circuit was but a mere strike away. Uncle Jerry cherished those male bonding trips to the Greenwood Bowling Center. The lanes awaited him, an imperfect game in his eyes could be the perfect score 10 frames later. I pulled for him, encourage him and cheered him on, even if the ball often found the gutters. But when he did get a strike or a spare, the expression on his face was priceless.

Now shooting hoops was his forte. Behind the utility room was his personal basketball court, paved with a regulation height rim and backboard. Hours on end he would hone his skills. In his yard he was the best dribbler, the most accurate shooter and a legend. Dressed in his Clemson jersey he mastered the universe, his universe, the one that counted the most. The heart of the Tiger reigned true. Uncle Jerry far outlived his life expectancy passing away in his 60's. The man child joined God in a heaven filled with those of common normalcy, free from ridicule and bullying, just one more angel among angels.

Jerry as actor in family Christmas production

Hub and Spoke

The definition of hub is the central part of a wheel, rotating on or with the axle, and from which the spokes radiate. It's the effective center of an activity, region, or network. A spoke is one of some number of rods radiating from the center of a wheel. These are Webster's spins on hub and spoke, not mine. I once had an Uncle Hub and I suppose I could have been called his number one spoke. I was maybe seven or eight years old, possibly slightly older but I vividly remember my time spent with Uncle Hub and Aunt Lorraine, Daddy's sister. He was hands down the best and most memorable uncle I have ever had. We had a connection, something special and almost unexplainable at the time to me. All I know is it was real, genuine, and unconditional, filled with love both ways. It's odd how I can so vividly remember the details of our relationship even to this day, a man on the backside of life.

Uncle Hub and Aunt Loraine rented an upstairs apartment just over a block from town on South Main. The house was next to what was then the Abbeville Post Office. They had a huge screened porch overlooking South Main. The house is long gone, and the post office eventually became the library and is something else now. I can remember watching the Christmas parade from that porch, the best seat in the house. The parade started on North Main, proceeded through the town square and ended a block from our location on Magazine Street. I only viewed one parade from that porch: not my choice though. I remember spending plenty of time with them. I guess it had to do with my parents working the second shift at Milliken textile mill. I suppose they enjoyed being fill-in sitters as much as I liked being the one needing a sitter.

Uncle Hub and Aunt Lorraine took me to my very first circus. It was in the old Greenville, South Carolina Memorial Auditorium. This was '**The**' circus, the Ringling Brothers and Barnum & Bailey Circus. I remember being mesmerized by the big cats, the elephants and that iconic clown car filled with what seemed to be a zillion clowns. Cotton candy and parched peanuts were on the kid menu. I'd like to believe that they enjoyed the experience as much as I did. I don't know if it was their first or not. It was for sure their first with me though. I can imagine that I probably entertained them with my antics. Uncle Hub was a big kid with a huge heart. Sorry, Aunt Lorraine, but men must embrace those male bonding moments. Girls don't always understand the significance. I loved you too, but in a different way.

Back in the day, the Winn family rented a two-story house on Edisto Beach. This was a stone's throw from Adams Run where Daddy's sister lived, The Newton clan. The rest of the family had some driving to get there. What did it matter to me? I was a rider. I got to play the part of the kid asking are we there yet. I, the little spoke was riding in Hub's convertible, Edisto bound with Aunt Lorraine. Top down, warm summer air and clear star-studded skies paved our way to our beach destination. To distract me from a kid's nagging questions and impatience, Uncle Hub perpetrated the perfect distraction. Every time we approached a billboard, he would honk the horn. For whatever reason this seemed hilarious and a bit magical. Who can explain what floats a young child's boat? Uncle Hub had a gift, a knack for connecting with little Tommy. We eventually arrived safely and with everyone's sanity in check.

Highlights from the vacation are still etched in my head. In the wooded area, when spot lighted by the automobile headlights, we'd see a multitude of deer roaming about. A kid like me had never seen wild deer, their eyes shining red, reflecting the lights. Edisto was filled with firsts. I witnessed my first blimp cruising just above the ocean under the brightness of the moon. I wasn't even sure what a blimp was at the time, but it was quite wondrous to behold. I can't explain why it was on our beach and ocean and where it was going. It did not have Goodyear emblazed on the side. Possibly it was a spy blimp if spies had blimps back then.

I wasn't a very good swimmer, especially in the angry waves of the ocean. Not to fear, Uncle Hub told me to hang on to his neck as he breached the waves and beyond. He swam along and I rode on his back, safe and secure. My relatives on the beach appeared miniature by comparison because we were so far from shore. This was another one of those male bonding moments, him swimming and me clinging. I've visited Edisto Beach as an adult, and it doesn't feel larger than life like it did back then. It's just a plain old beach, nothing special to it. That was not the case when the hub and spoke ruled the ocean. Some time later that year, Uncle Hub suffered a heart attack that landed him in the hospital. Another first, I had never known anyone who had suffered a heart attack. I didn't even comprehend the seriousness of it. Kids weren't allowed to visit people in the hospital for some reason. This was the same old white hospital that I had been born in. They had let me in then so why not now. It wasn't like I had never been there before. Not to worry, Mama and Aunt Lorraine snuck me in to see Uncle Hub. He looked normal to me, not sick at all. I don't remember much else about the covert visit but I'm so thankful I was able to see him. He died shortly there after. I documented my grieving in my memoir, 'The Caregiver's Son.'

Uncle Hub was gone! How could that be? I had only known him about a year, not much longer. The time I had spent with him was unforgettable. I wondered what would have happened if the heart attack had struck when we were in the ocean. It hadn't though. I'm a kid. What do I know about grief and anguish? I loved Uncle Hub and what was I going to do without him in my life. There would be a funeral, my first. I had no experience with funerals. Relatives and friends showed up. All my cousins had come. The family gathered at Granny Winn's house. Uncle Hub was elsewhere. My cousins were all into fun and games. Somehow having fun didn't seem quite right to me. I couldn't make them understand that I was not in a playful mood. Finally, I just couldn't take this circus like atmosphere. I retreated within myself and hid in a closet. No, this wasn't a case of playing hide and go seek. I needed to be alone, to think but to think about what. What did I do? I cried and remained hidden. Losing Uncle Hub was the most hurtful thing I had ever experienced. Another first, a kid shouldn't know this kind of pain. I was a lone spoke without my Hub. To this day I still miss him and wonder what it would have been like to have had him forever in my life. Sometimes life offers us no mulligan. Sometimes we must just hold onto those precious memories. Love is as forever as it gets.

Thinking about it now maybe this is why I never embraced the funeral experience. Possibly his death traumatized me; I just didn't realize this might be the root of me shying away from funerals. It makes perfectly good sense now that I reflect. The man that I loved more that life itself could have embedded this dread in me. Sometimes while traveling down the nostalgic highway revelations, deeply embedded memories surface. Mysteries are solved, explanations revealed. While looking back can often be sorrowful, it can often be eye opening. I will always cherish that short span spent with Uncle Hub and now possibly I understand the rest of the story.

**Little Spoke with Hub 1960
(One of the rare photos I have with him)**

Hail to the Heroes

I recently watched *The Longest Day* on television. I'm sure I've probably watched it before but this time I viewed it through the eyes of another. It took on a new perspective. The Longest Day was a 1962 black and white war epic movie about the landing at Normandy and the huge war effort of June 6, 1944 by the United States and its allies. The Nazis, led by Adolph Hitler, had to be stopped. Watching the movie this time I was amazed by how many stars or stars to be appeared in the feature, most dying valiantly. The list is huge and includes: John Wayne, Kenneth More, Richard Todd, Robert Mitchum, Richard Burton, Steve Forrest, Sean Connery, Henry Fonda, Red Buttons, Peter Lawford, Eddie Albert, Jeffrey Hunter, Stuart Whitman, Tom Tryon, Rod Steiger, George Segal, Robert Wagner, Don Adams, Gary Collins, Fabian, Edmond O'Brien, Tommy Sands, and Paul Anka. This was history on a horrific scale.

I say I viewed this with a new perspective, a better understanding, and a heartfelt thankfulness for those who gave everything, including their lives to defeat the evilest of evils. Heroes are real but reality never hit home until I met a real American hero. While researching history, following leads, and conducting interviews for Benji Greeson's and my book about Abbeville Football, we met some interesting people and learned much about our hometown pastime. We discovered we were on the brink of 100 years of its existence. We heard stories recapped by those who had played the game from recent to many years long passed. *It's All About the A* taught us the value of faith, family and football that our neighbors lived and breathed, and ensured that every generation that ever played the game understood these important life changing factors.

We began our search for the oldest living Abbeville Panther football player. Never in our wildest dreams did we realize where this journey would take us. The Tolbert sisters of Abbeville led us to the lead and the honor fell on me to contact this person and hopefully schedule an interview. Unknowingly I would be walking into one of the best experiences in my life. I called the phone number I had been given and contacted a man that I will never ever forget for many reasons. That man taught me the value of patriotism and faith in God. No. I didn't see this one coming. I was a newbie in the interviewing process and my simple goal had been to obtain the gentleman's perspective on Panther football as viewed from his generation of playing. I sought history and found a hero and undeniable wonderful friend. Oh, I did learn plenty about football of his era, but I was taught a history lesson I will never forget, one that made me understand the meaning of sacrifice and love of this country.

It infuriates me how generations of idiotic people today try to wipe the slate clean of history that they don't particularly like. It is history, good bad or ugly, evil or wonderful, wars waged, some won, and others lost. You can't change it. You can't pretty it up when it's ugly. You can't wish it away. And you can't tear down statues, destroy veteran gravesites, and disrespect the flag of our great nation and its people just because you think you know better than the rest of us. Read up on our history before you go off halfcocked and vigilante, how about it. Tearing down statues and disrespecting the United States Flag and those who gave their all to give us that right and protect us from evil is wrong on every level. Argue, scream and be violent if you must but you are wrong in doing so. Just that simple. Take time to sit down with a veteran and hear his or her side before you take a knee or burn our flag. Just maybe history will teach even you a valuable lesson. History, heroes and honor are powerful tools.

I cannot say I enjoyed learning history when I was in school. It was a necessary evil, classes we had to take, and I did not always fully understand the ramifications of the lessons teachers were trying to teach us. Some stuff I got. Other stuff I didn't. Even back then I knew I couldn't change any of the outcomes, whether I liked them or didn't. It's called history. It's really a simple concept. Love it. Hate it. You can't magically make it go away. D Day happened. We lost too many lives in a war effort to save the world from the cruelest of enemies, good versus evil. I heard firsthand what World War II meant from a man who was there on that beach June 6, 1944. I for one am thankful he was there, and I thank the Good Man above that he like so many didn't, did survive to tell us the truth and give us a valuable history lesson. He is a real American hero and we honored him with his very own chapter in our Abbeville Football book. We will get to this shortly.

My daddy served in the Korean War in the early fifties. I was born in 1953 after the war had ended and he had returned home. I never thought much about daddy and that war until many years later as a young man of maybe twelve, finding his army duffle bag in the attic. Without asking permission I rummaged through it. Mostly it just contained soldier uniforms, hats and such. He didn't appreciate that I had invaded his privacy, nor would he tell me anything about his time spent in Korea, North or South. All he ever told me was that he built temporary bridges but didn't elaborate on any personal experiences. I didn't know how to take that. My thoughts back then were that he didn't really fight the bad guys and just built these bridges. I had no idea why temporary bridges were required.

Later I would stumble into old family photographs including plenty showing daddy in his uniform along with others, his soldier buddies. He provided few explanations for the scenes depicted in the pictures. I learned as I got older that this seemed to be a common theme for those who served in war times. Few really wanted to talk about what happened. Mama simply told me that he had returned from Korea a changed man. She felt that the horrors of war had forever impacted him. Thomas Jefferson Winn lost his battle with Parkinson in 2004 so I will never know what really happened to him. Looking back now, I realize that he was a hero whatever happened had. He was equally a part of history, wartime history at that and like all veterans; I honor him for his service and sacrifices.

That brings me back full circle, doesn't it? Meeting a man that forever taught me what daddy could never share with me about the war he had experienced. WWII was a brutal war. Too many lost their lives, military and civilian, Americans and allies. For those of you who haven't read *It's All About the A* and the chapter about the Oldest Living Panther, it is worth picking up a copy to embrace Horace Beauford. I'm sure you will enjoy it and will be moved as much as I was from meeting the man, I now call my dear friend.

Me and Horace Beauford

This was written by Rene Beauford, Horace's daughter on his 95th birthday.

So many celebrations with this man with family & friends.... we are doing an early 95th birthday celebration at the Atlanta Braves game tonight. For all you Braves fans tune into game at 7:20 for a special birthday celebration

Dad has been chosen by the Braves to be "Saluted as Hometown Hero" of the game.

Couldn't think of a better 95th Bday present for a diehard Braves fan who is a Hero to everyone who knows him!!!

Dad, from the boy you were to the man you have become. Leaving your family behind 75 years ago to face the unknown, not knowing if you would ever come home, scared surrounded by 1000s but feeling alone.... you trusted God & put your faith in Him to keep you safe & bring you home...

You have lived your life in faith & trust of His leadership. Still today you live by that same faith. You share not only your life story but share the story of Jesus Christ. You go into schools talking to the children & youth of today about D-Day, but you never fail to give God the glory for sparing your life. God is not finished with you yet!!!

Love you Dad

My dear friend passed September 7th, at age 96, 2020 claiming another one of the special and beloved ones. His was not a Covid death.

Home of the Braves

It was in the early 60s and my family and the White family were taking a northerly vacation trip. We stopped over in Detroit for a few days to visit with the White's family. An added treat, we were going to go to a baseball game. I had never attended a professional baseball game. There weren't any baseball teams close to us in Abbeville. Maybe the closest at the time were in Cincinnati or Pittsburg. We were going to visit Detroit Stadium. Our seats were directly behind home plate and a double header was on slate against the California Angels. Mike White was a year younger than me, and as I discovered during our trip while bunking with him, he was a sleep talker. No, you heard it right. He didn't walk in his sleep. He would sit up and talk in his sleep and remember nothing the next day. It was fun and creepy. Just a weird little side story and it has nothing to do with me attending my very first baseball game.

Mike White and I developed a routine during the game. I'm not sure who came up with it, but that doesn't really matter now. When an opposing player, the Angels being the opposition, stood at home plate, we would yell swing when the pitch was thrown. We only did this for the Angels. I suppose the Tigers were our designated home team. We were in Detroit. I'm not sure if it ever worked but I bet it was quite annoying to the batter and the umpire. We probably had no outcome on the games. Detroit won the first game 1-0 and the Angels split the night by winning the second game 1-0. America's pastime had hooked and reeled me in, but what good was that going to do me with no teams near our home. On the trip I did visit my first country, Canada. We crossed the Canadian border in Michigan and later returned in Buffalo, New York at Niagara Falls. In 1969 I would visit my second country at age fifteen, walking across the border with my folks from San Diego to Tijuana.

Luck would be with us. The Milwaukee Braves relocated to Atlanta in 1966. We now had a professional team just three hours away. Daddy and I would tune in the AM station to listen to Braves' games. It was filled with static, the station fading in and out, but we were clued to the game. We had to adjust the antenna, strategically apply tinfoil, and stand on one foot to improve reception. Hank Aaron was the draw and reigning homerun king closing in on Babe Ruth's career homerun record. Atlanta Stadium was nicknamed 'The Launching Pad' because homeruns were in no short supply there. By '73 Aaron had upped his homerun total to 713, just one shy of Ruth. Phil Niekro was my favorite pitcher then, a knuckle ball pitcher. He was appropriately nicknamed 'Knucksie.' You never knew where that knuckle ball pitch might end up. I don't think he knew most of the time.

We began making a few weekend trips to Atlanta, most times seeing several games while staying there. Back then the Braves were losing so much you could practically sit anywhere in the stadium. Daddy tried to pick weekends when there would be double headers, more ballgames for your bucks. Plus, between games they would always have some sort of event to entertain us while we waited for the second game to start. Wrestling matches were not uncommon. Once we saw this old dude walk across the full width of the stadium on a cable. Karl Wallenda of the Flying Wallendas successfully pulled this stunt off. In 1978, at age 73, he would push his luck attempting to walk between the two towers of the ten-story Condado Plaza Hotel in San Juan, Puerto Rico. High winds and an improperly secured wire would cause him to lose his balance and fall to his death. Glad that didn't happen in Atlanta.

You remember how Daddy struggled behind the wheel when driving through Columbia and that time in Houston. Well, Atlanta was a big city posing more challenges. I think it is something about driving around capitols and domes. He would be unable to locate interstate 85 and we'd somehow find ourselves in downtown Atlanta circling the Atlanta Capitol Dome. Eventually a blind hog finds an acorn and we'd be on our way. A pitcher, Pascal Perez earned his nickname, Perimeter Perez when he couldn't get off the loop perimeter road around Atlanta. He drove until he ran out of gas. I think he and Daddy were kin.

The Los Angeles Dodgers were fearsome rivals. We attended a lot of Dodgers-Braves games. I can remember being at the park when things would get out of hand between the two teams and brawls would breakout. They would fight off and on throughout the game. Both teams would suffer many ejections. It was fun stuff to watch just the same. Ted Turner bought the team in 1976. He was a man with a new toy. Bizarre antics occurred under his watch. The commissioner didn't appreciate his hands-on ownership and gimmicks. The Braves had an Indian mascot, Chief Noc-A-Homa. Turner began broadcasting games on superstation WTBS, 'America's Team'. I acquired cable television just so I could watch the games. Eventually I moved into the country with no cable available. What did I do? I bought one of those ten-foot fiberglass dishes.

Bobby Cox was hired for his first stint as manager in 1978. Cox promoted a 22-year-old slugger named Dale Murphy into the starting lineup. Murphy hit 77 home runs over the next three seasons, but struggled on defense, positioned at either catcher or first base while being unable to adeptly play either. In 1980 Murphy was moved to center field and demonstrated excellent range and throwing ability, while the Braves earned their first winning season since 1974. My favorite Dale Murphy story occurred when my wife Shelby, Dale and Susan McCurry (rest in peace my two dear friends) attended a game. It so happened to be Dale Murphy baseball night and fans received a signed Murphy baseball. We were staying at the Stadium Hotel next to the ballpark. After the game we decided to take the stairs because the elevators were so crowded. Someone sprinted past us on the stairwell. I elbowed Beulah (Dale) telling him that the man looked like Dale Murphy. With a Murphy signed baseball in my hand I sprinted up the stairs behind him. He exited on a floor with me close on his tail. He dashed inside a doorway. I followed, only to be stopped at the door by a man telling me this was for Press only. Murphy heard the commotion and turned and smiled. He saw that I had the ball in my hand and came over, shook my hand and signed it again. What a class act he was. I was the envy of my trailing trio when I recapped what had just happened.

Who can forget the best pitching trio in baseball, the Cy Young Award winners of the 90s, Tom Glavine, Greg Maddox and John Smoltz. Glavine won two, 1991 and 1998. Maddox won three in a row, 1993-1995 and he had already won his first with the Cubs in '92. Smoltz won his in '96. I have a collector's plague of the 4 aces, the fourth being Steve Avery. The Braves finally won a World Series in 1995 beating another tribe, the Cleveland Indians. I knew they were going to win. Mister Joe Sanders, Judy's dad had lost his fight with cancer before the season began and I think he helped the boys win from the best seat in heaven. This Tomahawk Chop is for you, Mister Joe. Oh yeah, the PC police finally wore down the Braves organization in 1986, putting an end to the iconic Chief Noc-A-Homa.

There were so many memorable players over the years, too many to name them all. Here are some of m favorites: Aaron, Warren Span, Ralph Garr, the road runner, pitcher Al Hrabosky, the Mad Hungarian, Bob Horner, Rico Carty, Orlando Cepeda, Felipe Alou, Ron Reed, Felix Millan, Glen Hubbard, Rocker, Joe Torre, Gene Garber, David Justice, Ryan Klesco, Chipper Jones. Andrew Jones, Freddie Freeman and I could go on and one, but you get the point. I was a Braves loyal fan and still am. We got to see some of the upcoming Braves when they had a minor league franchise in Greenwood, S.C. When I first moved to Myrtle Beach in 2005, the Pelicans were a Braves franchise at the beach. I haven't attended a game yet at the newest stadium but did at the previous ones. Go Braves, forever loyal.

1992 Western Division Braves Coffee Mug and Autographed Baseball, and the Dale Murphey Autographed Baseball

**1992 National Champion Three Pitching Aces
Tom Glavine, John Smoltz and Steve Avery**

The Kudzu Palace

Anyone living in the south is fully aware of the dreaded creeping Kudzu vine. It's one of the few green foliage that can almost be seen growing without time-lapse photography. Historical fact: Kudzu was introduced to the United States as an ornamental bush and an effortless and efficient shade producer at the Philadelphia Continental Exposition in 1876. In the 1930s and 1940s, the vine was rebranded as a way for farmers to stop soil erosion. Workers were paid $8 per acre to sow topsoil with the invasive vine. The cultivation covered over one million acres of kudzu. What were they thinking? The concern today always hinges on the introduction of invasive species. Boy, nothing gets more invasive than this creepy crawling plant.

So, what exactly is Kudzu for those who have never interacted with the plant? It's called Japanese arrowroot. It was originally a climbing, coiling and trailing perennial vine native to eastern Asia. Kudzu climbs over trees, shrubs, most anything standing still long enough for it to overtake. It's supposed to be edible. I have not wrapped my taste buds around that fact though, thinking it might end up as an uncontrollable parasite inside, taking over and controlling you. Some positive benefits, it controls erosion and is supposed to enhance the soil by increasing nitrogen content. Those deep taproots transfer valuable minerals from subsoil to topsoil. To most this info is extremely irrelevant. It's a nuisance plain and simple.

Now that you have a grasp of the Mister Science version, I suspect that you are asking just what the heck is my nostalgic point, Mr. Rambling Man with all the psychobabble? It's really very simple. Back in my day it was virtually a kid's playground. The imaginary possibilities were endless. Let me paint the canvas for you. I lived on Hunter Street just behind Langley Milliken Grammar School. Just a block away on Moore Street lived Cousin Stevie. A short walk through the woods behind his house opened into a huge field overgrown with Kudzu. It seemed back in those days to reach as far as the eye could see. Everything had been consumed by the vines and its foliage. The trees were canopies of every size and shape. The landscape mimicked one from another planet, another world and we were the astronauts, explorers, ready to venture where no kid had gone before. Well at least not since the last visit there.

Our conquests and adventures varied. Sometimes we were on safari and taking on the creatures of Africa lurking among the overgrowth and challenging territory. The wooded area between Stevie's house and Kudzu world contained several large rock formations. Some of the smaller ones were just perfect to sub as elephants. We would mount them and ride our imaginary taxis toward the next frontier. No, the rocks stayed stationary, but our imagination didn't. The great outdoors was our only world and always at our fingertips. Video games had not been invented. We had only three television channels. Using our vivid imaginations gave us the perfect excuse to enjoy what nature had provided. Improvising was second nature.

Our weapon of choice might be a fully automatic Remington broom handle. It was guaranteed to never run out of ammunition if you could form the word bang on your lips or better still, mimic the actual sound of a gun shooting. Some of us were better than others at sounding like a gunshot. Never point the broom handle or any other stick at someone's eye though, so warned our parents. Today kids get expelled from school or arrested for just pointing a finger and saying bang or even drawing a gun. Back in my day kids weren't being murdered in school. It was torture to some of us to attend school though. I can't recall anyone ever being ruined for life or traumatized by bullies bad enough to flip us out and send us into a killing spree. We thought about beating the other kid within an inch of their lives but knew better. Bullies could usually take us even in a no rules fight. Sorry. I'm drifting away from the Kudzu narrative.

Sometimes the Kudzu covered trees became monstrous creatures, snagging us in their tentacles. We would have to fight for life and limb to free ourselves from its evil clutches. The landscape of Kudzu covered everything making the perfect place to play hide and go seek. Hiding places were limitless. If you didn't want to be found, usually you weren't, especially when the foliage was green and thick. I think it grew so fast it might have engulfed us without us realizing it. In the winter after a few hard frosts or freezes, Kudzu world took on a forbidding appearance. The vines became this grayish skeletal look of its former self. During this dormant time of the year the vines ceased their movement and virtual takeover. Suspended animation halted it until spring next arrived. It still held its firm grasp on the surrounding terrain. It was not going to relinquish the foothold at the mere drop of seasonal change and influence.

On the fringes of Kudzu world, in the woods on the other side of the field, flowed a creek offering more adventures for thrill seekers. We played in and around that creek with unbridled passion. Critter hunting was a pastime. In a blink of an eye we transformed into Mutual of Omaha's Marlin Perkins and his sidekick Stan, discovering and encountering what nature had to offer us. No, we never wrestled twenty-foot Anacondas but underneath rocks we found salamanders, crawfish and snails. Sometimes we captured them and brought them home to live in makeshift terrariums or aquariums. Seldom did they ever survive though. What did we know about having these creatures as pets? More times than not we just played with them there before freeing them. We were dam engineers, piling rocks, mud, tree limbs, whatever we could to construct a structure worthy of disrupting the water flow. Our creativity resulted in kid sized swimming holes. Nudity among friends treading the cold creek waters was a social function and fully acceptable. None of us were embarrassed by anatomical correct or incorrect differences. Fun knew no boundaries and we made up the rules as we saw fit. Our parents weren't always pleased when we returned, our clothing usually wet or worse for the wear.

Times were simple. Living the life was a joy. We had the world at our fingertips. The great outdoors was our playground. The possibilities were endless. Parents appreciated the fact that we could be self sufficient and entertain ourselves for hours. Close supervision in most cases was unnecessary. Out of sight and out of mind worked for them and for us. Physically and mentally we were in a better place than the kids are today. Our lives weren't crushed by something someone did or said. We didn't require therapy or a safe zone to deal with life's issues. We petted animals because we loved them and not because we were traumatized by something that didn't go our way. We were tough and resilient. We understood right from wrong, the consequences of choosing unwisely. The Kudzu Palace offered us the great escape, a plant woven castle perfect for the challenges of the day, fighting off aliens, dragons, lions and tigers, Indians, and army soldiers, all out to get us. Lost in the thick vegetation and our vivid imaginations shaped us for taking on life's real issues. We played hard and rested well at night. We didn't stress over what we couldn't control. In our minds we controlled our universe.

As an adult I encountered Kudzu on an entirely different level. At Abbeville's Flexible Tubing, as it was called when I worked there, Kudzu occupied the back forty so to speak just outside the doors of the lower level warehouse. As a matter of fact, someone dubbed it the Kudzu Warehouse. Discarded equipment, forklifts, machinery were stored there. Kudzu embraced their presence, eventually erasing all traces of their existence. The packman of the plant world devoured every morsel. Eventually the equipment vanished. It became undulated sections of the landscape, out of sight, out of mind, off the books. It was very cost effective with no need to dispose of the items in the traditional method. Magically it was no more, consumed by the miracle byproduct of Kudzu, introduced to the United States as an ornamental bush and an effortless and efficient shade producer.

Seeing Is Believing

Webster's meaning for believe: 1) to consider to be true or honest, 2) to accept the word or evidence, 3) to hold an opinion.

Everyone believes in something, right or wrong or indifferent. Just as many disbelieve what others consider as true or honest, whether it is considered opinion or factual with evidence to support their belief. I grew up like most kids fearing those things that we didn't understand, ghosts, the boogeyman, witches and unseen monsters to name a few. Horror movies fed our fears. In my era the monsters were pretty basic with the likes of Count Dracula, the Frankenstein monster, the werewolf, the mummy or something unknown and scary from outer space. If they were real on the silver screen or our televisions, there must be some basis for them existing. Somewhere, some place these things must have walked the earth or still did. Three movies scared the bejeebies out of me, The Creature from the Black Lagoon, King Kong and War of the Worlds. We didn't live near a lagoon or an island with monsters. Flying saucers had never landed in our backyard or town, not to my knowledge. Still, there had to be some basis for them being made into movies or television shows, right?

The lure of things that go bump in the night often occupied our adolescent fantasies back in the '60s and early '70s. We were teenage ghost hunters long before cable television and iconic series were developed for viewing audiences. Our little clique had it covered, from night vigils in cemeteries to visits at suspected haunted houses under the cloak of darkness. We were drawn to the aspect of the unknown. Our thought process didn't include just what the heck we might actually do if we encountered something unexplainable and paranormal. We were too enthralled by the thrill of the hunt to contemplate such an encounter.

Our team of investigators might be a mere handful or include two carloads of night stalkers on any given excursion. While safety in numbers seemed prevalent, we didn't rely on numbers to pursue our idiotic passion. When the mood struck us on any given night we reacted to the urge and spontaneity. Most of these occurred on Friday or Saturday nights unless we were in the middle of our annual summer reprieve from school incarceration. These were not preplanned excursions by any stretch of the imagination. Rarely were we packing the necessary equipment such as flashlights, cameras, or weapons; not that weapons would protect us from evil spirits or other unearthly encounters. We had youth and gutless prowess on our side for what it was worth. Plus, one only had to outrun the slowest team member to avoid unwanted interaction with vengeful apparitions. If you were the slowest then tripping was an option. Do what you must and face the consequences later.

I could change the names to protect the guilty but what fun would that be, right? I will exclude last names but those of this era can probably fill in the blanks. Plus, you've already seen them in other nostalgic shorts. Typical on our roster were Speed, Pete, Stanley, Larry, Glen, Jody, yours truly, but it might include the second string, Leroy, David, Donnie and Steve. As mentioned, this could often require a second vehicle, contingent on the number of brave participants. We were not a destructive lot. I suppose we sort of had an undocumented code of ethics and honor. We didn't set out to break windows or set fires or be stereotyped as juvenile delinquents or teenage renegades, marauding gangs out to establish reputations. We were just in it for the fun and twisted fellowship. What we did mostly remained among us. We surely didn't want parents or the authorities to catch wind of what we were doing. Trespassing was outside the boundaries of the law, enough said.

So, what did we target? Abandoned and secluded old countryside houses were high on the priority list, especially if they had a reputation for being haunted. If they didn't, we just figured any old house could be a home for spirits not of this world. It was all fun and games, so what did we really care. Cemeteries were another favorite on our agenda, especially if they included eerie tales of strange sightings and unexplained occurrences. We were full of piss and vinegar. Why not? We had encountered nothing to thwart our thinking and streak of unbridled bravery so far. That could change in the blink of an eye if ole Casper materialized and made believers out of us. Trash talk prevailed. We were bullet and ghost proof back in the day, stupid and naïve to boot.

The Rock House in Greenwood was a favorite on our touring list. It was a two-story building but not a huge structure. Indeed, the house was constructed from stone. As best I can remember there were four rooms on each level. A hole in the ceiling was where a long-ago spiral staircase had offered a portal to the second floor. Access could only be achieved by climbing trees that rested against the front of the house. Some of us were much better climbers than others of our party. Those unable to make the climb simply explored the first floor. That was seldom though because as brave as we were, nobody wanted to be left alone at any given moment. We did exercise our right to spook one another as much as possible. Ambushes, unworldly voices from secluded hiding places were all part of the experience. Scare tactics varied. Everyone was fair game.

For the record, we never encountered anything paranormal at the Rock House and not from lack of trying. We really wanted to or so we pretended we did. The Rock House does have a compelling back story about its origin and possible haunts, but we didn't have the luxury of the Internet or Google back then for research. We could only go on hearsay and our vivid and active imaginations. I cannot remember how many times we visited the Rock House, but I would say we frequented it at least once a year for several years. The participants varied. Good ole fashioned honest fun ensued.

Another ominous encounter was the (house on Cedar Springs Road). It was an octagon design. We didn't know that back then though, not the significance of the design or any history about the house. It was just old, empty and accessible. I confess, this one was one of the most forbidding houses that I ever visited. It was a one vehicle excursion and we only visited it one time. We parked the car further away than we preferred but the entrances were chained off, meaning that we weren't supposed to even try this. That didn't stop us though. Same as always, we were able to breach the house without breaking any windows. Breaking and entering, trespassing was still illegal as the day is long. We didn't consider the consequences, so it seemed; same rule as for ghostly encounters, be able to outrun the slowest in case of owner or police interference. We came better equipped for this one. We at least had a handful of flashlights.

This house felt like a potential haunted one. There was sparse furniture inside but the 1800's ambiance oozed loudly and clearly. If we were going to experience something paranormal, this sure seemed a likely candidate. Room to room, floor to floor, we spooked one another, always on guard that the real deal might get the last laugh eventually. Venturing as far as we could go upward, we found an old trunk. Thinking this might contain the Holy Grail, we couldn't pass up a peek inside. Cautiously we opened it but found only an empty cavity instead. We ascended the stairs, still hopeful this would be the ultimate experience, but we came up ghost-less.

There was one other place to explore, an old log cabin on the grounds. We didn't know it at the time, but this spot was that of a stagecoach stop. Again, we were not history buffs, nor did we have the resources or interest in researching our picks. While the log cabin was a quick visit on the exploration scale, I did find a unique book inside. It was signed and inscribed from the 1800's. Add thievery to our list of criminal accomplishments. I later handed this in to a teacher in exchange for credit on a class project. Hindsight, I should have kept it but what did I know about the historical value of things back then. Our best opportunity at spiritual intervention had us again coming up empty handed at this potentially perfect spook house. Ironically, many years later, the adult me would use this house and our antics as the backdrop and plot for my fictional book titled 'The Perfect Spook House.'

At a book signing on Trinity Street during Abbeville's Hogs and Hen festival, four ladies approached my table. One pointed to the book and said, "That's our house." I'm thinking lawsuit because I didn't get permission to use the house photo for the cover. Nice ladies they were. Sadly, they confirmed that they had never encountered anything paranormal at the old house. Then they all bought signed copies. One strange thing did happen at my first book signing in Georgetown, S.C. I had ordered fifty copies but hadn't opened either of the boxes until I was preparing for the signing. I opened the first box and retrieved a copy. Opening it I read the title on the first page. It clearly stated the title as 'Vanished', written by another author. I quickly flipped through the pages and my book content had indeed vanished. I was starring at this other author's book. Panic stricken I began opening other books, terrified now that I had no T. Allen books for those arriving. Lucky for me, this was the only misprint of the lot. It was a spooky premise just the same.

Our adventures were not restricted to old houses. We did venture into the sacred land of the undead. Surely a spiritual uprising could be uncovered in a cemetery. One drew us to it like flies on sugar. Ebenezer was located on what we called the old Anderson Highway in Anderson County. Supposedly there was a grave where a wicked old woman had been buried and at midnight the image of the devil would appear on her tombstone. If anything screamed our names, this one did. Of course, we didn't know the alleged woman's name, nor did we know the specific location of her grave. Ebenezer is a tiny graveyard compared to most, so how hard could it be to win the round of hide and seek. Game on, we picked a Friday night and made our way in that direction about an hour before the midnight hour.

We had to discreetly hide our car. Again, this was a one vehicle adventure with about four brave spook hunters. Well, at least we considered our bravery on the highest level. This was our first ever attempt at a rendezvous with the spiritual world at a specific time. Randomness and spontaneity better suited our demeanor. A schedule with destiny added just a tad too much creepiness for our own good. It was put up or shut up time for sure, upping our game so to speak. Four brave souls or so we reassured ourselves silently. We wandered around the graveyard scoping out the gravestones, best guessing which one might hold the key as the Devil's pick. One guess was just a good as the next, zeroing in on graves of elderly women. We commenced a countdown, every tick tock seemingly spanning a lifetime. We had to duck and hide when we saw headlights approaching on the roadway.

Finally, we were within ten minutes of midnight, the bewitching hour. Nothing but bad things happened at midnight in the movies. Toss in a haunted graveyard and we had the perfect recipe. Hey, that's what we wanted, right? This was a chance to live the dream or maybe nightmare in this case. Can't you feel the drama building? We had a flashlight but no camera or anything to ward off evil spirits in case things got out of hand. I'm not sure what protects you from evil spirits anyway. We were approaching five minutes to go. This was our moment. Piss and vinegar, young and bullet proof just didn't seem to be enough. We bolted to the car and hauled ass. We were that close to living out our ultimate fantasy and panicked. One thing for sure, there would be no razing one another. We simultaneously chickened out, not a brave soul among us willing to answer the call, myth or madness. Maybe the devil made us do it.

As I grew older, I became mesmerized by the premise that certain creatures might just exist. No. As a kid I never experienced any close encounters to justify my beliefs but that didn't quench the desire to believe. Ghosts were a favorite. We were paranormal investigators ahead of our time. Visiting old, deserted houses and cemeteries was common practice for the young ghost busters of our time. Did we have any major breakthroughs or discoveries? Not than I can recall. It wasn't for lack of trying to catch one red-handed. Now just what would we have done if we had encountered a spiritual entity is anyone's guess. We never went in search of vampires or werewolves. I guess we finally convinced ourselves that they weren't really real. Mummies fell into the same category. We were short on pyramids I suppose. Witches were a possibility, but we had no leads on any hags though. None of us had ever had a close encounter with a UFO of any kind. I don't remember us ever focusing on the pursuit of aliens.

You would think that one would outgrow such things. As an adult I think I became more interested with the premise that certain creatures might just exist. Hold your horses. I'm not an obsessed whacko. We're all entitled to our beliefs though. And no, the adult version hasn't gone out of his way to prove the existence of any specific cryptic or supernatural beings. There's nothing harmful in wondering why the unexplained can't be explained. UFOs for instance; even the government had Project Bluebook to investigate sightings and occurrences. There seems to always be an interest in alien encounters. I have experienced close encounters of the first kind. I was in my mid 30s and living in rural Abbeville when both encounters occurred. Encounters might be a bit melodramatic. They were unexplained sightings. My house was a split level atop a hill off highway 72 between Abbeville and Greenwood. The view from the back deck was unobstructed.

Sighting number one happened late one night when I was taking our dog outside. It was a crisp clear night filled with stars. For no reason I eased into a bit of star gazing. Something caught my eye, a single light like the size of the stars in the background moving south to north. My first thought, a plane. It was moving at the speed at which you would expect a plane to be moving. This was a single bright light, not blinking. Mostly I am accustomed to seeing blinking red or green lights on planes. Still, the sighting didn't really seem odd. That is until the light vanished and then no more than a couple of seconds reappeared. The light had made a 90 degree move and was moving in an entirely different direction. No plane could have changed directions in the manner I had just witnessed. That was a definite eye opener. I continued to watch it for maybe ten more minutes until it blinked out and never came back on. I don't know what I saw that night, but it wasn't a plane. That maneuver was something unexplainable.

The second one was weirder than the first. I can't recall the timeframe between it and the first. It could have been a year or so later. It happened from the same home. This time I was sitting in our den watching television. The den was on the backside of the house with sliding glass doors opening to the second story deck. That deck had made the perfect deer stand. I shot my very first deer, the ten-pointer from that doorway. It was night, pitch dark and the blinds had not been drawn. Something from the corner of my vision caught my attention. It was a series of multicolored lights just above the treetop level in the distance towards Greenwood. No houses were close by in that direction and there were no towers either. I eased out of my chair and walked to the door to get a better look. There were a dozen lights aligned left to right. None were blinking and they appeared to be stationary. I could latch onto no reasonable explanation to define what I was looking at out there on the horizon. To scale it in my view it was about 3 inches wide. Maybe a couple of minutes expired and then it began rotating until all the lights were aligned making it appear to be one single bright light now. As I remained glued to the sight attempting to figure out what I might be witnessing, the lights went out without warning and it was gone.

Planes have steady-burning red, green, and white lights. The red light is on the left wing, the green light on the right wing, and the white light on the tail. At night, another pilot can tell the direction the airplane is heading based on the color of lights he sees. On the ground, these lights serve to inform ground crew that a pilot is inside the cockpit. Strobe lights are bright, flashing lights on the wingtips. They serve to augment the airplane's visibility at night. They are the brightest airplane lights and are visible from miles away. They are turned off when operating in proximity to other aircraft, or in clouds, where the strobes can cause temporary blindness. They are not used on the ground for this reason. What I saw had way too many lights to be a plane. None were blinking and there were too many multicolored ones. You tell me. What did I see? I have no reasonable explanation for this one either. I experienced no other encounters while living there and it wasn't from lack of looking every opportunity I had.

Then there are ghosts, paranormal experiences, poltergeist, or things that just go bump in the night. I always wanted to see one. One thing I learned though. You cannot will a spiritual encounter. My wife at the time did encounter a spiritual hitchhiker. I have documented that one in my short, 'Rider in the Storm' that was featured as a bonus story in the book, 'The Hardwood Walker of Port Harrelson Road.' The Hardwood Walker is also based on a true story as told to me by a coworker in Conway. It happened in Bucksport.

As previously stated, as kids we ventured into old, deserted houses and allegedly haunted cemeteries but found no ghosts willing to play with us. As an adult though, I had a friend that lived in a supposedly haunted house. His house was in Greenwood. He and his wife had told me stories about a spirit that visited and played with their daughter. They had heard voices and witnessed lights turning on and off when no one was in the rooms. They had appropriately named the entity 'Ghosty'. They had also witnessed an apparition enter the doorway in their kitchen and then disappear behind an island as if it was going down steps. Slave quarters had been in a basement in the home's original floor plans. Once, my friend even heard footfalls on the wrap around porch stopping short of the front door. When he looked outside, no one was there.

He and his wife participated in Civil War reenactments. He wore authentic confederate attire. His wife dressed in clothing for the women of that era. We once attended a Christmas party at their home and as usual they entertained the guests with spooky stories. Whenever I ventured for a bathroom break, I would encourage the ghosts to appear to me. Summoning ghosts is probably quite foolish on numerous levels. I even placed his confederate hat on my head and taunted them. I don't know what I expected to happen, but nothing did. That might have been a blessing looking back now. Okay, so I can't lay claim to having seen a ghost but that doesn't mean I haven't experienced weird and unexplainable stuff. We'll start with the house where the UFO sightings happened and then backtrack to two previous homes.

I had read the Amityville Horror long before we had relocated to the house on the hill. And I had experienced several unexplainable events in my previous home inside the city limits of Abbeville while married to my first wife. We will go there next. The kitchen was located on the front of the house overlooking the hill and highway 72. A door opened from the kitchen and lead down steps to the second level. One morning as I prepared for work and walked into the kitchen, I was taken aback by a smeared blood trail leading to the closed second level doorway. I have no logical explanation for the blood and why it led to a closed door. Neither I nor my wife had suffered an accident. I'd never heard any stories of our house on the hill being haunted. That was it, just the single event. Well, that and my stepdaughter claiming she heard voices in her bedroom. Her hearing voices in any room are not a stretch though. I'll just leave it at that.

Now let us digress to my previous home in Abbeville. I was in the middle of reading the Amityville Horror when three consecutive nights I woke to look at the digital clock on my nightstand. It always displayed the same time as the time had been displayed in the book when the spirits became restless. Weird, mere coincidence or subliminally implanted, who can say. Remember in the book and the movie when the priest came inside to bless the house and those large green flies swarmed him. This was in the dead of winter when I was reading the book. I came home from work one day and about thirty green blow flies were on the inside of the kitchen window overlooking the sink. Tell me where in the heck they came from in cold weather and how they got in the house. My wife at the time claimed she was going into the attic looking for something and found a Ouija Board sitting on the floor open and the pull chain for the attic light tied in a noose. I didn't see either when I investigated. You tell me, fact or an overactive imagination.

One last unexplainable event happened when same first wife and I lived in a rental house after we were first married. We had just seen the movie the Exorcist with another couple and I had just begun reading the book, the Exorcist. What can I say? I'm a sucker for horror. If you've seen the movie or read the book, then you will remember the mention of something scratching and rustling about in the attic. They thought they had rats and the butler was setting traps in the attic. Well. We began hearing scratching and clawing sounds too. Ours were underneath the bathroom tub. Did I go underneath the house to investigate? Nope. You would think I would, me the one wanting to encounter something potentially paranormal. Not a chance.

That brings me to Bigfoot. No, I have never seen a Sasquatch, but I have always been intrigued by the possibly of their existence. I do have a friend who told me that his niece and her friends claimed they saw a Bigfoot one night in a park area in Michigan. That's about as close as my encounters go, third hand. I have written a fictitious trilogy about Bigfoot though. The first has been published, titled 'Foot, Rock Throwers and Tree Knockers.' Books two and three, 'Another Foot, What Really Happened to D.B. Cooper' and 'Final Foot, Willow Creek' will see the light of day soon enough. But before I had published book one, I had an opportunity to check something off my Bigfoot list. In 2016 we took a trip out west with the Cannons. We flew to San Francisco for a two day stay before retrieving our rental car and driving up the coastal California highway in route eventually to Lake Tahoe, Nevada. We ventured as far north as Eureka, California, then took a right turn to head to my must-see place, Willow Creek, birthplace of Bigfoot. I kept a wishful eye on the landscape as Cuz navigated us toward our destination. Nope, I didn't catch a glimpse of an illusive Sasquatch, camera readied to capture a blurry image. We did visit the Bigfoot museum there, my dream fulfilled.

Ole T. Allen with The Legendary Patterson-Grimlin Bigfoot

Ole T. Allen at Willow Creek Museum

Next on my must-see list will happen August 2019. I had written a fictitious story based on historical and haunted events of the Lake Shawnee Amusement Park in Princeton, West Virginia. The story appeared in our Beach Author Network book titled 'Shorts' and is titled, 'For Your Amusement.' I penned this one based on Google research. I had the opportunity to visit the defunct Shawnee Amusement Park when we spend a couple of nights there before heading to Baltimore for a 9-day cruise August of 2019, years after publishing the story. I hope to investigate another potential story when I take an ex-coworker's invite to visit a place, he calls The Devils Dinning Room located near Conway in Horry County. Haunted events have been experienced and sighted there.

My friend has shared a personal encounter with me. Seeing is believing, right?

Lake Shawnee Ferris Wheel

Lake Shawnee Swings where Young Girl Died and now Haunts Park

Is That You Marilyn?

Living on the Grand Strand for fifteen years now, we still pretend to be tourist from time to time. Funny though, when you live just minutes from the ocean, you don't seem to be drawn to it like when we lived 4 ½ hours away and cherished the visits here. Every year are so we attend the Alabama Theater or Carolina Opry, often it is when they offer local discounts, buy one ticket, get one free. When we have company visiting, we take on the tourist persona and venture to the boardwalk and sometimes ride the Sky Wheel. Brookgreen Gardens is a favorite venue, especially during the Christmas season and Nights of a Thousand Candles.

If you visit the beach often then you'll remember the Palace Theater that anchored a corner near Broadway at the Beach. Sadly, it no longer exists. Hurricane Matthew did significant damage to the venue a few years ago and now it has been leveled. It still holds one of my fondest memories though. Inside the theater there used to be a smaller theater just off the main entrance and near the souvenir shop. This is where we first attended the Dino Variety Show. It was exactly what its namesake insinuated. The set was a mockup of the Dean Martin television show that aired 1965 – 1974. It featured an assortment of weekly guests and the dancing Golddiggers. An impersonator, Larry Tanelli, pulled off a believable Dean Martin.

The room was small, seating its audience at tables, giving the feel you were in a nightclub. Besides Dino, they had others impersonating Phyllis Diller, Granny from the Beverly Hillbillies, Dolly Pardon, Judy Garland, the genie of I Dream of Jeannie fame and my favorite, Marilyn Monroe. The female impersonators also pulled off amazing renditions of the Lennon, Andrews, and McGuire sisters. It was an authentic throwback show for sure. Audience participation was a big part of the show. Dino serenaded an unlucky 'volunteer'.

Eventually the show must have completed its run and closed. Later I discovered that the Dino show popped up again. This time it was in a small theater further south at Litchfield by the Sea in Pawley's Island. We had family and friends planning to pay us a visit and were looking for something special to do with them. I contacted the Dino show via their website and began exchanging emails with Cindra Marshall. I conveyed to her that I would like to do something special for the group I'd be bringing, Big Jerry. The sting, the set-up was put in motion. I fed Cindra an assortment of tidbits about the crew that I would be bringing. She particularly loved the fact that there would be a Jerry, a Big Jerry, and a

Little Geri in the group. Fun facts were covertly shared. Game on. Might I remind you, I had never met Cindra prior to this little ruse.

Entering the lobby Cindra just so happened to be one of the greeters. Somehow, we made eye contact and realized we were the ones in cahoots. I discreetly pointed out the victims. She assured me she would make this an unforgettable experience. The twinkle in her eyes told me this was going to be good. Ladies and gentlemen take your seats. The show of all shows is about to begin. I had no idea what to expect but I knew it was going to be good. As it would turn out, it far exceeded my wildest expectations. The first part of the show was as we had previously experienced at The Palace. Dino did his thing. The Golddiggers performed. Various guests would knock on the door and Dino would grant them access and then a comedic monologue would be next. I wasn't sure when it was going to happen or how it was going to happen. But it was going to happen.

Marilyn Monroe appeared at the door. A skit between Dino and the blonde bombshell left the audience in stitches. Then, out of the blue, Marilyn Monroe began working the crowd, mingling with the audience. She approached our row and began asking our names. 'And who might you be?' Jerry Solomon replied, 'Jerry.' Who might you be she continued and Big Jerry said, 'Jerry'? She eventually got to Little Geri and there she found her third, three Jerry's out of six. The set-up was in progress. She began telling the three Jerry's personal things and episodes that she shouldn't know. Mouths open and wide eyed, they smelled a rat. Marilyn even got in a few jabs at me. She then invited the birthday boy, 'Big Jerry' on stage. She seated him on the couch beside her and then began singing a sexy and provocative song to him. She ran her hands through his hair, landed a red lipstick kiss on his forehead and continued her foreplay with Big Jerry who was eating it up. Cindra Marshall, 'Marilyn' and I instantly became friends after the perfect prank had been pulled off flawlessly. We were Facebook friends afterwards also. She is responsible for introducing me to Shelia Suggs-Little of Grapefull Sister's Vineyard in Tabor City, N.C. Sheila and her sister Amy are the owners of the vineyard. Jacquelyn, Sheila's granddaughter did the front cover artwork for my Mr. Twix book.

This wouldn't be the last of our little coconspirator pranks. I would later invite two coworkers and their wives to attend the Dino show while it was still being performed at the Litchfield by the Sea location. They two would be targeted by Marilyn. Cindra and I were getting good at this. Eventually they would close out the show at this location. She and I continued to stay in touch. Next, they would open the show back on the north end of the Grand Strand. This time they would be performing at the 2001 Night Club.

Game on again. We invited beach friends Harry and Marge to join us. Harry was Cindra's mark this time. She played him like a fiddle. A twist I hadn't been expecting though; Dean Martin singled out wife, Judy and positioned her on the coach with him. In true Dino fashion he serenaded her and gave her the full Dino. It wasn't over yet. I was chosen to join the crooner on stage. He sang some silly song about a donkey and I had to make jackass sounds when prompted. I certainly made the perfect jackass of myself, thank you very much, Cindra.

The Dino show completed its run at the 2001 location and sadly closed for good this time. The following is an excerpt that was featured in the Sun News in December of 2012 by Steve Palisin. It is an interview with Cindra.

Cindra Marshall enumerated a list of artists and TV stars to whom they've paid tribute, besides the show's namesake, Dean Martin and his Golddiggers: Louis Armstrong, Sammy Davis Jr., Willie Nelson, Doris Day, Phyllis Diller, Judy Garland, Ethel Merman, Marilyn Monroe, Dolly Patron, Dinah Shore, Nancy Sinatra, Jeannie from "I Dream of Jeannie," Granny and Ellie May Clampett from "The Beverly Hillbillies," and sister troupes in the Andrews, Lennon and McGuire names.

Cindra was asked what tribute artist role had been most respected and she said that all the show's characters had gone through an evolution during its years in the area. She singled out Dean Martin as possibly the strongest in growth. She was asked which artist had connected the most with the audience. She graciously responded saying it really depended on the audience. She did go on to say that Marilyn Monroe tended to always get a huge response. She was so iconic. The Marilyn routine was fun and popular for all ages. Judy Garland was another unforgettable character.

She was asked how Dino's originated on stage. She explained that it was a spin-off from 'The Rat Pack' that had appeared at the Palace. She and the character that played Dean Martin discussed the premise of the Dino show. Cindra had been a background singer for 'The Rat Pack.' They decided to take it to anew level. Cindra's husband Hank got involved and added special affects and screens. The shows ran for eight years. In might come as a surprise to know that Cindra performed, and her husband produced shows around the world before they settled at the beach. Their last three years they performed on the road almost exclusively for the USO.

As mentioned previously, Cindra and I developed a wonderful friendship. After Dino, she opened a show in a theater in Surfside featuring the

Marvelous Wonderettes. We attended that show of course. Cindra's daughter was one of the featured Wonderettes along with her. We visited with her and the cast before and after the show. Rhonda Singleton, my Judy's daughter, taught both of Cindra's children in school. Small world. Cindra is an avid supporter of the Red Cross. She also poses as the Fairy Godmother for the annual Princess Gala to benefit the Red Cross. She is a wonderful and giving person and I am proud to have her as a friend.

Here are a few iconic Marilyn Monroe quotes.

I'm selfish, impatient, and a little insecure. I make mistakes, I'm out of control, and at times hard to handle. But if you can't handle me at my worst, then you sure as hell don't deserve me at my best.

Imperfection is beauty, madness is genius and it's better to be absolutely ridiculous than absolutely boring.

I never wanted to be Marilyn – it just happened. Marilyn's like a veil I wear over Norma Jeane.

Cindra Marshall as Marilyn Monroe

Cindra as Jeannie with Larry Tanelli as Dean at the Dino Variety Show

Sadly, Larry Tanelli, at age 71, died of Covid July 17, 2020.

Do-Overs Are Not for Dummies

In 2019 I published The Endless Mulligan, Short Shots from the Golf Whomper. This was a collection of over 50 golfing short stories spanning at least 45 years. If you ever played golf with me, you were probably in one of these shorts, especially if you did something unorthodox or unforgettably funny. I had started collecting and writing new stories for a second release titled Do-Overs Are Not for Dummies but instead decided to include most of them in this release. In the endless mulligan I explained how some of my partners seem to think anytime they make a bad shot during the round, they can declare a mulligan and then score using the best shot between their first and second one replayed. Our group usually allows one mulligan per nine holes; not as many as you feel appropriate to end with a descent score. Do-overs are not mulligans. A do-over can be claimed for almost any reason, some well beyond reason. Someone was talking while you were hitting your ball on the tee. Someone on another fairway was talking or someone in their back yard might have spoken too loudly; do-over. You were talking, do-over. A lawnmower, a weed eater, a leaf blower, hammering, dogs barking, birds chirping, a sneeze, a cough, an airplane, a shadow, most anything imaginable can justify a do-over. Once I called a do-over as I was in mid swing when Marvin yelled something about a hawk. He had just witnessed the bird of prey snatch up a squirrel. My do-over ended up no better that my first attempt. Funny though. Those same things can happen when the shot is a good one and no do-over is claimed. Time to tee it up and if the shot is a bad one, do-over please. FORE!

My favorite nephew, Brian Adams could use a do-over after his tee shot on The Fox's #6 hole at River Oaks in Myrtle Beach placed him was a challenging second shot. Oh yeah, and that is a fire ant mound.

Ed McMenamin, the founding father of the Tupelo Bay Boys earned his wings May 31, 2020 at age 77. He and his friend Martin, seeing that I was playing solo behind them, asked me to join them on the 3rd hole at Tupelo. Then began a friendship that spanned from February 2016 until his passing and weekly play at Tupelo Bay. We usually played two or three times weekly there with a 10:10 standing starting tee time. The Tupelo Boys miss Eddy. I included stories about him in the first book. For this one though, let me begin with a bit of 'Eddieology'. Ed had some unique terms and bit of quirkiness.

I noticed him adding a S on some of the holes beside his score. These signified he had been doomed by a sand trap shot. Over the years I began noticing S's with circles around them. I asked Ed why he had started circling the S's. These he explained stood for 'Stupid', meaning he had made a stupid shot on the hole. Too many 'stupids' made for a bad round. I interpreted these notations as Rain Man moments.

Ed was a tad bit superstitious. He warned me numerous times to never claim that my round had so far consisted of no three putts. If I did, I would surely three putt and his prophecy, a Grasshopper learning moment, usually came to pass. Ed believed that if you continued doing the same thing you would continue having the same results. Makes sense.

If I rode in the cart with Ed, it was guaranteed that he would be the driver. I do not think he knew how to miss potholes on the cart path or fairways. In wet conditions he seemed to always park the cart so that I either stepped into a mud hole when exiting the cart or a deep puddle rested behind the cart at my golf bag. Intentional? Ed tended to pull close to the greens and had been warned many times by the rangers for doing so. He sported at handicap flag on the cart that warranted him a few liberties, but Ed took to the max despite the frequent warnings. Eventually in early 2020 during a round I had missed, the club pro and gold course manager had finally reached that last straw and revoked his handicap privileges and would no longer issue him the flag. He blamed me for kidding him in front of some of workers. I would have none of that telling him he had been caught too many times disobeying the warnings. Most courses would have kicked him off after two or three times if ignoring them. Ed was Ed. What can I say?

Ed always had some joke to tell, old school most of them. He once proclaimed that he had not talked to his wife in six months saying he didn't want to interrupt her.

Ed believed in trying what supposedly worked for others. Golf professional Moe Norman had struck his fancy. Be like Moe. He had perfected a swing that Ed tried to mimic. His version of the Moe swing unfortunately more ended up like Moe Howard of the Three Stooges. He got on a Ben Hogan kick once as well. Ben there, did not work as illustrated. Moe, Ben and Curly Ed, stooges on the fairways.

Playing partners Marvin, Carl and I were playing golf at Tupelo one morning without Ed. He had just gotten home from the hospital after leg surgery, an infection, and an extended stay. Marvin received a text from an Ed family member stating Ed had just died after experiencing breathing problems that had sent him back to the hospital. The time was 11:40 that morning. We all wondered if Ed had taken his last breath at our usual 10:10 starting time. Ed loved playing the game. It was his only outlet. We still miss our dear friend.

My last Photo of Ed 2020 @ Tupelo Bay before his Illness and before the Covid Outbreak

Judy (John's wife), Jersey John and Ed Selfie 2020 @ Tupelo Bay

August 13, 2020, we played the memorial Eddy round at Tupelo Bay. In his memory we did a morning tee time. While sad, we payed our respect to the Tupelo Bay Boy's founding father. It was a bit of a double-sided sword for me as this would also be the final round playing with fellow member Marvin Jose, slated to move to West Virginia later in the month. Bloody Carl and Dodd Smith rounded out our foursome. Only our friend, Jersey John could not make it for the last ride because he was in New Jersey. Still in the middle of the pandemic and golf's adaptation of protective measures, Marvin and I broke rank after the round and shook hands one last time. Tupelo will never be the same. See you on the other side Ed.

These next ones are snippets from various rounds. Worth mentioning just because I want to so say I. One round that didn't go my way occurred on a Sunday afternoon. I proclaimed it the Black Sabbath Round, dark times, and equally devilish errant shots. I even added one to my bucket list by hitting a light mounted high on a pole. I have hit almost anything one can hit on or near a golf course: people in other groups, people in my group, cars, condos, swimming pools, tee markers, birds. My longest drive was a Tin Cup moment my ball bouncing down highway 544, a four-lane road at the beach. No telling where it ended up if a vehicle didn't jump in its way.

Bloody Carl earned his nick name for being a free bleeder if he got a nick or scratch. We elevated the nickname status when he forgot to change from his street shoes to his gold shoes. He was wearing his white tennis shoes that day. It must have brought him instant good luck. He sunk a putt from many yards off the green for a par. Other miraculous shots were so noted during the round. Billy White Shoes reincarnated. I must also add that Carl is a certified head banger. Nope. Music had nothing to do with it. He tends to bang his head often during the rounds getting in or out of the golf cart. His record stands at five times for one round. You will find Carl numerous times in many chapters in the Endless Mulligan. Worth reading, I must admit.

At River Oaks we found ourselves with a rare fivesome. While waiting for his son-in-law and nephew to arrive, Dodd explains how he now buys his reading glasses at the Dollar Tree because he is always misplacing them. He used to purchase them in 8-packs until he discovered the cheaper dollar versions. His son-in-law arrives and as if choreographed, hands Dodd a pair of reading glasses he had left in his truck. Bloody Carl lays claim to using a Miracle Club after several save shots. I told him he needed a miracle worker to help with his round. Dodd hoped for a goose save as his ball headed toward the lake. Not to be though. It is tough to keep up with a fivesome on the fairways, but with temperatures in triple figures heat index wise, we managed to survive the round.

Do-overs can be quite hurtful as we learned on the River Oaks' Bear course. I was standing over my chip shot to the green on a par 3 when

Bloody Carl strolls into my path as I hit the ball. Perfect shot foiled by his butt. Same hole, a minute later, we waved a single through. I yelled for Carl to stay put where he was on the opposite of the green. Nope. He walks across the green as the golfer is tagging his tee shot. Yep. You got it. The ball hits Carl in the top of his head. Seeing stars, he has now been hit twice on the same hole, butt then head, a new record. Death lurks at every turn and shot. On a previous round, Tom Marsh almost runs me over with a cart, pressing his foot on the gas instead of the brake as he approached me. Payback, later during round I nailed him with a line drive chip shot while he was standing where he shouldn't be standing, by a greenside bunker directly ahead of me. Luckily for me, he assisted with a sand save the ball careening off his foot. Yes, there are hazards on golf courses. Not all can be categorized as bunkers and ponds.

I now move to the foggiest round I have ever played. No. I am not referring to my state of mind. Wachesaw East golf course had been the scene of the Category 4 short story in the Mulligan book. This time an even eerier occurrence set the stage for the round. It was December 9, 2019, playing partners Jersey John and Marvis Jose (Tupelo Bay Boys) and Marvin's nephew waited out a first ever fog delay. Rain delays, frost delays, yes but a fog delay, never. Our original morning start drifted as did the fog into a new PM tee time. Even then, the afternoon fog remained thick and hugging the ground. I am estimating that our ball disappeared into the blanket a mere 40 or 50 yards off the tee box. This posed issues, unable to see the best or worst shots. I thought that a production crew might be filming reboots of *The Fog* or *The Mist*. Something foreboding and ominous might be lurking in the fairways, something more terrifying than bunkers or water hazards. The song Werewolves of London humming inside my head. The fog didn't begin to lift until the back 9, midafternoon. Jersey John developed a new technique that day, first addressing his ball with an affectionate 'I love You' before striking it. Later he demonstrated to us a unique way to hold his putter while chipping, resting it in his butt crack, earning him a new nickname, Mister Butt Tuck. Later a local meteorologist remarked how an odd weather pattern had introduced the weird fog phenomenon to the Grand Strand.

Jersey John Teeing it up in Breaking Fog

And then there was the Great American Oreo Challenge. I met West Virginian Tom Marsh in 2019 during our church's annual sponsorship for Snowbirds and Seagulls. This is a program for winter vacationers (Snowbirds) on the Grand Strand to have fellowship with locals (Seagulls) from our church, First Methodist, located near the ocean. Our church is known as the church with a heart in the heart of Myrtle Beach. We have eight Tuesdays of golf starting in January and a Thursday brunch program that lasts through March for visitors and church members. Tom and I became friends, more like brothers. We began playing weekly days other than the Tuesday events. Friendly competition warranted an equally friendly wager. But I must recap the setup as previously documented in the Mulligan book. Tom provided a wealth of material for it.

During the first round he and I ever played together Tom broke out a pack of Oreos in the back nine at the Arrowhead Golf Course. He was my riding buddy. As he finished his cookies, he looked over at me and asked if he had any Oreo residue in the corners of his mouth, further explaining that it seemed to accumulate there. I nodded and reached over, like mama used to do me, and wiped it from his mouth with my fingers. Is that bonding or what? That incident became a running joke, told numerous times, and documented in the book. Later that year we took a trip to Princeton, West Virginia where Tom and I played a golf round on his home turf. It was then that he sprung the mirror on me. He had started carrying a compact in his golf bag so that he could inspect for cookie crumbs. Yes. That's in the book as well.

In 2020 when he and Laura returned to the beach for three months, I suggested that we up our little friendly competition. The one who won the most rounds during their stay would win the ultimate prize, Double Stuff Oreos. We began our first round at Beachwood Golf Couse accompanied by Bloody Carl and Little Gooberhead. You must read the Endless Mulligan to see how Eric earned this nickname. I won the first outing. Next up, Tupelo Bay and Tom Marsh was up by 3 strokes at the turn. I mounted a challenge parring one hole and birding two to tie with two holes remaining. I made a double bogey on #17 as he made boggy to take a one stroke lead into the last hole. We both greened our tee shots on the short par 4. He two putts for a bird and I one putt for an eagle tying the round. As rounds progressed, I had built a 3-1-1 lead.

Next, we are at a course at Sunset Beach in North Carolina. This is where we discover a new form of do-over. Bloody Carl claims one of our shadows distracted him during his tee shot and takes a do-over. Carl, attempting to be helpful, moves our cart and his to greenside while we are in the fairway. After completing the hole, he drives off in our cart. Do-over! Don, another west Virginian has joined us. Don is a die hard republican and Carl is as liberal as they come. Don does his best during the round to distract and convert Bloody Carl. Tom Marsh takes the round. My lead is shrinking.

River Oaks offers more opportunities. Again Carl, Don and Tom are my playing partners. Don explains the game of golf stating that golf is a mere acronym for Gentleman Only Ladies Forbidden. Glad no women were around when he did. Don also expanded on the decision that landed him the name Donald 'Duck'. He was named by his grandmother in 1943 just five years after Walt Disney introduced Donald Duck to the world. On the first tee box, Tom Marsh loses the grip during his backswing sending the club dangerously in our direction. Luckily, no casualties. Not to be outdone, on the 18th fairway Don parks his and Tom's cart to the left and ahead of me. What do I do? I tag a widow maker 3 wood sailing it over their cart. We survive the round thankfully, but Tom has now taken a 4-3-1 advantage in the Oreo Championship.

We managed a few more rounds before Covid-19 struck with two weeks remaining before Tom headed back to West Virginia. I did squeak out a win at Shaftsbury Glenn. Tom Marsh, now leading by two rounds 6-4-1, I conceded and awarded him the winning trophy. I took a hiatus from golf for 3 ½ months while Covid transformed and destroyed the world. When I did decide to play again, golf had undergone changes to ensure our safety. One person per cart, load your own golf bag, do not remove the flag on the greens, no rakes in sand traps and no cart girl.

Tom Marsh and Oreo Trophy

Red Jeep on the Beach
A Hurricane Dorian Mystery

September 6, 2019 as Hurricane Dorian approached Myrtle Beach, we became national news and not because of the hurricane. A red jeep was spotted on the beach, abandoned as Dorian approached the coast. It remained on the beach until the hurricane passed. Onlookers and news hounds alike embraced the perilous predicament of the jeep. Social media was abuzz with photographs and scenarios for the beached jeep. A bagpiper arrived on the scene after the storm and played Amazing Grace and then Taps. It was portrayed as the greatest vehicle incident since the slow-moving pursuit of O.J. Simpson in the white Bronco. Hours upon hours of national coverage were shown as the jeep was battered in the ocean surf. Many spoofs were presented on social media. One stood out; a kid reporter pretending to be on the scene with his toy vehicle. Speculation on how the jeep became stranded ran the gambit. Eventually, the owner came forward and claimed a cousin had borrowed the jeep and had decided to drive onto the beach to snap photos of the sunset and had gotten stuck. The cousin abandoned it when emergency personnel refused to tow it due to the pending hurricane. The infamous red jeep was finally rescued and went on tour traveling to local businesses to raise money for hurricane victims. The red jeep instantly obtained celebrity status.

Sleeping Beauties Caught in the Act

I have had this knack for capturing nappers on camera. Don't know why but I have always been fascinated with these little gems, life caught in precarious situations. These are some of those pictorial nostalgic moments caught in still frame spanning probably pert near fifty years if I had to take a guess. Some nappers are better than others as you will soon see in my little montage.

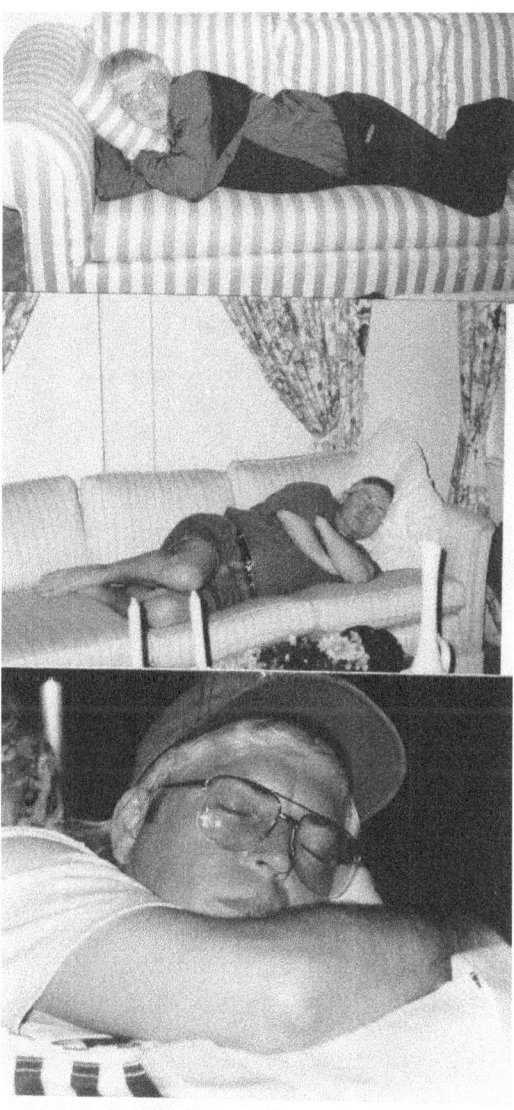

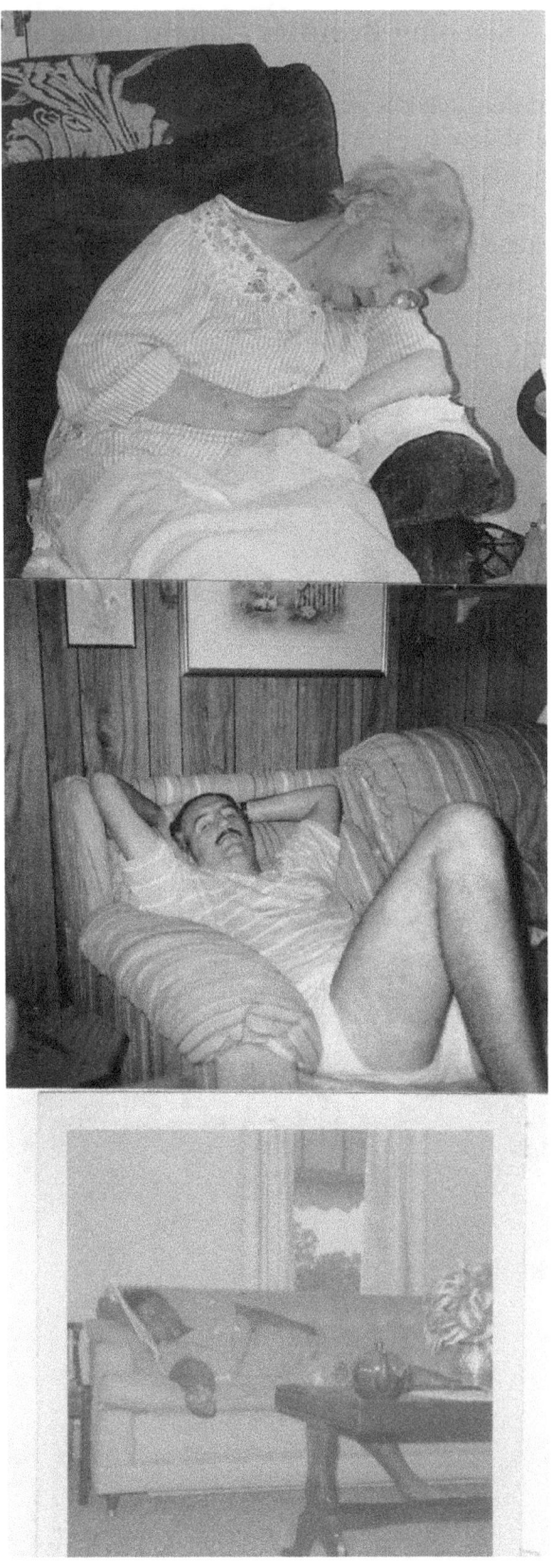

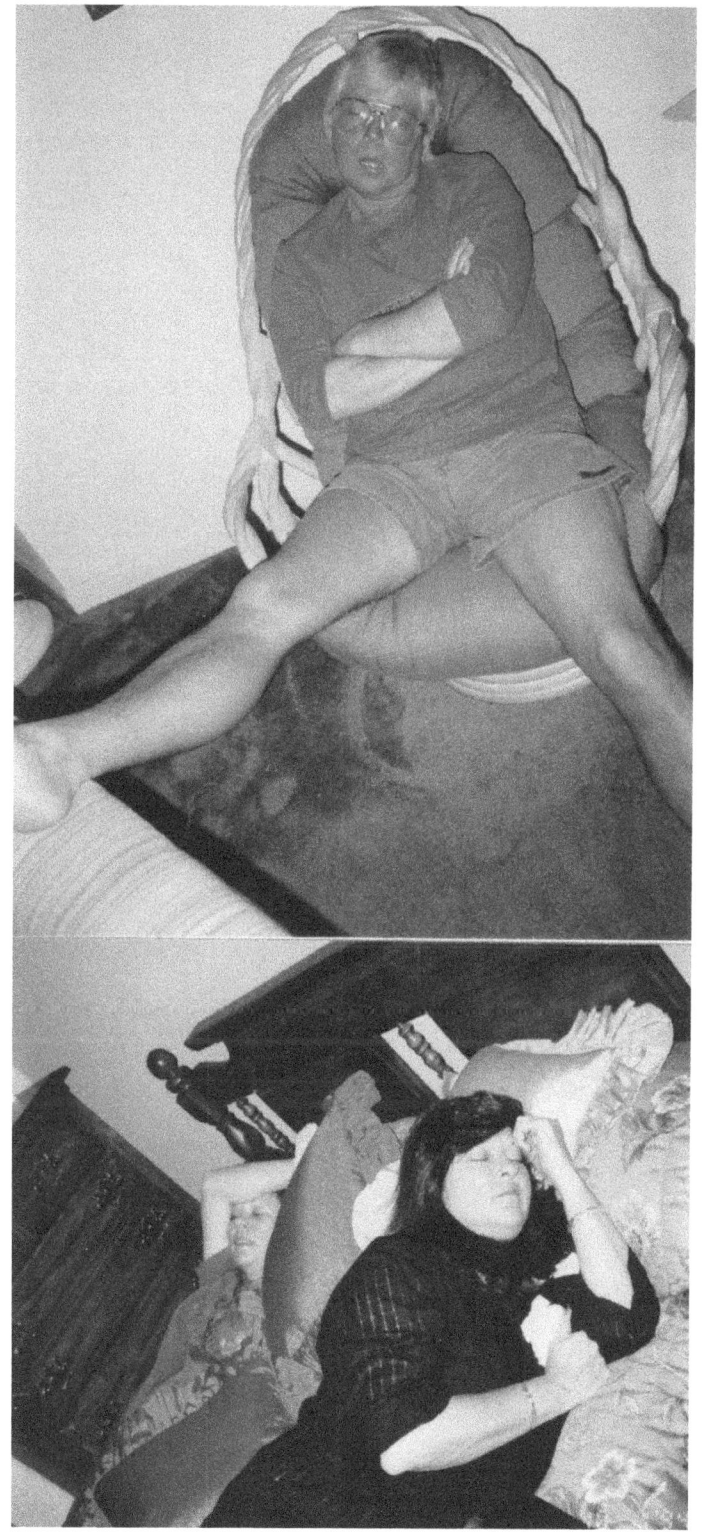

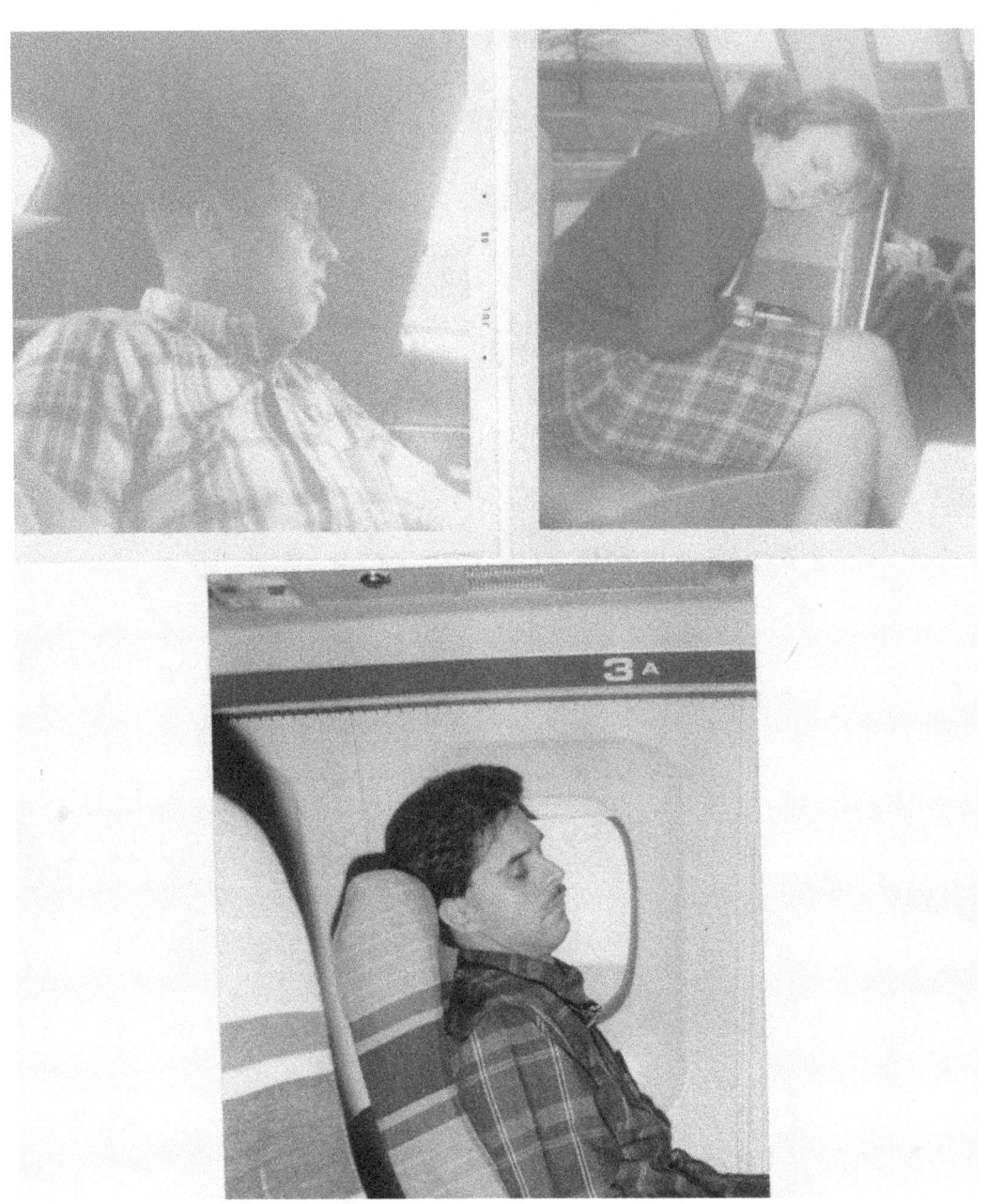

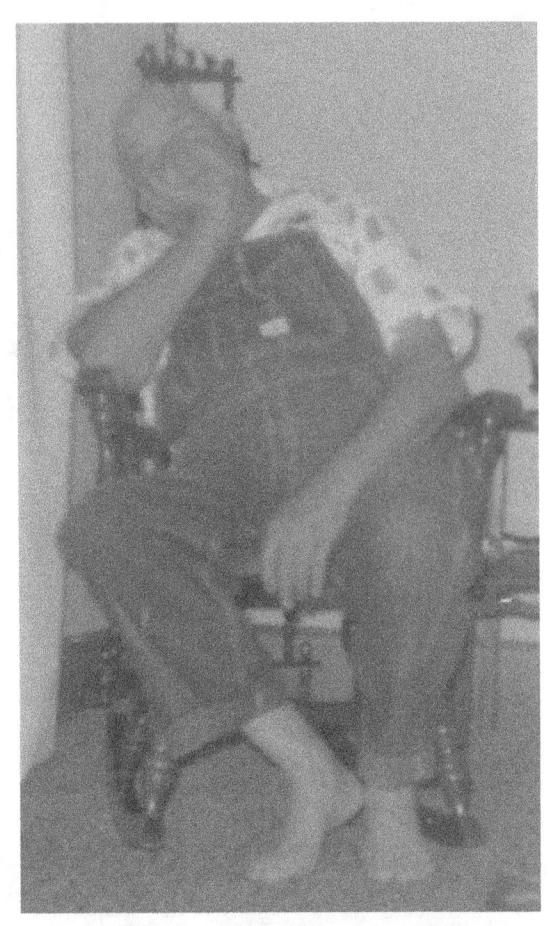

Perfect Pair, Nice'uns in their Day

Things come in pairs for a reason. You need both to complete the set. One is typically not enough without the other. Try wearing just one shoe all day. While pants and underwear are often referred to as pairs, they equal just one item a piece, not two. Hats and shirts for instance; you wouldn't wear a pair of hats or shirts, would you. Doesn't exactly roll off your tongue, does it? Gloves come in pairs but so does a pair of glasses. Makes you want to scream if you really think about it.

Okay. I confess. This isn't exactly a nostalgic moment, but it is something most of us can relate to from any generation and walk of life. Call it author preference or something. Hang with me. It might be helpful in an ole T. Allen twisted way. If not, my bad, but it is what it is as my friend Mike says.

New House Rule: When doing the laundry and one shy of a pair of socks shows up in the dryer, leave the one sock on the dryer until its matching one shows up. It seems easy enough to digest if you maintain low expectations. Soon there are three pairs of pair-less socks resting on the dryer. None match the other, so mixing and matching is not a viable option; that is unless you decide to become a trend setter and raise the fashion bar.

Question: Are you sure both socks entered the washer and made a similar trip to the dryer?

Yeah, maybe, sort of…I wasn't really paying attention. Matching them up and/or pre-counting is not part of the equation. Checks and balances happen after due process of the cleaning and during cycles. Can a sock exit the washer via the drain line? I have no proof or evidence to support it. Facts, just give me the facts. It seems to me that if this were possible, the manufacturers would have fixed the flaw by now. Or maybe they are part of the conspiracy. Appliance manufacturers and sock distributors are in cahoots. It boosts the economy or something. Same applies to purchasing golf balls. You really just rent them. Sooner or later you will lose them too.

Plausible Deniability:

Black holes, worm holes, time warps or parallel dimensions could hold the key to the mystery. These theories don't hold up in court though. Why don't these phenomena snatch up other articles of clothing? I for one am not missing any pants, shirts or underwear. Towels, sheets nor wash clothes ever vanish into thin air. Does this mean that the entity only has insatiable appétit for socks or is the hole too small for other objects to pass through? Process of elimination, the washer or dryer is guilty until proven innocent. Either that or we're back to black holes, worm holes, time warps or parallel dimensions. Days have passed and searches haven't revealed the location of those missing in action. Sock disappearances are the perfect scenario for episodes of *In Search Of, America's Most Wanted, Myth Busters, and Stranger than Truth or* maybe *Finding Big Foot and My Other Sock.*

Observation: Why is it always those socks that perfectly match a specific pair of pants that go AWOL? Both pants legs are in one piece, even though the dryer has this uncanny ability to turn one or both inside out. What's with that? Same thing happens to shirts. Landry devices possessed or possessing a superior intelligence; possibly they are even **extraterrestrial life forms.**

Is it possible that Captain Kirk from the Star Trek's Enterprise is having socks transported on board but, if so, why not beam up the pair, Scotty? Maybe our socks are being traded to Klingons. Miss matched foot apparel deters from an ugly puss of a face, cloaking equally ugly feet. Sometimes you just must reach for the stars when seeking explanations.

Explanation: Maybe this is nature's way of culling the thread worn and hole riddled socks. The weak are supposed to be weeded out to make for a healthier herd. Not buying it, one surviving sock contributes nothing to the quality of other socks residing in the ole sock drawer. Good or new socks do go missing, don't they?

Corporate Intervention: Each pair of socks is designed with a unique genetic code and an embedded expiration date. When the pair reaches their life cycle, one dissolves or disintegrates. This is a sure thing insurance policy for sock manufacturers, guaranteeing the customer will initiate a new purchase. Back to that conspiracy theory concept, maybe detergent makers are responsible, some secret ingredient that can dissolve one sock per load.

I Don't Know: Someone or something is obviously responsible for the missing socks. *I don't Know Who* did it is the pat answer.

Easier Solution to the Evil: Jeopardy Category…socks for $200…take the pair, please, the complete pair each time; not one from each. Oddly, have you ever had that happen before? I can never ever remember both pairs of the sock going missing while washing and drying a load of laundry. You would think that at some point it should happen. Possibly it has. Think about it. Would you really pay any attention if the pair disappeared? One there, one not, is usually the tip-off there is something rotten in Denmark. Sure, eventually you might notice the pair missing but you would never blame it on the laundry eaters. You'd shrug and think they'd eventually show up, maybe in another drawer.

Prevention through Innovation: Staple, tie, affix each pair together before allowing them to undergo the vicious, merciless process. Just as I got my entrepreneur inventive juices flowing, a quest to design and develop such an item, patent it and then make a fortune, I inquired through Google first. To my shock, several items existed on the internet to do just that. I might just have to purchase one of these options, a way to preserve my sanity and a save matching socks. My gut tells me that the same ones responsible for stealing them probably came up with the solution. Remember radar to apprehend speeders and radar detectors to beat the system and detect those hiding in ambush. Some say both devices were made by the same company.

Make a Joyful noise: Not to worry, the Calvary is on the way. I'm going to bite the bullet and buy some of those new-fangled sock clips. A fine pair mine will make, nice'uns anchoring each foot once again. Real men never discard socks until the holes appear above shoe level or toss underwear until the elastic is shot and it ends up below our butt cheeks inside our britches making us have that commando feeling. Underwear, another story…don't even get me started.

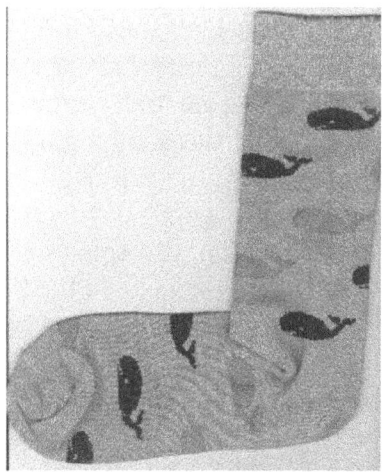

Sole Survivor or Maybe a 'Save the Whales' Moment

Politically Incorrect

WARNING---READERS BEWARE!

This is an editorial from my most inner thoughts. Mine may not agree with yours, but I guess that's more your issue than mine. Mine are not meant to influence yours. They are mere opinions and my spin on the subject matter. Last chance! Cease your reading now or continue and humor me. Be advised though, my thoughts are not intended to provoke any violence or retaliation. There's already enough hatred being spewed out there. My opinions, the way I choose to view things and live my life is my choice. Yours are yours. I'll not attack you physically or verbally. Free speech, free country does not give you or me the right to attack anyone who doesn't believe what we believe. With that, this is your last chance. Stop or continue to read, your choice. And again, this isn't exactly nostalgia, but it is closer to being so than the sock it to me round you just finished reading.

My life was much less complicated and freer of stress when I didn't follow politics and allow it to dominate my world. What changed you might ask. I did. I allowed politics to slither through a crack in my otherwise closed door and mind. For the first forty-seven years of my life I remained on the sidelines, a nonparticipant and nonvoter in our democracy. My choice, I just wasn't interested in politics or the political process. I never voiced my opinion one way or the other in local or federal government. My thinking was simple. If I didn't cast a vote, then I didn't have the right to grumble and moan about the political winds blowing debris in my face. Fact, I shied away from debates, discussions and the hoopla surrounding which party did what and why and the impact it might have on our welfare. I was neutral, neither a democrat nor republican nor any one of those other parties claiming this or that. I don't think the far right or left existed in my time before politics. I do not recall liberalism or conservatism, but I really wasn't paying that much attention. Seems I do recall socialism and communism being tossed out in some of my high school classes. Back then they taught the truth, actual history. Teachers did not make a political stance and try to sway our way of thinking.

My humble opinion remained the same. Toss the democrats and republicans in a paper bag and shake it up thoroughly. Empty the contents and try to tell one from the other. I don't think you can. Promises made, most not kept. My interaction in the political arena really went no further than these thoughts. And no, I wasn't going to bring it up or defend my position. I just left well enough alone. Thinking back now, I'm not even sure which side of the political isle my parents resided. I have no real memory of politics being openly discussed around the dinner table, the den or any place in my upbringing. It didn't interest me, so I never asked. I don't recall my folks encouraging me to register to vote when I reached voting age. It just seemed to be a nonissue. Maybe that's why the urge to vote never struck me. My life revolved around me and the stuff I enjoyed doing. Politics never invaded my thought process. Life was good for the most part without it.

No, my life was not perfect growing up as a kid in the 50s and 60s but I lived it normally as far as I remember. I played with toy guns and shot a lot of my friends. None of them died. In fact, I was shot more times than I can count too. Sometimes I was the bad guy. Other times I was the good guy. Bad and good were equal in the imaginary playground. Sometimes I was an Indian. Other times I was a cowboy. I liked being the Indian. There was nothing bad or disrespectful about being an Indian, even when I got shot by the cowboys. Often, we were soldiers, fighting other soldiers on our backyard battlefield. Dirt clods were our grenades. Oh yeah, and they hurt if you were hit by them. We mouthed imaginary explosions and died valiant deaths. We didn't receive Bronze Stars or Purple Hearts, but then again, we sprung back to life to participate in the next war on the battlefield when playing soldier was the flavor for the afternoon.

In school those who excelled were recognized as being the smart ones. I was not offended by the categorizing and pecking order. It was an equal opportunity situation. Study hard, and you, too, would be recognized. Be a flunky and live the life of a flunky. Or just ride down the middle of the road like me and not worry much about how others perceived me. It wasn't politically incorrect to be who you chose to be. Teachers mostly divvied out the grades you deserved. If you deserved an 'A', you got one. Those who got the failing grades earned them as well. Kids weren't lumped into one noncompetitive category. We were and are still all different. I wasn't raised to expect to get stuff handed to me on a silver platter. If you wanted it badly enough, you better be prepared to work for it. Life wasn't fair and it wasn't intended to be. Merit meant something. Being a winner wasn't an evil concept. Those choosing to be slackers weren't given a free pass, and those without the ability to excel weren't rewarded to keep from hurting their feelings. The world didn't implode because of these differences.

I didn't choose to wear the 'in clothes', the name brands, the preppy look; and not because my folks couldn't afford it if I would have asked. It wasn't important to my existence and me just being me. Clothes didn't make the boy as far as I was concerned. As I grew older, I remained true to these values. As a teenager and now as an adult my preferences haven't changed. I'm a bargain hunter and if the price is right, I make the purchase. What I end up with has nothing to do with making a statement or trying to wow somebody. Take me or leave me. It's really your choice and not mine. I don't require friends determined by clique rules. I never participated in cliques while in high school. Being in one did not make me a better person or instill a sense of feel good superiority. To each, his own, I say; as in politics, I just stayed out of the theatrics. I avoid drama at all cost.

I didn't attend college. Not because I couldn't. Instead, I decided to try marriage. I took a few courses at the local technical school. Lack of securing a degree of some sort didn't derail me. I just progressed the old fashion way, by merit and worth. I started my full-time trek into the world of the working within the walls of the manufacturing industry. I became a slitter, a mere machine operator and quickly became good at it. A few years later I tossed my hat in the ring for an open quality inspector position. After the interviewing process I was chosen over the others who had applied. I eventually worked my way from the night shift to the day shift and became recognized unofficially as the inspector that would train new inspectors. Hard work positioned me for assuming the role of quality technician, a newly created position. This would eventually be the steppingstone for me becoming the official leader, a quality supervisor. My peers now reported to me. Sometimes that can be a difficult transition but, in my case, I just treated it as any other opportunity. What does this have to do with being politically correct, you might ask. It doesn't.

That's the point. I wasn't promoted through these various positions because I was a college graduate or because I was affiliated with a workforce clique. I demonstrated that I was willing to work in each position and the folks I worked for saw my worth based on experience and work ethics. I lobbied this into positions elsewhere as a quality manager and quality engineer and even served as an operations manager. I was hired or promoted based on my experience. I have always said that I never hung my hat on job titles. In fact, it is my opinion that throughout my working career within the quality circle, I have done a little bit of everything and all positions required some combination of it. In the world of the politically correct that is now taboo, sad but true. It's frowned upon if you excel and can afford the creature comforts you have worked so hard to get. Those choosing not to carve their own path feel entitled to portions of mine or those who have succeeded in life. Politicians are eager to take our money and give it to others while they are exempt to the laws they pose on us.

I make this point, referring to the silver platter analogy. To survive or excel in this world means you must compete and show those who grade you that you are worthy. Sorry, cupcakes, this means that there are winners and yes, losers. Everyone doesn't get or deserve a passing grade, a participation trophy or free path to the next round. Real coaches play their best players. They do this to win, not to be fair to all the other players on the roster. Today though a society of entitled are being nurtured. They can't face disappointment, failure or interaction with others who don't share their opinions. The sensitivity level is off the charts. The PC police are out to get everyone. Phrases, words, symbols ending in feeding frenzy reactions, violence and this incredible desire to rewrite or wipe out history simply because they don't like it or agree with how it happened. Suck it up. It happened. Tearing down monuments, statues, ripping apart books and recognized symbols do not change anything except in your fragile little minds. History has good and bad points. Learning from the past is what makes us stronger. Hugging up to a lama or a pony are just placebos on the grandest scale for those wishing to live in a perfect and make-believe world.

I am just getting started, snowflakes. I only use this term because this is the term that labels those who can't cope with a world of opinions. God is being pushed out of every aspect of our lives. He has been booted out of school. In my time long forgotten, Wednesdays were a day we assembled in the gymnasium to listen to a different minister from one of the town's churches. We didn't have a meltdown or rave and rant because religion was being crammed down our throats. It didn't matter if the affiliation was that of Baptist, Methodist, Lutheran or any other, we listened and remained respectful. There was no war waged against Christianity, at least not where I lived. In an era before it had a name, the world of the politically correct were already sowing their seeds. Those on the politically incorrect side of the fence envisioned where this was heading.

In school we started our mornings standing for the flag in each classroom and pledging our allegiance while our national anthem blasted over the speaker system. No one took a knee or remained seated. First of all, we just didn't. Second of all, we knew better. Free protest, I don't think so. Our teachers would have delivered just punishment and then our parents would have finished what the teacher had started. I can't recall a kid ever disrespecting the flag, the pledge and for which it stands. I was a Cub and Boy Scout. We did our pledges there too. And yes, boys were scouts. The girls had their Brownie and Girl Scout equals. We knew the difference and didn't want to be in the one where we didn't belong. I am spewing rhetoric that most have heard, when those listening allow it to be heard. That's just it. We are supposed to live in a world of free speech and free opinions. We deserve the right to agree or disagree but not to attack those who don't believe as we do.

There is nothing wrong with protesting in an organized and safe manner. Wearing masks, burning property, and attacking those who don't believe as you do are wrong on every level. I say those who wear mask and promote violence are cowards or should be labeled terrorists. Those condoning this behavior or not speaking up to call out those who do make you as bad, if not worse, than those perpetrating the crimes. And yes, I call these crimes. Setting fires, beating people and cursing with hateful rhetoric are just that. You can't pretty it up and you can't justify the actions.

Christmas, where do I begin? Those who do not believe in it want the rest of us not to believe in it or support it. Years ago, they tried instilling in us that we should call it X-mas, crossing out the Christ part. Fat chance that was going to work, right? Then the new politically correct approach began. They tried to convince us to just say Happy Holiday and not Merry Christmas. The Christmas tree should be the holiday tree to make it more acceptable to everyone. It's the Christmas holiday not the Holiday holiday. Even the diehards knew better than to pursue canceling Christmas as a paid holiday. You really want to see a bunch of angry Americans. Try taking away their Christmas holiday and time off from work. Then nativity displays became offensive for those too sensitive to embrace Christ's birth. God forbid if anything Christian or Christmas related was discovered on government property. As kids, we looked forward to exchanging Christmas cards and gifts but in schools today, but children cannot embrace this concept today. Saying Lord in the wrong venue will set the crazies off. Simple phrases such as giving out a cordial 'bless you' after a sneeze derails those who are set on removing all references to religion. And yes, I called these people crazy. Sorry, I don't live in that world of incredible and undesirable sensitivity. I do not have to reach out to a little lama or visit a petting zoo if my opinions unleash stressful and unbearable emotions. Oh, give me back those days of my youth.

Now, those who don't wish for us to have our beliefs or opinions are attacking Christmas and other longtime favorite stories, movies, Disney flicks, various songs and any symbolic references that just launch them into a hissy fit. *Peanuts, Charlie Brown* and his gang's Thanksgiving special are racist. The *Rudolph the Reindeer* animated feature promotes bullying. Disney's *The Little Mermaid, Cinderella* and *Snow White*, along with the song Baby *It's Cold Outside*, somehow degrade women. Where's the outcry for video games promoting killing and worse. Why was there no outrage for the reindeer that ran over grandma? *Homer Simpson* is an acceptable iconic cartoon. Mean Birds doesn't disturb those who flip out over something as trivial as Animal Cracker animals being depicted in cages. Heaven help us for saying "beating a dead horse" or "bringing home the bacon'. Horses and pigs are not protesting our use of these phrases. The PC police really do need to get beyond overusing their sensitivity meters. We stay out of your business. Why not practice staying out of ours? In American we have the right to be different without persecution.

I might as well cover all the sensitive topics while I'm at it in my nonintrusive, nonviolent, good old fashion, tell it like it is format. Please don't read my thoughts if they offend you, send you over the edge or instill in you a sudden urge to harm and maim me. You do have the right to disagree though. I respect your right. Here goes. I was raised to understand that there was a difference in girls and boys, men and women, males and females. No, not all of us are created equally but the differences are obvious, size put aside. I was taught to read the signs and placards on the restroom doors. Men use the ones designated for them. Females follow the same rules. There is no place for opposite sexes in the other restrooms. I'm sorry. There really aren't a zillion other species in the human world. Fine, some feel they are this or that and have a need to dress in clothing that defines them. A male feeling like a female is still a male and he does not belong in the women's restroom. Same goes for a woman insistent on being a man. And you can choose the mate that best suits your lifestyle. I will stay out of your business and you can do whatever floats your boat. I require no details of your relationships, straight or gay. What you do and how you live your life is your choice, not mine. I simply draw the line when you feel it is your right to force your beliefs, your lifestyles on me. I don't need your business being part of mine and I promise I will not share mine or flaunt it in your face. And for goodness sake, get over this belief that your way is the only way we are supposed to view the world. My opinion and choices are mine. Yours are yours. It's really no more complicated than that.

I keep forgetting, I am living in the past, in that world before the PC Gestapo arrived. Okay, let's paint the canvas the way many wish to portray it. Let's say the world as we know it no longer exists because those who think they should determine how we think, how we live and what we can and can't do have totally ruined it. Here's a glance into our future if we don't band PC now.

A Jurassic style electrical fence on our Mexico and Canada borders with armed guards prevent USA citizens from leaving the country. No longer is anyone trying to come into this United States. They are already here and the changes they have made have doomed them. Military patrol both coasts to keep defectors from escaping. Our President is a Chinese-Hispanic American and the VP is Venezuelan-American. Socialism reigns strong. China owns us financially. Redistribution of wealth is a mere fantasy. There are no wealthy left. The government has bled them into extinction. Healthcare for all has imploded. Governmental panels monitor individuals and cull those who are no longer healthy or beneficial for the greater good. Retirement, enjoying the best years of your life doesn't exist. The life expectancy is thirty. Opposite sex marriage or interaction is against the law, punishable by death. Over population is a thing of the past. Prayer of any kind is prohibited. You are allowed to worship those who have taken everything you once had. The collapse of society is a joyful phenomenal, no money, no personal weapons, no fast food joints. Sounds like a glorious ending, a script played over too often in the movies. Forget the zombies. The flesh eaters exist already in politics.

My life was so simple and less stressful before I allowed politics to ruin it. I voted for the first time when I was forty-eight, 2001 and for the second George Bush. I suppose that could make me a republican. I think I'm sticking with the lesser of two evils. I really don't fully trust anyone in government. Sadly, in 2001 I began for whatever reason, paying attention to some of the political rhetoric. Many of the movers and shakers made me nervous. If it's not broken don't try to fix it. Everything isn't perfect and it never will be, but I stand by my convictions. Things are not served on that silver platter. If you want it bad enough, you earn it. You are not entitled to anything. Oh, and by the way, there's no free stuff from the government. Government enjoys taking a hefty share from those who work giving it to those who don't. They take and they take, and they take even when it isn't theirs to take. Can you say social security, the money paid in for our future? They couldn't keep their greedy little hands off it. If we stole, we'd be in jail. The politicians make the rules and pass the laws that don't apply to them. Isn't this why the United States distanced itself from England? Boy, how soon we have forgotten the premise of government. I say toss them all out and start over. Those who force themselves on us passed laws on presidential term limits, yet they stay in office until they become feeble drooling feigns.

Oh yeah, walls, fences, and barriers work. Why are there walls and fences around all these rich and mighty Hollywood types and politicians? What are they afraid of? Walls and fences are used to keep criminals inside prisons. Walls and fences would help deter criminals from entering our country. But some argue they are just seeking a better life. Hey, when they cross our border illegally that labels them criminals. Once in, government gives them everything without earning the right to have it. There are legal means to entering this country. And let's embrace those who curse this country, toss rocks and other projectiles at those defending out borders. That really makes plenty of sense. Let these people in. We love all people. Give me a break. Oh yeah, let's forward this narrative by offering the criminal protection in sanctuary cities. If I were an American criminal I would be suing for equal rights. This is discrimination, plain and simple. Let's focus on the humane condition of criminals sneaking over our borders and forget the Americans who are harmed by this encroachment. Politicians are elected to promote and protect our interest, not to ensure illegal folks have more rights that we do. Shame on you who put them first and us second. Double shame on you who think we are bad because we feel we should be at the front of the line, not them. Quit giving them our money.

I suppose I was a bit too naïve, allowing myself to be pulled into the world of politics. I thought I was voting for presidents and politicians that represented us, the people of the United States. I was led to believe that they worked for us and their job was to ensure we lived in a safe and prosperous country. Something has gone terribly wrong with those we elect to political office who now think that people who are not citizens and enter our great country illegally deserve the benefits that we Americans pay for as our promised rite. If all you must do is sneak across the border and automatically be rewarded with free government support and welfare, then why aren't we as American citizens demanding the same treatment? I'm sorry. Paying for illegal personnel does not support what I was taught. We have people who struggle to make ends meet, many living month to month on their social security checks. We give it to the illegal ones without them having to earn it. Hey elected officials of this country, do you support and work for us or them? If the answer is both or you can't answer the question asked, then you do not deserve to be paid quite well to represent us, the American public. No, I'm no expert on politics but common sense tells me that we have a bunch of folks in Washington and local government that no longer work for us. Heck, they spend years serving and can't even make simple decisions or balance a budget. They steal our social security then worry how they are going to fund it. Oh yeah, they fund it by raising our taxes to pay for what they stole. If we did this or couldn't pay our debts, we would be behind bars. When they open their mouths, most just spew more false promises and blatant lies. Yep, I am politically incorrect and proud of it.

I admit that I watch too much news, tossed at me 24/7. I have heard the same crap from both sides of the aisles. These people can't compromise, can't balance a budget and want more and more of our money. I say let them live by the rules and laws they enforce on us. If they had to do this, I bet the process would run smoother and be better for all of us. As long as they have immunity from everything they see fit to punish us for, they'll continue to get away with murder. Yep, allowing politics in my life altered everything. Sometimes not knowing is better. Voting is a privilege. Promises by those seeking our votes shouldn't lie to us. Shake them up in that sack and what comes out looks the same and acts the same, no difference in my book. That's it for me, not because there is nothing else to say. It's just pointless and doesn't change a thing in the life of one already beat, battered and ruined. There will be no bloodletting, no violent actions and no f-bombs threatening those who do not share my opinions. Live your lives peacefully and I'll live mine the same. May the best one win? Oops, I forget, winning is not an option in the world of those who only wish to participate equally and have a free ride. Free, meaning that they don't have to pay for their luxuries. Those who work and the politicians who continue to tax and take are the ones who serve up heaps of helpings on that silver platter.

If I offended anyone, remember I warned you. You should have stopped reading this segment at the reader beware warning and at *my life was much less complicated and freer of stress when I didn't follow politics and allow it to dominate my world.* God bless American and those who just don't get it. Yeah, I said the 'bless' word and I do believe in God. If you don't, you don't know what you are missing. But that's your choice, isn't it? If ever you change your mind you have an open invitation to my church, no strings attached. Like the iconic commercial goes, 'Try it. You might like It.' Just a friendly invitation. I'm not forcing my beliefs on you. I've not always had a relationship with God either. But when I did finally see the light, I knew God was Good. Life is Good too if you learn to really enjoy it. There's nothing more miserable than being miserable all the time. Life is too short to not embrace and enjoy it. My opinion, my life, you do what floats or sinks your boat. Please refrain from harming or abusing those that don't meet your narrative. Love thy neighbor isn't a bad concept. Forgiveness is a wonderful concept too. Okay. I'm done for now and return you to your regularly scheduled program.

This concludes more of my nostalgic nonsense. I love who I am and the life I have lived, the good, the bad and the ugly. Could I have done better? Sure. We all can if we choose to do so. Life is full of choices and options. That's why I now declare this 'The End' No, not the end of the world as we know it but the end of this book. 'The End' will happen when it happens. Be ready for it; my choice, not yours.

Well, maybe is not quite the end of my ending after all with the zombie apocalypse upon us or it's the version the new media is painting. Before closing this chapter and book, I find myself sitting here pondering catastrophic consequences. It's March 17, 2020 and the world as we have known has come to a screeching and unexpected halt. No, zombies haven't decimated our world but something just as deadly, at least by the painted consequences, has all but consumed us. To be determined how this one will play out, but for now it has impacted everything. Every sporting event even the sports themselves have been canceled indefinitely. No more PGA, NCAA Basketball Tournament, no NASCAR racing, absolutely no sports are being played, period! Churches have canceled services. Schools and colleges are closed as well. Many restaurants and bars have closed. The travel industry has come to a full stop. The domino effect is unfathomable. And of all things, the crazies are hoarding toilet paper, paper towels and sanitizers. The stock market has plummeted daily, record lows; not something a retiree wants to witness.

This is an epic event, something out of a sci-fi horror movie, the end of the world as we know it. Can mankind survive? Scary is getting scarier by the day. Oh yeah, politics and news media frenzy are not helping an uncomfortable situation. I don't know where this might end and if it will end before I publish this book. Sadly, it is real and not something on the wishful nostalgic list. People are asked to stay away from people. Don't congregate in crowds larger than ten. Wash your hands wash your hands, wash your hands. COVID-19, the coronavirus that apparently originated in China has brought us to our knees. Speaking of, while on our knees, it's the perfect time for praying. Leaving this crisis in God's hands might be the only hope we really have.

Hopefully, we will look back on this and appreciate the lessons learned and we will have made the necessary adjustments to prevent it from happening again. Or, at the least, we will be better prepared. Nostalgia isn't always the product of a perfect childhood or wonderful memories. This one is indeed an ugly one with a yet to be determined ending. Again, I pray for the best. God is Good and works in mysterious and righteous ways and only He knows the outcome of this new virus wreaking havoc on a world ill prepared for it. I hope now that 'The End' means only the book's ending. For now, though, it is far from being over.

This is a little taste of Papa Tommy's poetry written in the 1988 nostalgic timeframe. I am no poet and indeed I know it. It was a bit of fun and silliness shared with these boys I so loved while spending time with them when life was much simpler.

For Greg Thomas (aka Sam), the boy who possessed so many identities then. Who would have ever guessed that he would transform into Sam, a name he didn't like in those days?

> Some people call me Sam.
> Some people call me Rat.
> Some people call me Greg.
> Let's put an end to that.
>
> What you may call me,
> May not be important to you.
> But I care what I am called
> And it's time you did too.
>
> Do I look like a Sam?
> I know I don't look like a rat.
> Why do you prefer to call me
> Names of this and that?
>
> Wonder if I called you
> Just any old name?
> Would you still like me,
> Or would you feel the same?
>
> So, let's get it straight
> For the very last time.
> My name is just Greg.
> Any other name is a crime.

For Scott Thomas, 'Eat Till You Pop' was written because this young man had a ravenous appetite and was quite proud of poking out his belly and patting it to flaunt it to everyone else. It was in no way meant to be cruel even though his brothers had affectionately nicknamed him Hog-Pig.

Food is this thing in the world
Says a Thomas Boy named Scott.
Eat two plates of food each meal
To see if your belly will pop.

It doesn't matter if you're hungry.
That's not why you neat so.
It's to see how big your belly is,
And can you really make it grow.

His stomach hangs over his pants,
And is hard and big as a rock.
He's proud of it when it's full.
And so sad when it is not.

Someday when he's grown,
And has a tummy still big.
He won't think he's so cute,
When other kids call him Hog-Pig.

Scott better learn to eat much less
Unless he wants to be that hog.
He'll be so huge and round
That he'll roll like a log.

It's not how much you eat,
But to simply eat right.
Eat small single portions
And not every single bite.

For Brandon Scott, the cousin to the Thomas boys, I wrote this little ditty in December 21, 1988. It was at the peek of reports from Bishopville, South Carolina of this legendary Lizard Man creature that had been allegedly spotted in the area. The creature had been wreaking havoc, attacking vehicles in yards at night, biting chrome fenders and bumpers. It had chased a young lad when he had stopped at night to change a flat tire. I had customed my poem numerous times and had addressed it to many other coworker's kids. This one was addressed to Brandon and was another version titled 'A Lizard Man Christmas'. He had received the letter via the mail and the tale had terrified him; enough said. I included a sketch of Lizard Man.

Santa is said to know
Who is naughty or nice.
For those who are naughty
Let me give you this advice.

Don't look for any presents
Underneath the Christmas Tree.
Keep your sneakers on your feet
And make the preparations to flee.

Only one creature will be heard
Stirring in your house that night.
With a mouthful of yellow teeth
You'll make a meal in a single bite.

It wears no fluffy red suit,
Only two glowing red eyes.
It has no flying reindeer
But when it runs it can fly.

From the corner of its mouth
There rests no smoking pipe.
Instead there's some chrome
From its last fender fight.

It has two hug green feet
That make tracks in the snow.
And once you have seen them
To Grandma's house you will go.

You might use jingle bells
To try to keep it away.
But it will be a silent night
If it decides it will stay.

Leaving milk and cookies
Will not do the trick.
It has those eyes on you
Because sweets make it sick.

Don't scream for your mama
Once you're in its sight.
It will take Mike Tyson
To help you with this fight.

All dressed in scales of green
From its ugly head to it toes.
It might grab you by your hand
And try to get you to go.

Unless you prefer a life
Of a fugitive on the run,
Best you refuse its invitation
And shoot it with a gun.

If all fails.
And you've done all you can.
Have a Merry Swampy Christmas
With Jolly Old Lizard Man.

Original Lizardman as drawn back then.

For Dale Thomas, the oldest and the best critter catcher of the bunch. I had tutored him well in the art of snatching up things that crawled, jumped or flew. It is titled 'Lizards and Frogs'.

Once there was a critter catcher,
that would catch lizards and frogs.
He would find them under rocks,
Or underneath some hollow logs.

This catcher of wild critters
Was big and had ad blonde hair.
His hair was worn in a spike
And he had a grip like a bear.

By day, no lizard was safe,
As he'd catch them with speed.
At night, came the frogs,
That he could grab with ease.

He'd collect all these creatures
In a terrarium made of glass.
It had rocks, shells and sand
That looked of the land of the past.

The problem with their new home
Was not the lack of a bed.
They had rocks and sand for this,
The trouble was they were not fed.

There was a creature of the woods
That had heard this sad tale.
It knew it was left up to it
To get them out of their glass jail.

This creature had cold green skin,
Sharp teeth and glowing red eyes.
It preferred chrome at meal time
Instead of bugs or house flies.

It knew it was up to it alone
To free his friends from Dale.
This catcher of all critters
May end up in his own glass jail.

Through the cloak of darkness
The rescue attempt began.
This was its job to do,
The one they called Lizard Man.

He watched as his Dale
Was outside and turning over rocks.
With swift and silent speed
It has its sharp claws cocked.

Lizard Man smiled at him
As it turned to carry him away.
"I've got a glass house for you,
And it's there you will stay.

Before carrying his blonde critter
To his new glass terrarium home,
He freed the lizards and frogs
To their life to hop and roam.

Deep in the depths of the swamp
You can hear a young boy's cry.
"Please give me grasshoppers and bugs
I'm so hungry I could die.

So, remember all of you kids,
Before you neglect any pets.
Lizard Man is watching you
And it'll get you, you can bet.

For Andy Thomas, second oldest and the most inquisitive of the bunch. He could wear me out questing everything under the sun. This piece is titled 'The Boy was a Why Monkey.' I often still call Andy 'Why Monkey' when we communicate on Facebook.

On a house resting on a hill
There lives a boy named Andy.
He as a very few front teeth
From earlier days of eating candy.

He wants to be a grow up
And repeats what grow-ups say.
He will mock them as they yell
And for this he must pay.

He loves to ask why this
And will always ask why that.
He wants to know all the answers
At the drop of a hat.

By asking so many why questions
He may soon look very pale.
Because where his hinny used to be
He may soon grow a monkey's tail.

For all his why questions
A boy he may no longer be.
Instead, he will like bananas
And become a Why Monkey.

He should learn to accept
The way things usually are.
To always ask a question
Can carry things a bit too far.

Next time you feel the urge
To ask the question why.
Reach back and feel your tail
And kiss your human hinny goodbye.

About T. Allen Winn T. Allen

Winn began writing in 2003 while being cooped up in hotels during business travel. Completing a 650 page so called novel he became hooked. The homegrown Abbeville, S.C. boy embraced the experience completing one novel and then leaping into the next one, fun and therapy at the time. That changed in 2011 when a chance encounter brought stranger and new neighbor Bob O'Brien to his Pawley's Island doorsteps. Bob didn't realize the neighborhood home had been sold and apologized when Tom greeted him instead of the man he had expected to see. Book in hand, Bob had just published his first novel, The Toppled Pawn and explained the previous neighbor had shown interest in writing. Tom remarked he dabbled in writing to which Bob asked, do you have a manuscript? Tom replied ten. Bob had just started Prose Press, a publishing company and suggested publishing one. You can't make this stuff up.

T. Allen Winn's first novel, Road Rage joined the ranks of the published a few months later, and he owes a special thanks to Bob O'Brien for making this possible. His first seven books were published by Prose Press. In 2016, T. Allen Winn established Buttermilk Books, his publishing company and has now published twenty books under the brand. He and his wife reside in Myrtle Beach, South Carolina.

Ole T doesn't write under any specific genre. He writes what strikes his fancy. If you don't see something that fits your reading wheelhouse, just tell him what you like, and he might just write it for you.

Books are available on Amazon or online where books are sold. Select books are available at Southern Succotash on Washington Street in Abbeville, S.C. and in Tabor City, N.C. at Grapefull Sisters Vineyard. Or *Message* T. Allen Winn on Facebook to arrange delivery of signed copies.

Fiction from T. Allen Winn

The Detective Trudy Wagner series

Road Rage
North of the Border
Tithes and Offerings

Bigfoot Trilogy

Foot, Tree Knockers and Rock Throwers
Another Foot, What Really Happened to D.B. Cooper

More Fiction from T. Allen Winn

The Perfect Spook House
Dark Thirty
Lou Who
Raw Ride, a Wild West Zombie Apocalyptic Shoot'um Up
The Man Who Met the Mouse
Mister Twix Mystery, a Cat Scene Investigation
Come Here, Getouttahere, Tyler's Tail Wagging Tale
The Tenth Elemental
Last Stand on the Grand Strand
The Lord's Last Acres

Non-Fiction from T. Allen Winn

Being Bentley, A Dog Like No Other
It's All About the 'A', Faith, Family, Football and Forever to Thee
with coauthor, Benji Greeson
It's All About the Angels in the Backfield, Dawn of a Dynasty
with coauthor, Benji Greeson
December's Darkest Day, While I Breathe, I Hope
The Hardwood Walker of Port Harrelson Road (based on true events in Bucksport, S.C.)
Cuz, My Brother, Life is Good, God is Good

Memoirs

The Caregiver's Son, Outside the Window Looking In
Cornbread and Buttermilk, Good Ole Fashion Home Cooked Nostalgic Nonsense
Don't Sit Naked in a Grits Tree, More Nostalgic Nonsense Vol 2
The Endless Mulligan, Short Shots from the Golf Whomper

Biographies

Clay Page, Somewhere In Between
Screw It, Let's Ride, The Legend Bub Lollis

Short Stories

For Your Amusement featured in Beach Author Network's book titled 'Shorts'

Ciled Me a Bar featured in friend and author, Danny Kuhn's Headline Book's *Mountain Mysts*, Honorable Mention in Fiction at the 2015 London Book Festival and the book is endorsed by *Joyce Dewitt* of the sitcom *Three's Company*

Short story about Granny Bowie in friend and author Robert Sharpe's book, *The Heart and Soul of Caring*, about caregivers and their challenges

www.ingramcontent.com/pod-product-compliance
Lightning Source LLC
Chambersburg PA
CBHW081506040426
42446CB00017B/3411